D1124068

TWENTIETH CENTURY VIEWS

The aim of this series is to present the best in contemporary critical opinion on major authors, providing a twentieth century perspective on their changing status in an era of profound revaluation.

Maynard Mack, *Series Editor*
Yale University

DOSTOEVSKY

NEW PERSPECTIVES

Edited by
Robert Louis Jackson

Learning Resources Center
Santa Fe Community College
P.O. Box 4187
Santa Fe, New Mexico 87502

Prentice-Hall, Inc. A SPECTRUM BOOK *Englewood Cliffs, N.J. 07632*

Library of Congress Cataloging in Publication Data

Main entry under title:

Dostoevsky: new perspectives.

(Twentieth century views)
"A Spectrum Book."
Bibliography: p.
Includes index.
  1. Dostoevsky, Fyodor, 1821–1881—Criticism and
interpretation—Addresses, essays, lectures.   I. Jackson,
Robert Louis.   II. Series.
PG3328.Z6D629 1984   891.73'3   83-17737
ISBN 0-13-218586-5
ISBN 0-13-218578-4 (pbk.)

To the memory of my mother,
Ella Fred Jackson

Quotations from *The Double* by Fyodor Dostoyevsky are from Dostoyevsky's *Notes from the Underground/The Double*, translated by Jessie Coulson (Penguin Classics, 1972), copyright © Jessie Coulson, 1972. They are reprinted by permission of Penguin Books Ltd.

Quotations from Dostoyevsky's *The Devils*—translated by David Magarshack (Penguin Classics, revised edition, 1971), copyright © David Magarshack, 1953, 1971—are reprinted by permission of Penguin Books Ltd.

Quotations from *The Brothers Karamazov* by Fyodor Dostoyevsky are from the Random House, Inc., edition, which was translated by Constance Garnett.

Editorial/production supervision by Elizabeth Torjussen
Wood engraving © 1984 by Vivian Berger
Manufacturing buyer: Edward J. Ellis

© 1984 by Prentice-Hall, Inc., Englewood Cliffs, New Jersey. A SPECTRUM BOOK. All rights reserved. No part of this book may be reproduced in any form or by any means without permission in writing from the publisher. Printed in the United States of America.

10 9 8 7 6 5 4 3 2 1

ISBN 0-13-218586-5

ISBN 0-13-218578-4 {PBK.}

PRENTICE-HALL INTERNATIONAL, INC. *(London)*
PRENTICE-HALL OF AUSTRALIA PTY. LIMITED *(Sydney)*
PRENTICE-HALL CANADA INC. *(Toronto)*
PRENTICE-HALL OF INDIA PRIVATE LIMITED *(New Delhi)*
PRENTICE-HALL OF JAPAN, INC. *(Tokyo)*
PRENTICE-HALL OF SOUTHEAST ASIA PTE. LTD. *(Singapore)*
WHITEHALL BOOKS LIMITED *(Wellington, New Zealand)*
EDITORA PRENTICE-HALL DO BRASIL LTDA. *(Rio de Janeiro)*

Contents

Introduction

by *Robert Louis Jackson*

The French critic E. Halpérine-Kaminsky wrote in 1888 that Dostoevsky "will only be truly understood when the rising nerve-storm of our century has reached its apogee." The twentieth century has given us ample opportunity to ponder Dostoevsky's art and his special appeal to our disjointed times. To speak of Dostoevsky's relevance to our century has become a cliché. Indeed, the notion of the contemporaneity of Dostoevsky has been a constant refrain in literature and criticism almost from the time of his death in 1881. Few are the important writers or works that have not felt the impact of Dostoevsky's images, ideas, the very forms and rhythms of his artistic processes. Thomas Mann's *Dr. Faustus*, Kafka's *The Trial*, Gide's *The Immoralist*, Faulkner's *The Sound and the Fury*, Zamyatin's *We*, Gorky's *Life of Klim Samgin*, Bulgakov's *Master and Margarita*—to mention only a few—all bear witness to the presence of Dostoevsky. For the writer as for the reader, what is at issue is not only the specific opinions or conclusions of Dostoevsky as they may be culled from his writings, but also the manner in which he managed to focus on and dramatize, through literary types and images, fundamental moral, psychological, social, and philosophical questions that have become insistent in the life of both individual and society in the one hundred or so years that followed his death. These questions, of course, are not confined to the nineteenth or twentieth centuries, nor are they exclusively posed in Dostoevsky's works; but they find special application to these times and attest to the capacity of the great artist, in Dostoevsky's words, "to guess a type *on time* and present him *in time*."

In his seminal study, *Dostoevsky's Legend of the Grand Inquisitor* (1894), the Russian critic and philosopher V. V. Rozanov sought to define the specifically historical as well as universal grounds for the surge of interest in Dostoevsky. His emphases are broadly psychohistorical but with an important aesthetic dimension. Commenting on the "strange disharmony of life" that has characterized human existence for thousands of years, Rozanov argued that in all of world

1

literature no writer had examined "so penetratingly the causes of this disharmony" as had Dostoevsky. He did so with "a passionate love for everything that suffered." His works speak of the "unbearable sufferings of human nature and of the absolute impossibility of enduring them and of the need to find some way of escaping them. Hence the febrile tone of all his works, the absence of external harmony of parts in them. . . . " All this, Rozanov observed, imbues Dostoevsky's works with "their eternal meaning, and undying significance."[1]

The story is different, he maintained, with Turgenev's art. Declaring it an anachronism to analyze the characters in that writer's works, Rozanov argued:

> [These characters] responded to the interests of their moment, were understood in their time and now have left behind an exclusively artistic attractiveness. We like them as living images, but we find nothing left to puzzle out in them. It is quite the opposite with Dostoevsky. The anxiety and doubts that flood his works are our anxieties and doubts, and they will remain such for all times. In those epochs when life flows along particularly smoothly or when people are not conscious of its problematic nature, this writer may even be quite forgotten or not read. But whenever anything on the paths of human history arouses a sense of distress, when the people moving along these paths find themselves stunned or thrown into confusion, then the name and image of the writer who thought so much about these paths of life will awaken with unabated force.[2]

It is the unhealthy custom to praise one Russian writer at the expense of another. We may in any case firmly dissociate ourselves from Rozanov's dismissal of the extraordinary Turgenev, a writer who, for complex cultural and historical reasons, has been vastly underestimated. Nonetheless, Rozanov's invidious comparison of Turgenev with Dostoevsky was, and continues to be, characteristic of the dominant trend in Russian and Western criticism; it is therefore of great interest in any assessment of the psychology and taste of both the late nineteenth-century and twentieth-century readers of Dostoevsky and Turgenev. It was neither the artistry of Dostoevsky nor the feeling

[1]V. V. Rozanov, *Legenda o velikom inkvizitore F. M. Dostoevskogo* (Berlin, 1924), pp. 39, 40.
[2]*Ibid.*, p. 41.

that his characters were living images in a strictly aesthetic sense that drew the reader to Dostoevsky. Indeed, the cliché of Dostoevsky as an inferior artist, but a profound writer, and of Turgenev as a "pure artist," but lacking in depth or universal relevance, has been one of the most tenacious and (at least as far as Turgenev is concerned) largely unchallenged notions in criticism. Yet Rozanov's observations with respect to the special appeal of Dostoevsky are entirely to the point: the twentieth century reader of Dostoevsky identifies with and is drawn to a tragic literary world whose inhabitants are "stunned or thrown into confusion," are without moral pivot, and obsessed with destruction and apocalypse.

"In our times," Dostoevsky wrote as the editor of a journal in the early 1860s, "all is in confusion . . . everywhere people are quarreling over foundations, principles." "Skepticism and the skeptical view are killing everything, even the very view itself in the final analysis." "Who among us in all honesty knows what is *evil* and what is *good*?" These issues are at the center of the important works Dostoevsky wrote after he returned from his Siberian exile: *Notes from the House of the Dead* (1860–1862), *Winter Remarks on Summer Impressions* (1863), *Notes from the Underground* (1864), *Crime and Punishment* (1866), and *The Gambler* (1866). The "crisis of nihilism," of which Nietzsche was to speak so brilliantly nearly a quarter of a century later, was already apparent to Dostoevsky. And like Nietzsche, though without the latter's dissent from the specifically Christian values of European civilization, Dostoevsky's works are filled with ominous forebodings and prophesies about the future of Russian and European society.

Both *The Idiot* and *The Devils* are apocalyptic works. A spirit of confusion and madness seeks to dominate in the worlds of these two novels. Dostoevsky's macabre tale, "Bobok" (1873), is a grim admonition, a warning of total disintegration of the moral and social fabric. It was his critics, Dostoevsky wrote in his notebook to *The Raw Youth* (March 22, 1875), who were

> . . . ignoring facts. They do not observe. There are no *citizens*, and nobody wants to make an effort and compel himself to think and observe. I cannot tear myself away, and all the cries of the critics that I am not depicting real life have not dissuaded me. There are no *foundations* to our society, no principles of conduct that have been lived through, because there have been none in

life even. A colossal eruption and all is crumbling, falling, being negated, as though it had not even existed. And not only externally, as in the West, but internally, morally.

These notes of warning echo throughout Dostoevsky's *Diary of a Writer* in 1876–1877. "Everybody is in a state of suspense," he writes in connection with the "Eastern Question" in the September 1876 issue of *Diary of a Writer*. "Everybody is alarmed; some kind of general madness is moving upon us." Europe is changing from hour to hour, he writes in November 1877: "The fact is that we are just now on the eve of the greatest and most shocking events and upheavals in Europe, and this is said *without any exaggeration*." He writes again in 1877,

> The point is, that, to my way of thinking, the present age, too, will end in old Europe with something colossal, that is, with something perhaps not literally identical with the events which brought to an end the eighteenth century, nevertheless just as colossal—elemental and dreadful, and also entailing a change in the face of the whole world, or, at least, in the West, of old Europe.

Writing his novels in Russia in the 1860s and 1870s—a tumultuous period of social and economic transition when Russia was experiencing its own rationalist and materialist "Enlightenment" and the birth of its own uncertain forms of revolutionary Socialism—Dostoevsky grasped the inner content and movement of a vast historical epoch, its critical tensions and, above all, its potential for catastrophe and change. The drama of the eighteenth century culminating in the explosion of the French Revolution and the apocalyptic drama of the nineteenth century (one ultimately "entailing a change in the face of the whole world")—here is the grand, epic historical frame for Dostoevsky's extraordinary art and intuition.

Intuition in Dostoevsky (at least as a political thinker) often went hand in hand with idiosyncratic and even grotesque conceptions and formulations. Much that he anticipated, however, came to pass, though much that he hoped for did not occur; and what came to pass did not always occur when and where he expected it. Dostoevsky was an artist. He painted what he saw, but he saw in depth. It is noteworthy that he conceived of art as concerned with "ends and beginnings," as a guessing or divining of the "subsurface, unexpressed future Word." Indeed, few artists have been more preoccupied than Dostoevsky with the future in the sense of mankind's general destiny. The Russian writer and satirist M. E. Saltykov-Shchedrin, a contemporary of Dostoevsky, noted this special facet of that writer's genius:

> In the profoundity of his intent, in the breadth of the moral problems contained within his vision, this writer occupies a place apart in our literature. He does not only admit the right to existence of those interests which most concern contemporary society, but goes even further and enters into that sphere of foresight and premonition that constitutes the aim not of our immediate, but of mankind's most distant quests.[3]

Yet with Dostoevsky the problems of mankind are never presented abstractly (it is the fate of his heroes, not the novels they inhabit, to be swallowed up in the abstract or purely intellectual dimension). Life in Dostoevsky's novels is almost always disclosed and experienced in the cross-section of the moment, and with an acute sense of social and historical specificity and detail. The glass through which the most universal and timeless moral and philosophical concerns are refracted is always the sufferings, crises, spiritual strivings, and fate of human beings in his own time—in the first instance, those of his fellow Russians. It is surely Dostoevsky's own concern we sense when, speaking of cruel and debasing exploitation in factories, Father Zosima cries out: "There must be no more of this, monks, there must be no more torturing of children, rise and begin preaching this, and make haste, make haste!" Wholly characteristic of Dostoevsky's concerns are his remarks in *Diary of a Writer* in 1876: "I do not want to think and live other than with the faith that all of the ninety millions of us, Russians (or however many there will be) will some day all be educated, humanized and happy."

The special place of Dostoevsky in any confrontation with Russian history and consciousness is indisputable. His art engages some of the most problematic aspects of Russian historical life just as it embodies some of the most lofty and transcendent qualities of the Russian spirit. Maxim Gorky (1868–1936), whose life and work mirror in an exemplary way the tortuous complexities of Russian history and cul-

---

[3]Saltykov-Shchedrin in *F. M. Dostoevskii v russkoi kritike*, ed. A. A. Belkin (Moscow, 1956), p. 231.

ture in the first half of the twentieth century, was obsessed with the psychohistorical character of Dostoevsky's art. He emphasized the Shakespearean dimensions of Dostoevsky's art. But Dostoevsky, for him, was above all Russia's "memory," the painful record of all the cruelties and humiliations endured by the Russian people and history from the time of the Mongol invasions. "A man had to appear who embodied in his soul the memory of all those human sufferings and gave expression to that fearful memory," Gorky wrote in 1909. "That man was Dostoevsky."[4] Dostoevsky, in Gorky's view, was an intimate part of that fearful memory—the evil genius of Russian culture. Reading him "you feel his endless fright at the dark depths of his own 'soul'."[5] Gorky reproached Dostoevsky for emphasizing only the "negative aspects" of life. He "fixes them in the memory of man, always depicting him as helpless in the chaos of dark forces." All this "can lead man to pessimism, mysticism, etc."[6]

Gorky was deeply responsive to Dostoevsky's anguish over evil and suffering, and his contribution to an understanding of Dostoevsky should not be underestimated. The negative and pedagogical aspects of his reaction to Dostoevsky at the same time represent a despairing effort to find a way out of the morass of Russian life (and out of the dark depths of his own soul). He wished to cultivate in the Russian masses a healthy and positive attitude toward life. But the impact of Gorky's Dostoevsky criticism on the Soviet cultural scene of the 1930s and 1940s was not a positive one. Limited in its emphases, it encouraged suspicion and hostility toward Dostoevsky. As Soviet power under Stalin sank to some of the worst excesses of violence in Russian history, his establishment quite naturally (though for motives very different from Gorky's) sought to distance itself from Russia's "memory," Dostoevsky. Yet memory and Dostoevsky, as Gorky rightly perceived, are joined indissolubly in Russian cultural consciousness. The recovery of the first, in the post-Stalin period, inevitably led to the rehabilitation of the second.

Dostoevsky was at no time a forgotten figure in Soviet literary consciousness. The Russian Marxist scholar V. F. Pereverzev, whose

[4]Gor'kii, *Istoriia russkoi literatury. Arkhiv A. M. Gor'kogo* (Moscow, 1938) I, 251.
[5]Gor'kii, *O literature* (Moscow, 1953), pp. 511–12.
[6]*Op. cit.*, p. 250.

pioneering sociological study of Dostoevsky's art first appeared in 1912, observed in 1922 that all of modern literature "follow[s] in the footsteps of Dostoevsky." He spoke, too, of the special relevance of Dostoevsky for contemporary revolutionary Russia:

> Dostoevsky remains a contemporary writer. Our times have by no means outlived the problems he takes up in his work. For us to speak about Dostoevsky still means to speak about the most painful and rooted problems of our contemporary life. Caught up in the whirlwind of a great revolution, buffeted about amid the problems posed by it, passionately and painfully responding to all of the revolutionary tragedy, we find in Dostoevsky our very own selves; we find in the way he poses the problems of revolution the kind of passion and intensity we might expect to find in a writer who was passing through the revolutionary storm with us.[7]

Pereverzev had in mind specifically Dostoevsky's novel, *The Devils*, a work whose relation to the revolution he examines from a sociological point of view. Pereverzev, of course, was only one of many Russian writers, critics, and thinkers—both in Russia and in exile—who felt that in his fictional works Dostoevsky had anticipated the "revolutionary tragedy." Dostoevsky is a "prophet of the revolution in the most exact sense of the word," the Russian philosopher Nicholas Berdyaev wrote in his study of Dostoevsky in 1923. Berdyaev continues: "The revolution took place the way he said it would [*po Dostoevskomu*]. He disclosed its ideological foundations, its inner dialectic and gave it form. He grasped the character of the Russian revolution from the depths of the spirit, from internal processes, and not from the outward circumstances of empirical reality around him."[8]

Early Soviet literature—the works of Leonov, Olesha, Zamyatin, Fedin, Platonov, Ehrenburg, Pilnyak, Bulgakov, and many others—was saturated with Dostoevsky and made use of his imagery and ideas to define the problematic nature of revolutionary experiences and transformations and to explore the intelligentsia's own complex and very often ambiguous relationship to Soviet power. Many of the characters in these works seem to emerge from Dostoevsky's novels. "Whenever he read Dostoevsky he felt ill," Ilya Ehrenburg writes of

[7]V. F. Pereverzev, *Tvorchestvo Dostoevskogo*, 2nd ed. (Moscow, 1922), p. 4.
[8]N. Berdiaev, *Mirosozertsanie Dostoevskogo* (Paris, 1923), pp. 134–35.

his anti-hero Volodya Safonov in his novel *The Second Day* (translated as *Out of Chaos*, 1934). "Those were not books, but letters from a man intimately related to him." At the same time that many Soviet writers in the 1920s and early 1930s were trying to assess Soviet reality partly with the aid of a Dostoevsky lens (he was not the sole Russian writer, of course, who made his presence felt), scholars from various schools of criticism were producing a rich crop of writing on Dostoevsky. Apart from ideologically oriented criticism, important critical, stylistic, and historical studies were written by such outstanding scholars as M. P. Alekseev, M. M. Bakhtin, Arkadi Dolinin, Leonid Grossman, V. L. Komarovich, A. S. Skaftymov, V. V. Vinogradov, and others. Throughout the 1930s and 1940s some important scholarly work was accomplished and the heritage of Dostoevsky, his significance to the new revolutionary society, was the object of debate in ideologically oriented criticism. But the works of Dostoevsky were published in very small numbers. After a brief period of rehabilitation during World War II, the name and work of Dostoevsky were sharply assailed. The lowest level of the attack on Dostoevsky in these last years of Stalin's rule was reached, no doubt, by the party stalwart, D. I. Zaslavski who stigmatized Dostoevsky as the "spiritual father" of "double-dealers and traitors." The Legend of the Grand Inquisitor was dubbed by Zaslavski (not without some literary astuteness) "The Legend of the Grand-Agent Provocateur."[9]

Yet as one Soviet scholar rightly observed many years later, "even in quarrelling with Dostoevsky, even in refuting him, even in renouncing him, Soviet writing could not get away from him." "The relations between F. M. Dostoevsky and Soviet literature," the writer concluded with considerable understatement, "have always been dramatic."[10] That drama has lost none of its intensity or interest, though its nature has changed radically.

[9]Zaslavski's comments are cited by Vladimir Seduro in his study, *Dostoyevski in Russian Literary Criticism 1846–1954* (New York, Columbia University Press, 1957), pp. 279, 280.

[10]E. V. Starikova, *"Dostoevskii i sovetskaia literatura (k postanovke voprosa),"* in *Dostoevskii: Khudozhnik i myslitel'* (Moscow, 1972), pp. 603, 615. For an earlier discussion in English of Dostoevsky and Soviet literature, see Robert L. Jackson's *Dostoevsky's Underground Man in Russian Literature* ('S-Gravenhage: Mouton and Co., 1958; 2nd ed., Westport, Conn.: Greenwood Press, 1981), pp. 127–216.

The 1960s and 1970s witnessed a striking increase in interest in Dostoevsky on the part of readers, scholars, and Soviet publishing houses. "Today we read Dostoevsky, we read him as we never read him before," wrote B. Bursov (*Voprosy literatury*, No. 11, 1971), the author of a book on Dostoevsky, on the one hundred and fiftieth anniversary of Dostoevsky's birth. "A real renascence is taking place," wrote the critics T. Guralnik and S. Dmitrenko in a review of Dostoevsky scholarship in the literary journal *Voprosy literatury* (No. 5) in 1982. The output of Soviet scholars has been large and fruitful. Noteworthy in the twenty-five years following Stalin's death was the scholarly, critical, and editorial work of numerous writers: M. S. Altman, S. V. Belov, B. Bursov, A. V. Chicherin, F. I. Evnin, G. M. Fridlender, Yu. F. Karyakin, V. Kirpotin, V. V. Kozhinov, D. S. Likhachev, Yu. M. Lotman, V. S. Nechaeva, L. M. Rozenblium, V. Shklovsky, V. A. Tunimanov, V. E. Vetlovskaya, and I. S. Zilberstein—to mention only a few. Publication of a monumental thirty-volume edition of the complete works of Dostoevsky's *belles lettres*, notebooks, journalism, critical writings, and letters under the direction of the doyen of Dostoevsky scholars, G. M. Fridlender, has provided an important impetus to the development of Dostoevsky scholarship, not only in the Soviet Union but throughout the world.

While Dostoevsky's religious and philosophical outlook stand in sharp contrast to the ideology of Soviet Marxism, Dostoevsky scholarship "in the field" enjoys a surprising degree of independence. It has begun to reexamine and reevaluate many of the larger issues that aroused so much anguish in Stalinist-oriented criticism: Dostoevsky's political conservatism (particularly as manifested in his journalism); his critical attitude toward revolution and socialism; his rejection of materialism; his deeply Christian outlook; his tragic (though not pessimistic) view of human nature. In an effort to overcome the excesses and crudities that marked quasi-official attitudes toward Dostoevsky in the Stalin period, one notes here and there a tendency on the part of some publicists to harmonize or smooth over problematic and sometimes disagreeable aspects of Dostoevsky's writing, such as anti-Semitism and chauvinism. Efforts to popularize Dostoevsky or to enlist him in new causes (whether an all-purpose bland humanism or Russian neo-Slavophilism) account for some of these tendencies.

On the whole, Soviet scholars tend to be as polyphonic on most of the complex questions in Dostoevsky's work as scholars in any other part of the world. Dostoevsky's novel, *The Devils*, for example, has been variously viewed as a lampoon on the revolution (Gus), an "anatomization and criticism of ultra-left extremism" (Suchkov), and as the "tragedy of a whole people. . . . In *The Devils* we are on the eve or at the beginning of the Apocalypse" (Karyakin). The increasingly intense interest in *The Devils*, moreover, has been a mark of the deepening post-Stalin ferment in Soviet Russian intellectual consciousness. As Guralnik and Dmitrenko noted in *Voprosy literatury*, the interest in *The Devils* was further stimulated by the "difficult fate of a novel which reached the reader after years of biased presentation and at times complete rejection."

Soviet criticism and scholarship after Stalin's death underwent a process not only of reassessment but rediscovery of earlier Russian and Soviet interpretations of Dostoevsky (for example, the work of M. M. Bakhtin and N. M. Chirkov). Although the Dostoevsky studies of such important and provocative émigré Russian thinkers as Leo Shestov, N. Berdyaev, and V. I. Ivanov have never been published in the Soviet Union, their works have been the subject of criticism and discussion.[11] The republication in 1963 of a revised and expanded edition of M. M. Bakhtin's major study, *Problems of Dostoevsky's Poetics* (originally published in 1929) was a signal event. This study, with its focus on the "dialogical nature of the word" and the "polyphonic character of the text," constituted, as in 1929, an important widening of horizons for the general reader as well as for the specialist. Bakhtin's criticism, in particular his theory of the polyphonic novel, continues to carry with it a certain extra-literary significance. Thus, the Soviet critic Pyotr Palievsky, in his introduction to a round-table discussion of Dostoevsky (*Soviet Literature*, No. 12, 1981) finds the key to an understanding of Dostoevsky in the latter's "capacity to recognize truth wherever he came across it," and, most importantly, in the "polemical technique" he used to reach truth, that is, "the way he would suddenly begin to argue not against, but for an idea which had been declared alien to him." In this sense, Palievsky

[11]Apart from these thinkers, Russian émigré culture has been rich in Dostoevsky scholarship. Here one may mention, in the early post-revolutionary period, Yury Nikolsky, A. Steinberg, A. L. Bem, I. I. Lapshin, and Fyodor A. Stepun; in the post-World War II period Konstantin Mochulsky, Nikolai Lossky, and Lev Zander, among others, have made important contributions to the development of Dostoevsky studies.

concludes, no figure is more suited than Dostoevsky "to inaugurate real communication between people, I mean the modern kind of communication where you get so many differing opinions." Palievsky does not mention Bakhtin, but his point of reference is clear. Bakhtin's book, drawing in important ways upon Russian and Soviet studies of Dostoevsky, surely represents a major achievement in Dostoevsky scholarship in the realm of literary theory. It has stimulated fruitful argument and counterargument. As Bakhtin himself acknowledged in a letter to his disciple and colleague, V. V. Kozhinov, in 1961, his position on the polyphonic novel "has more than anything else given rise to objections and misunderstanding."[12] One of the crucial areas of uncertainty for many scholars has been Bakhtin's exact understanding of the relation of Dostoevsky the author to "the plurality of independent and unmerged voices," those "free people who are capable of standing beside their creator, of disagreeing with him and even rebelling against him." Responding to this critical inquiry, Bakhtin insisted in his notes "Toward a Reworking of the Dostoevsky Book" (1961) that "our point of view in no way asserts a passivity on the part of the author, who would then do no more than assemble others' points of view, others' truths, completely refusing his own point of view." Bakhtin affirms

a completely new and special interrelationship between the author's and the other's truth. The author is profoundly *active*, but his activity is of a special *dialogic* sort. [This is the] activity of God in His relation to man, a relation allowing man to reveal himself utterly (in his immanent development), to judge himself, to refute himself. This is activity of a higher quality. It surmounts not the resistance of dead material, but the resistance of another's consciousness, another's truth.[13]

Polyphony in the Dostoevsky novel clearly did not imply for Bakhtin passivity, indifference, or absence of judgment on the part of the author. Yet his major emphasis is not upon the nature of Dostoevsky's judgment or the way it is concretely manifested throughout the play of voices, but upon the relative independence of the voices in the Dostoevsky text. The "misunderstanding" of the reader with respect to Bakhtin's position on the polyphonic novel is surely rooted in

[12]M. M. Bakhtin, *Estetika slovesnogo tvorchestva* (Moscow, 1979), p. 404.
[13]*Ibid.*, p. 310.

Bakhtin's unwillingness (or inability for political reasons) to integrate
his discussion of the poetics of the Dostoevsky novel with a detailed
consideration of authorial activity and point of view (and authorial
"point of view," as Dostoevsky once insisted in some remarks on the
improvisation in Pushkin's story "Egyptian Nights" "is the main
thing"). A more holistic approach to the Dostoevsky text or novel
would not only have clarified Bakhtin's position, but quite possibly
would also have led to important modifications in some of his formulations. In any case, polyphony for Dostoevsky is not so much a ruling
principle as a problem to be solved in the interrelated realms of consciousness, ideology, and aesthetics. The problem was posed in *Notes
from the Underground*. "In the confession of the Underground Man,"
Bakhtin writes in *Problems of Dostoevsky's Poetics*, "we are struck by an
extreme and sharp internal dialogizing: there is in it literally not a
single monologically firm, undisintegrated word."[14] Such is the "disease of consciousness" (Dostoevsky's words in his notebook in 1864)
with which the Underground Man is afflicted and of which he gives
such eloquent account in *Notes from the Underground*:

> Where are my primal causes on which I can rest, where are my
> foundations? Where can I find them? I exercise myself in
> thought, and consequently with me every primary cause imme-
> diately draws another one after itself, even more primary, and so
> on into infinity. Such is precisely the essence of all consciousness
> and thought. (I,5)

Such is precisely the essence of all truth or reality in the world of
dismantled consciousness. Such would be the essence of truth in a
statically conceived polyphonic novel. But in his great novels Dostoevsky not only explores the "disease of consciousness," that is, discloses its social, psychological, and spiritual causes, but he also masters
it aesthetically in the dramatic form of the controlled polyphonic
novel. Truth in the Dostoevsky novel, as in the Tolstoy novel, is always
multivalent. But here we are not involved with truths spinning independently in a void. These truths are embedded in an artistic structure, constitute a dialectical unity, and give expression in their interaction to the author's highest vision of human experience.

One must distinguish, then, between the endless sense of life's

[14]Bakhtin, *Problemy poetiki Dostoevskogo* (Moscow, 1963), p. 306.

complexities, contradictions, and ambiguities that works of art like *The Brothers Karamazov* or *Anna Karenina* arouse in the reader, and the vision or focal point of view that the work itself constitutes as art; that is, as a living aesthetic form giving movement and design to reality. Here is the "activity of a higher quality" or the "work of God in His relation to man" of which Bakhtin spoke in his notes "Toward a Reworking of the Dostoevsky Book." Interpretation that ignores this level of higher activity at which the artist's point of view ultimately manifests itself, that gets mired in the bog of dismantled consciousness, that confuses the constructive task of criticism with dismantling literary consciousness "and so on into infinity"; such interpretation not only ignores the work of art, but systematically denies its essence. This was not the direction of Bakhtin's Dostoevsky criticism, to say nothing of his personal philosophy. He had to exclude much from his criticism that was anathema to official Soviet ideology. But he in no way shared the crisis of consciousness and culture that Dostoevsky so brilliantly depicted in his novels and that he, Bakhtin, so acutely perceived to be a major shaping factor in the development of that great writer's novel-form.

Bakhtin's discussion of *The Double*, the first chapter in this volume, provides important insight into "the dialogical nature of the word" in Dostoevsky's work. *The Double*, though not entirely successful by the standards of Dostoevsky's later work, anticipated some of the most important developments in his art. The polyphonic novel, or important aspects of it, may be perceived here in embryonic form. "This is not yet polyphony," remarks Bakhtin, "but it is no longer homophony."

No form, perhaps, was more congenial to Dostoevsky than that of first person narration. The feuilleton, a genre popularized in France in the 1830s and in Russia in the 1840s, afforded Dostoevsky a freedom for play and paradox, for dialogues with himself and the reader, and a possibility for merging fiction and reality. But as Joseph Frank also points out in his fine discussion, "The Petersburg Feuilletons," the genre afforded Dostoevsky an opportunity for oblique social criticism, broad historical meditations, the exploration of certain social and psychological types, such as the dreamer, as well as a chance for commentary on his literary work in progress.

So congenial was the feuilleton form that Dostoevsky returned to it in the beginning of the 1860s and, most importantly, in his *Diary of a Writer* (1873, 1876–1877, 1881). In his important essay, "Reading between the Genres: Dostoevsky's *Diary of a Writer* as metafiction, Gary Saul Morson projects Dostoevsky's work as challenging our definition of literature: "A self-conscious anomaly, it violates the conventions of literature to make us aware of what those conventions are. . . . The *Diary* does not exist on the boundaries of art: it dramatizes them." Morson's discussion opens up broad questions of literary theory with respect to both Dostoevsky's work and the literary tradition that he responded to in *Diary of a Writer*.[15]

Few works in Dostoevsky are more resistant to one-sided interpretation than *Notes from the Underground*. Set in the field of moral and spiritual coordinates that dominate Dostoevsky's work at large, the Christian design of *Notes* is clear and evident; but perceived in the blindingly paradoxical terms of its narrator, this same work—much like Tolstoy's later *Kreutzer Sonata*—leaves the reader with a disturbing sense of unresolved authorial tensions. In our essay "Aristotelian Movement and Design," we define the inner movement toward catastrophe in Part Two of *Notes* as Aristotelian. Yet we ultimately perceive this Aristotelian element as in tension with Dostoevsky's Christian design.

The elusiveness of the narrator is nowhere more clearly observed than in the confessional form. "In Dostoevsky's work the truth will out in various ways," Robin Feuer Miller observes in her thoughtful essay on Dostoevsky and Rousseau, "but rarely finds unadorned release through the mode inherently concerned with the utterance of truth: the confession." This is true of the Underground Man through whom Dostoevsky explores, among other things, the dynamics of confessional deception and self-deception. In her essay Miller explores the use of the confessional form in Dostoevsky's work at large and contributes to an understanding of Dostoevsky's complex relationship to Rousseau.

In the Dostoevsky novel, what appears as background is always relevant foreground. Petersburg in his novels, for example, is not the setting for tragedy; Petersburg, as Dostoevsky himself once observed,

---

[15]For a further elaboration of these questions, see Morson's *The Boundaries of Genre: Dostoevsky's* Diary of a Writer *and the Traditions of Literary Utopia* (Austin, Tex.: University of Texas Press, 1981).

is a tragedy. The city in all its aspects is part and parcel of the life and drama of Raskolnikov. In "Raskolnikov's City in the Napoleonic Plan," Adele Lindenmeyr deftly brings out the manner in which the problems of urban reforms and city planning—in the "background" the Napoleonic plan for Paris's renovation—enters into the dialectic of consciousness of Raskolnikov in the last moments preceding his murder of the pawnbroker.

Among the works of Dostoevsky that have received the least attention is one of the most brilliant and rewarding: *The Gambler*. As with the important *Notes from the House of the Dead* with which it is closely related on the philosophical plane, for example, the problem of fate and freedom,[16] the tendency has been to discuss it as a simple extension of Dostoevsky's own personal experiences. But as D. S. Savage points out in his fine essay on Dostoevsky's novel, "behind *The Gambler* is no mere scandalous revelation of personal history but, as is usual with Dostoevsky's work, a dominating and shaping *idea*, to which everything in the action is related." Savage's examination of this idea places *The Gambler* directly in the ideological context of *Notes from the Underground* and *Crime and Punishment*.

In his provocative essay, "Gaps in Christology: *The Idiot*," Michael Holquist argues convincingly that the central metaphors of *The Idiot*, in contrast to those of *Crime and Punishment* (the Lazarus story, rebirth) are execution and apocalypse; not a sudden beginning of life, but rather its abrupt end. He perceives *The Idiot* not in the usual terms of characterological likenesses between Myshkin and Jesus, but as tragedy, as a "pattern for failed epiphanies." Holquist's excellent essay is of particular interest for its integration of questions of interpretation with issues involving the theory of the novel.

The two essays devoted to *The Devils* constitute a stimulating introduction to a complex and much-debated novel. V. A. Tunimanov's "The Narrator in Dostoevsky's *The Devils*," excerpted here from a larger study under the same title, is a fine close-to-the-text analysis of narrative techniques in *The Devils*. Tunimanov, one of the leading Soviet Dostoevsky scholars, sensitively and patiently foregrounds the

---

[16]For a discussion of the works and the problem content that joins them, see Robert Louis Jackson, *The Art of Dostoevsky. Deliriums and Nocturnes* (Princeton, N.J.: Princeton University Press, 1981), particularly chapters V and VIII.

elusive narrator-chronicler and the manner in which Dostoevsky uses him to dramatize and develop action and character in the novel. Tunimanov convincingly concludes that *The Devils* "is one of the strongest and most artistic works of Dostoevsky."

In a finely worded and persuasive essay, "Stepan Verkhovensky and the Shaping Dialectic of Dostoevsky's *Devils*," Gordon Livermore argues for the artistic unity of Dostoevsky's novel. He locates the central dramatic conflict in the novel in Stepan's idealist sensibility and his consistent impulse to leap from "lower" to "higher" reality, *a realibus ad realiora* (Livermore employs Vyacheslav I. Ivanov's terms). Stepan's fatal tendency to negate reality is matched by his son Pyotr. In the final pages of this rewarding essay, one marked by a close attention to the interaction of language, imagery, and idea, Livermore reminds us that the novel's two moments of epiphany, given to the two idealists Stepan Verkhovensky and Shatov, constitute "moments of renewed contact with reality, experiences in which *realiora* and *realia* are at least briefly united."

The Brothers Karamazov turned out to be the last and, in the view of many, the crowning achievement of Dostoevsky's artistic career. Yet as V. A. Vetlovskaya reminds us in her fine discussion, "Alyosha Karamazov and the Hagiographic Hero," Dostoevsky conceived of *The Brothers Karamazov*, as we know it now, as only the first of two parts. It was in the second volume that Alyosha Karamazov was to occupy the position of central hero of the novel. Vetlovskaya carefully shows how Dostoevsky anticipated in the first novel the subsequent development of Alyosha in the second. Yet the main contribution of Vetlovskaya's fine essay is her thorough exploration of the hagiographic dimension of Alyosha as a character. Again and again, Dostoevsky links his hero Alyosha with the central figure of one of Russia's most popular *vita*, that of Aleksey Man of God. Vetlovskaya's discussion contributes much to our understanding of Dostoevsky's intentions in *The Brothers Karamazov*. Her work as a whole, like Tunimanov's, attests to the continuation in the Soviet Union today of the best traditions of Russian and Soviet Dostoevsky scholarship.

Dostoevsky wrote directly about literature, art, and aesthetics as a critic and journalist. At the same time, his art is rich in literary and aesthetic subtext. This is the focus of Victor Terras' fine and ranging discussion, "The Art of Fiction as a Theme in *The Brothers Karamazov*."

"Throughout *The Brothers Karamazov*, aesthetic categories are unhesitatingly applied to the phenomena of life." Terras shows, for example, how each main character in the novel is a "different type of *homo aestheticus*," but also explores Dostoevsky's rich and paradoxical play with fact and fiction in the novel. Terras's discussion of the duel between the prosecutor Ippolit and the defense attorney Fetyukovich is particularly provocative. Apropos of Fetyukovich, Terras remarks: "Dostoevsky assigns the voice of truth to the man with the greatest imagination . . . and he does so regardless of the man's moral qualities."

In his perceptive and informative contribution, "Memory in *The Brothers Karamazov*," Robert L. Belknap foregrounds a phenomenon and device in Dostoevsky's art of enormous philosophical, moral, and psychological importance. Belknap not only brings out the central role of memory in Dostoevsky's last novel, but also gives considerable attention to the literary and scientific context in the eighteenth and nineteenth century of Dostoevsky's thought on memory (Diderot, Taine, Claude Bernard, and others).

In the final essay of the volume, "The Paradox of the Legend of the Grant Inquisitor," the noted French Slavist and Dostoevsky scholar Jacques Catteau explores the complex dialectic of the Legend of the Grand Inquisitor in *The Brothers Karamazov*. Catteau poses the question of his essay as follows: "Could the Legend of the Grand Inquisitor be the eclipse of hope, the imprisonment of hope, or does it leave the door open to some ray of hope?" He analyzes the Legend against the background of the literary tradition in which it finds itself and in the light of various readings. The conclusion of his metaphysically informed essay is that at the conclusion of the Legend "all is tragically renewed, all becomes possible again in a new legend: hope is both extended and released."

The present volume brings together only a sampling of Dostoevsky scholarship in the East and the West. Soviet Russian scholarship, as we have noted, is abundant. In the United States the work of Robert L. Belknap, Roger L. Cox, Donald Fanger, Joseph Frank, George Gibian, Robert Louis Jackson, Ralph Matlaw, Robin Feuer Miller, Gary Saul Morson, Nadine Natov, Nathan Rosen, Ellis Sandoz, Vladimir Seduro, Victor Terras, and Edward Wasiolek, among many others, attests to the leap of American scholarship in the past twenty-five

years. It is an advance matched in other parts of the world by such
scholars as Jacques Catteau and Dominique Arban (France), Sven
Linnér (Finland), Sigurd Fasting (Norway), Richard Peace and
Malcolm Jones (England), Horst-Jürgen Gerigk, Hans Rothe, and
Wolf Schmidt (West Germany), Ettore Lo Gatto and Anna Maver Lo
Gatto (Italy), Ryszar Przybylski (Poland), Gyula Kiraly (Hungary),
Konrad Onasch (German Democratic Republic), Slobodanka Vladiv
(Australia), Toyofusa Kinoshita (Japan), Rudolf Neuhäuser (Au-
stria), Carl Stief (Denmark), and Jan van der Eng (the Netherlands),
to mention only a few. Taken together with the resurgence of Dostoevsky scholarship in the Soviet Union, one can justly speak of a real
renascence in Dostoevsky studies. It is hoped that this volume will
provide further impetus to the development of interest in Dostoevsky
throughout the world.

   To facilitate reference to Dostoevsky's work for readers using any
of the available texts or translations, I have followed quotations with
parenthetical notes indicating the part (uppercase Roman numeral),
chapter (Arabic numeral) and, if any, subchapter (lowercase Roman
numeral) in which the passage occurs.

The Dismantled Consciousness:
An Analysis of *The Double*

by Mikhail M. Bakhtin

In *The Double*, the characteristic feature of consciousness and speech that we have examined in Dostoevsky's first novel, *Poor Folk*—the anticipation of another person's word—achieves extremely sharp and clear-cut expression, more so than in any other work by Dostoevsky. The tendencies already imbedded in Makar Devushkin are developed here with extraordinary boldness and consistency, carried to their conceptual limits, on the basis of the same deliberately primitive, simple and crude material.

We cite below the semantic structure and speech profile of Golyadkin's discourse in a parodic stylization done by Dostoevsky himself, in a letter written to his brother while working on *The Double*. As in any parodic stylization, there is an obvious and crude emphasis upon the basic characteristics and tendencies of Golyadkin's discourse.

> *Yakov Petrovich Golyadkin* holds his own completely. He's a terrible scoundrel and there's no approaching him; he refuses to move forward, pretending that he's not ready yet, that for the present he's on his own, he's all right, nothing is the matter, but that if it comes to that, then he can do that too, why not, what's to prevent it? He's just like everyone else, he's nothing special, just like everyone else. What's it to him! A scoundrel, a terrible scoundrel! He'll never agree to end his career before the middle of November. He's just now spoken with his Excellency, and he just may (and why shouldn't he) be ready to announce his retirement.[1]

"The Dismantled Consciousness: An Analysis of *The Double*" [editor's title], by Mikhail M. Bakhtin. From Bakhtin's *Problems of Dostoevsky's Poetics*, Caryl Emerson, trans., (Minneapolis: University of Minnesota Press). Copyright © 1983 by the University of Minnesota.

[1]A letter to Mikhail Dostoevsky, October 8, 1845 (translator's note).

As we shall see, *The Double* itself is narrated in this same style, parodying the hero.

The influence of another person's words on Golyadkin's speech is absolutely obvious. We immediately sense that his speech, like Devushkin's, gravitates neither toward itself nor toward its referential object. Golyadkin's interrelationships with the other's speech and the other's consciousness are, however, quite different from Devushkin's. And for this reason the traits in Golyadkin's style produced by the other's discourse are of a different sort.

Golyadkin's speech seeks, above all, to simulate total independence from the other's words: "He's on his own, he's all right." This simulation of independence and indifference also leads to endless repetitions, reservations and long-windedness, but here they are directed not outward, not toward another, but toward Golyadkin's own self: he persuades himself, reassures and comforts himself, plays the role of another person vis-à-vis himself. Golyadkin's comforting dialogues with himself are the most prominent trait of the whole story. Along with a simulation of indifference, however, goes another attitude toward the other's discourse: the desire to hide from it, to avoid attracting attention to himself, to bury himself in the crowd, to go unnoticed—after all, "He's just like everyone else, he's nothing special, just like everyone else." But in this he is trying to convince not himself, but another. Finally, there is a third attitude toward the other's discourse: concession, subordination to it, a submissive assimilation of it, as if Golyadkin thought the same way himself and sincerely agreed with it: "If it comes to that, then he can do that too, why not, what's to prevent it?"

Such are Golyadkin's three general lines of orientation, and they are complicated by other secondary but rather important ones. Each of these three lines in itself gives rise to very complex phenomena in Golyadkin's consciousness and discourse.

We shall concentrate primarily on his simulation of independence and composure.

The pages of *The Double* are filled, as we have said, with the hero's dialogues with himself. It could be said that Golyadkin's entire inner life develops dialogically. We quote two examples of such dialogue:

> "Will it be all right, though?" went on our hero, stepping out of his carriage at the porch of a five-storey house on Liteiny Street,

beside which he had ordered the vehicle to stop; "will it be all right? Is it a proper thing to do? Will this be the right time? However, does it really matter?" he continued as he mounted the stairs, breathing hard and trying to control the beating of his heart, which always seemed to beat hard on other people's stairs; "does it matter? I've come about my own business, after all, and there's nothing reprehensible in that. . . . It would be stupid to try to keep anything from him. So I'll just make it appear that it's nothing special, I just happened to be driving past. . . . He will see that's how it must have been." (I)[2]

The second example of interior dialogue is considerably more complex and pointed. Golyadkin conducts it after the appearance of the double, that is, after the second voice has already become objectified for him within his own field of vision.

Thus Mr. Golyadkin's delighted mood expressed itself, but all the time something went on nagging away at the back of his mind, a kind of ache, which sometimes so drained his spirits that Mr. Golyadkin did not know where to turn for consolation. "However, we'll wait a day, and then we can be happy. Still, what does it amount to, after all? Well, we'll think about it, and we'll see. Well, let's think it over, my young friend, let's discuss it. Well, he's a man like you, to begin with, exactly the same. Well, what of that? If that's what he is, ought I to weep over it? What's it got to do with me? I'm outside it; I just whistle, that's all! Let him work! Well, it's something strange and queer; just like the Siamese twins, as they call them. . . . Well, why them, the Siamese twins?—all right, they're twins, but even the very greatest people have seemed a bit queer sometimes. Why, even in history, it's well known the famous Suvorov crowed like a cock. . . . Well, but that was all for political reasons; and great generals . . . but why talk about generals? I go my own way, that's all, and I don't want to know anybody, and in my innocence I scorn my enemies. I am no intriguer, and I'm proud to say it. Honest, straightforward, orderly, agreeable, mild. . . ." (VI).

[2]Passages from *The Double* cited from Fyodor Dostoevsky, *Notes from Underground and The Double*, translated by Jessie Coulson (Penguin Books, 1972). The translation has been slightly amended where necessary for accuracy or tone (translator's note).

The first question that arises concerns the function of this dialogue with the self in Golyadkin's spiritual life. The question can be briefly answered thus: The dialogue allows him to substitute his own voice for the voice of another person.

This substituting function of Golyadkin's second voice is felt in everything. Without understanding it we cannot understand his interior dialogues. Golyadkin addresses himself as if addressing another person ("my young friend"), he praises himself as only another person could, and he verbally caresses himself with tender familiarity: "Yakov Petrovich, my dear fellow, you little Golyadka you, what a nice little name you have!"[3] He reassures and encourages himself with the authoritative tone of an older, more self-confident person. But this second voice of Golyadkin's, confident and calmly self-satisfied, cannot possibly merge with his first voice, the uncertain timid one; the dialogue cannot be transformed into the integral and confident monologue of a single Golyadkin. Moreover, that second voice is to such a degree unable to merge with the first, it feels so threateningly independent, that in place of comforting and encouraging tones there begin to appear teasing, mocking, and treacherous ones. With astonishing tact and artistry Dostoevsky transfers—almost imperceptibly to the reader—Golyadkin's second voice from his interior dialogue to the narration itself: it begins to sound like an outside voice, the voice of the narrator.

Golyadkin's second voice must compensate for the inadequate recognition he receives from the other person. Golyadkin wants to get by without such recognition, wants to get by, so to speak, on his own. But this "on his own" inevitably takes the form of "you and I, my friend Golyadkin," that is, it takes dialogic form. In actual fact Golyadkin lives only in another, lives by his reflection in another: "Will it be all right? Is it a proper thing to do?" And this question is always answered from the possible and presumed point of view of another person: Golyadkin will pretend that nothing is the matter, that he just happened to be driving by, and the other person will see that "that's how it must have been." In the reaction of the other person, in his discourse and his response, the whole matter lies. There is no way that the confidence of Golyadkin's second voice can rule all of him, nor

---

[3]The name in Russian suggests *golyada*, "tramp" or "beggar," derived from the adjective *golyi*, "naked, bare" (translator's note).

can it actually take the place of another real person. For him, another's words are the most important thing.

> Although Mr. Golyadkin had said all this [about his independence—M.B.] with the utmost possible distinctness and clarity, confidently, weighing his words and calculating their probable effect, nevertheless it was now with anxiety, with the utmost anxiety, that he gazed at Christian Ivanovich. Now he had become all eyes, and awaited Christian Ivanovich's answer with sad and melancholy impatience (II).

In this second excerpt of interior dialogue, the substituting functions of the second voice are absolutely clear. But here there appears in addition a third voice, the direct voice of the other, interrupting the second merely substitute voice. Thus elements appear here that are completely analogous to those we analyzed elsewhere in Devushkin's speech—words of the other, words partially belonging to the other, and the corresponding accentual interruption:

> Well, it's something strange and queer; just like the Siamese twins, as they call them. . . . Well, why them, the Siamese twins?—all right, they're twins, but even the very greatest people have seemed a bit queer sometimes. Why, even in history, it's well known the famous Suvorov crowed like a cock. . . . Well, but that was all for political reasons; and great generals . . . but why talk about generals? (II).

Everywhere here, but especially where ellipses appear, the anticipated responses of others wedge themselves in. This passage too could be unfolded in the form of a dialogue. But here it is more complex. While in Devushkin's speech a single integrated voice polemicized with the "other person," here there are two voices: one confident, even too confident, and the other too timid, giving in to everything, capitulating totally.[4]

Golyadkin's second voice (the voice substituting for another person), his first voice hiding away from the other's word ("I'm like everyone else"; "I'm all right") and then finally giving in to that other word ("in that case, I'm ready") and, finally, that genuinely other voice forever resounding in him, the three voices are so complexly interrelated that they provide adequate material for the entire intrigue and

[4]There were, as well, rudiments of interior dialogue already in Devushkin.

permit the entire novel to be constructed on them alone. The actual event, namely the unsuccessful courting of Klara Olsufievna and all the circumstances accompanying it, is in fact not represented in the novel at all; they serve only as the stimulus setting inner voices in motion, they make immediate and intensify that inner conflict which is the real object of representation in the novel.

Except for Golyadkin and his double, no other characters take any actual part whatsoever in the intrigue, which unfolds entirely within the bounds of Golyadkin's self-consciousness; the other characters merely provide raw material, add, as it were, the fuel necessary for the intense work of that self-consciousness. The external, intentionally obscure intrigue (everything of importance has already taken place before the novel begins) serves also as a firm, barely discernible frame for Golyadkin's inner intrigue. The novel tells the story of Golyadkin's desire to do without the other's consciousness, to do without recognition by another, his desire to avoid the other and assert his own self, and what resulted from this. Dostoevsky intended *The Double* as a "confession"[5] (not in the personal sense, of course), that is, the representation of an event that takes place within the bounds of self-consciousness. *The Double* is the first dramatized confession in Dostoevsky's work.

At the base of the intrigue, therefore, lies Golyadkin's attempt—in view of the total non-recognition of his personality on the part of others—to find himself a substitute for the other. Golyadkin plays at being an independent person; his consciousness plays at confidence and self-sufficiency. The new and acute experience of collision with another person, at the dinner party where Golyadkin is publicly humiliated, intensifies the split in his personality. Golyadkin's second voice overexerts itself in a desperate simulation of self-sufficiency, in order to save Golyadkin's face. It is impossible for this second voice to merge with Golyadkin; on the contrary, treacherous tones of ridicule grow louder and louder in it. It provokes and teases Golyadkin; it casts off its mask. The double appears. The inner conflict is dramatized; Golyadkin's intrigue with the double begins.

The double speaks in Golyadkin's own words, bringing with him no

[5]In a letter to Michael Dostoevsky, January or February 1847, Dostoevsky writes to his brother: "But soon you shall read *Netochka Nezvanova*. It will be a confession, like *Golyadkin*, although of a different tone and sort."

new words or tones. At first he pretends to be a cringing Golyadkin, Golyadkin surrendering. When Golyadkin brings the double home with him, the latter looks and behaves like the first and uncertain voice in Golyadkin's internal dialogue: "Will it be all right, is it a proper thing to do," and so on.

> The visitor [the double—M.B.] evidently felt highly embarrassed and extremely shy; he humbly followed his host's every movement and caught his every look, apparently trying to guess his thoughts from them. All his gestures expressed something meek, downtrodden, and cowed, so that at that moment he was, if the comparison is permissible, like a man who for want of his own clothes is wearing somebody else's; the sleeves have crept halfway up his arms, the waist is almost round his neck, and he is either constantly tugging at the too-short waistcoat, or sliding away somewhere out of the way, or striving to find somewhere to hide, or looking into everybody's eyes and straining to hear whether people are talking about his plight and laughing at him or ashamed of him; and the poor man blushes, he loses his presence of mind, his pride suffers.... (VII).

This is a characterization of the cringing and self-effacing Golyadkin. The double speaks, too, in the tones and style of Golyadkin's first voice. The part of the second voice—confident and tenderly reassuring in its relation to the double—is played by Golyadkin himself, who this time seems to have merged totally with that voice:

> "Well, you know, Yakov Petrovich, you and I are going to get on well together," said our hero; "you and I, Yakov Petrovich, will get on like a house on fire, we'll live together like brothers; the two of us will be very clever, old chap, very clever we're going to be; we'll be the ones to intrigue against them ... intrigue against them, that's what we'll do. After all, I know you, Yakov Petrovich, I understand what you're like; you blurt out everything straight away, like the honest soul that you are. You just keep away from all of them, old man." (VII).[6]

But later on the roles change: the treacherous double takes over the tone of Golyadkin's second voice, parodically exaggerating its af-

---

[6]Not long before Golyadkin had said the same thing to himself: "That's just like you!... You go plunging in, you're delighted! You guileless creature."

fectionate familiarity. At their very next meeting in the office, the double has already assumed this tone, and he sustains it until the end of the story, now and then himself emphasizing the identity between expressions from his own speech and Golyadkin's words (the words spoken by him during their first conversation). During one of their meetings at the office the double, familiarly poking Golyadkin, said to him:

> ... with a smile full of the most venomous and far-reaching implications: "Oh no, you don't, Yakov Petrovich, my little friend, oh no, you don't. We'll dodge you, Yakov Petrovich, we'll dodge you." (VIII).

Or a little later, before their face to face confrontation in the coffee-house:

> "You've talked me over, my dear boy," said Mr. Golyadkin junior, climbing down from the cab and shamelessly clapping him on the shoulder, "you're such a good sort; for you, Yakov Petrovich, I'm willing to take a side-street (as you so rightly remarked that time, Yakov Petrovich). You're a sly one, you know, you do whatever you like with a man" (XI).

This transferral of words from one mouth to another, where the content remains the same although the tone and ultimate meaning is changed, is a fundamental device of Dostoevsky's. He forces his heroes to recognize themselves, their idea, their own words, their orientation, their gesture in another person, in whom all these phenomena change their integrated and ultimate meaning and take on a different sound, the sound of parody or ridicule. In *Crime and Punishment*, for example, there is one such literal repetition by Svidrigailov (Raskolnikov's partial double) of Raskolnikov's most intimate words, spoken by him to Sonya, a repetition with a meaningful wink. Here is the passage:

> "Ah! you sceptical person!" laughed Svidrigailov. "I told you I had no need of that money. Won't you admit that it's simply done from humanity? She wasn't 'a louse', you know" (he pointed to the corner where the dead woman lay), "was she, like some old pawnbroker woman? Come, you'll agree, is Luzhin to go on living, and doing wicked things or is she to die? And if I didn't help them, Polenka would go the same way."

He said this with an air of a sort of gay winking slyness, keeping his eyes fixed on Raskolnikov, who turned white and cold,
hearing his own phrases, spoken to Sonya. (V, 5)

Almost all of Dostoevsky's major heroes have their partial double in
another person or even in several other people (Stavrogin and Ivan
Karamazov). In his last work Dostoevsky again returned to the device
of fully embodying the second voice, this time, to be sure, on deep and
more subtle grounds. In its externally formal plan Ivan Karamazov's
dialogue with the devil is analogous to those interior dialogues that
Golyadkin conducts with himself and with his double; for all the dissimilarity in situation and in ideological content, essentially one and
the same artistic task is being solved here.

Such is the manner in which Golyadkin's intrigue with his double
unfolds—as the dramatized crisis of his self-consciousness, as a
dramatized confession. The action cannot go beyond the bounds of
self-consciousness, since the *dramatis personae* are no more than isolated elements of that self-consciousness. The actors here are the
three voices into which Golyadkin's voice and consciousness have been
dismantled: his "I for myself," which cannot manage without another
person and without that person's recognition; his fictitious "I for the
other" (reflection in the other), that is, Golyadkin's second substituting voice; and finally, the genuinely other voice which does not recognize Golyadkin and yet is not actually depicted as existing outside
Golyadkin, since there are no other autonomous characters in the
work.[7] What results is a peculiar sort of mystery play or, rather, morality play, in which the actors are not whole people but rather the
spiritual forces battling within them, a morality play, however,
stripped of any formalism or abstract allegorizing.

But who tells the story in *The Double*? What is the positioning of the
narrator and what sort of voice does he have?

In the narration too we do not find a single element that exceeds
the bounds of Golyadkin's self-consciousness, a single word or a single
tone that could not have been part of his interior dialogue with himself or his dialogue with his double. The narrator picks up on Golyadkin's words and thoughts, intensifies the teasing, mocking tones embedded in them, and in these tones portrays Golyadkin's every act,

---

[7]Other autonomous consciousnesses appear only in the novels.

every gesture, every movement. We have already said that Golyadkin's second voice, through imperceptible transitions, merges with
with the voice of the narrator; one gets the impression that the narration is dialogically addressed to Golyadkin himself; it rings in Golyadkin's own ears as another's voice taunting him, as the voice of his
double, although formally the narration is addressed to the reader.

This is how the narrator describes Golyadkin's behavior at the most
fateful moment in his escapades, when he tries, uninvited, to gain
entrance to the ball at Olsufy Ivanovich's:

> Let us rather turn to Mr. Golyadkin, the real and sole hero of
> our true to life story.
>   The fact is that he is now in a position that is, to say the least,
> extremely strange. He is here too, ladies and gentlemen, that is
> to say not at the ball, but almost at the ball; he is all right, ladies
> and gentlemen; he may be on his own, but at this moment he
> stands upon a path that is not altogether straight; he stands
> now—it is strange even to say it—he stands now in the passage
> from the back entrance of Olsufy Ivanovich's flat. But that he is
> standing there means nothing; he is all right. He is standing,
> though, ladies and gentlemen, in a corner, lurking in a much
> darker, if no warmer, place, half concealed by an enormous
> cupboard and an old screen, among every kind of dusty rubbish,
> trash, and lumber, hiding until the proper time and meanwhile
> only watching the progress of the general business in the capac-
> ity of casual looker-on. He is only watching now, ladies and gen-
> tlemen; but, you know, he may also go in, ladies and gentle-
> men . . . why not? He has only to take a step, and he is in, and in
> very neatly (IV).

In the structure of this narration we observe two voices interrupting each other, and the same merging of two rejoinders that we had
earlier observed in the utterances of Makar Devushkin. But here the
roles have changed: here it is as if the other person's rejoinder has
swallowed up the rejoinder of the hero.

The narration [in the text at large] glitters with Golyadkin's own
words: "He is all right,"; "He's on his own," and so on. But these
words are uttered by the narrator with ridicule and somewhat with
reproach, directed at Golyadkin himself and constructed in a form
meant to touch his sore spots and provoke him. The mocking narra-

tion imperceptibly passes over into the speech of Golyadkin himself.
The question "Why not?" belongs to Golyadkin himself, but is given in
the teasing, aggressive intonation of the narrator. Even this intonation, however, is not in essence alien to the consciousness of Golyadkin himself. All this could ring in his own head, as his second voice. In
fact the author could at any point insert quotation marks without
changing the tone, voice, or construction of the sentence.

Somewhat further he does exactly that:

> So there he is now, ladies and gentlemen, waiting for the chance
> to do things quietly, and he has been waiting for exactly two and
> a half hours. Why not wait? Villèle himself used to wait. "But
> what's Villèle got to do with this?" thought Mr. Golyadkin.
> "Who's Villèle, anyhow? And what if I were to . . . just go
> through . . . ? Oh, you bit player, you!" (IV).

But why not insert quotation marks two sentences earlier, before
the words "Why not wait?"—or even earlier, changing the words "So
there he is now, ladies and gentlemen" to "Golyadka, old boy," or
some other form of address by Golyadkin to his own self? Of course,
the quotation marks are not inserted at random. They are inserted in
such a way as to make the transition especially subtle and imperceptible. Villèle's name appears in the narrator's last sentence and in the
hero's first. Golyadkin's words seem to continue the narration unin-
terruptedly and answer it in an interior dialogue: "Villèle himself
used to wait. 'But what's Villèle got to do with this!' " These are, in
fact, detached rejoinders in Golyadkin's interior dialogue with himself: One side entered the narration, the other remained with Golyadkin. A phenomenon has occurred that is quite the reverse of what
we had observed earlier, when we witnessed the interruption-prone
merging of two rejoinders. But the result is the same: a double-voiced,
interruption-prone construction with all the accompanying
phenomena. The field of action is the same, too: a single self-
consciousness. Authority in that consciousness, however, has been
seized by the other's discourse, which has made its home in it.

We shall quote another example with the same vacillating borders
between the narration and the hero's discourse. Golyadkin has made
up his mind and has at last entered the hall where the ball is going on,
and finds himself before Klara Olsufievna:

There is not the slightest doubt he could most gladly have sunk through the floor at that moment without so much as blinking; but what's done can't be undone ... no, indeed it can't. What was he to do? "If things go wrong, stand your ground, if all goes well, stand firm." Mr. Golyadkin, of course, was "not an intriguer, nor was he good at polishing the parquet with his shoes...." Well, now the worst had happened. And besides, the Jesuits were mixed up in it somehow.... However, Mr. Golyadkin had no time for them now! (IV).

The passage is interesting because it contains no grammatically direct discourse belonging to Golyadkin himself, and thus there is no justification for setting off words in quotation marks. The portion of the narration in quotation marks here was set that way, apparently, through a mistake of the editor. Dostoevsky probably set off only the proverb: "If things go wrong, stand your ground; if all goes well, stand firm." The next sentence is given in the third person, although of course it belongs to Golyadkin himself. Further on, the pauses marked by ellipses also belong to Golyadkin's inner speech. The sentences preceding and following these ellipses, judging by their accent, relate to each other as do rejoinders in an interior dialogue. The two adjacent sentences with the Jesuits are completely analogous to the above-quoted sentences on Villèle, set off from each other by quotation marks.

Finally, one more excerpt, where perhaps the opposite mistake was committed: quotation marks were not inserted where grammatically they should have been. Golyadkin, driven from the ball, rushes home through a snowstorm and meets a passerby who later turns out to be his double:

It was not that he feared this might be some bad character, he was simply afraid. "And besides, who knows?"—the thought came unbidden into Mr. Golyadkin's mind—"perhaps this passer-by is—*he*, himself, perhaps he is here and, what matters most, he is not here for nothing, he has a purpose, he is crossing my path, he will brush against me." (V).

Here the ellipsis serves as a dividing line between the narration and Golyadkin's direct inner speech, which is structured in the first person ("*my* path,"; "brush against *me*"). But they are merged so closely here that one really does not want to insert quotation marks. For this sentence, after all, must be read with a single voice, albeit an internally dialogized one. Stunningly successful here is the transition from the narration to the hero's speech: We feel, as it were, the wave of a single speech current, one that carries us without dams or barriers from the narration, into the hero's soul, and out again into the narration; we feel that we are moving essentially within the circle of a single consciousness.

One could cite many more examples proving that the narration is a direct continuation and development of Golyadkin's second voice and that it is addressed dialogically to the hero, but even the above examples are sufficient. The whole work is constructed, therefore, entirely as an interior dialogue of three voices within the limits of a single dismantled consciousness. Every essential aspect of it lies at a point of intersection of these three voices, at a point where they abruptly, agonizingly interrupt one another. Invoking our image, we could say that this is not yet polyphony, but no longer homophony. One and the same word, idea, or phenomenon is passed through three voices and in each voice sounds different. The same set of words, tones, and inner orientations is passed through the outer speech of Golyadkin, through the speech of the narrator and through the speech of the double, and these three voices are turned to face one another, they speak not about each other but with each other. Three voices sing the same line, but not in unison; rather, each carries its own part.

But these voices have not become fully independent real voices, they are not yet three autonomous consciousnesses. This occurs only in Dostoevsky's novels. In *The Double* there is no monologic discourse gravitating solely toward itself and its referential object. Each word is dismantled dialogically, each word contains an interruption of voices, but there is not yet an authentic dialogue of unmerged consciousnesses such as will later appear in the novels. Already, the rudiments of counterpoint are here: it is implied in the very structure of the discourse. The analyses of the sort we have offered here are already, as it were, contrapuntal analyses (speaking figuratively, of course). But these new connections have not yet gone beyond the bounds of monologic material.

Relentlessly ringing in Golyadkin's ears are the provocative and mocking voice of the narrator and the voice of the double. The narrator shouts into Golyadkin's ear Golyadkin's own words and thoughts, but in another, hopelessly alien, hopelessly censuring and mocking tone. This second voice is present in every one of Dostoevsky's heroes, and in his final novel, as we have said, it again takes on an independent existence. The devil shouts into Ivan Karamazov's ear Ivan's very own words, commenting mockingly on his decision to confess in court and repeating in an alien tone his most intimate thoughts. We shall not take up here the actual dialogue between Ivan and the devil. But we shall quote the passage immediately following this dialogue, Ivan's agitated story to Alyosha. Its structure is analogous to the structure of *The Double*. The same principle obtains for combining voices, although to be sure everything here is deeper and more complex. In this story Ivan passes his own personal thoughts and decisions simultaneously through two voices, he transmits them in two different tonalities. In the quoted excerpt we omit Alyosha's side of the dialogue, for his real voice does not yet fit into our scheme. What interests us now is only the intra-atomic counterpoint of voices, their combination solely within the bounds of a single dismantled consciousness (that is, a microdialogue).

"He's been teasing me. And you know he does it so cleverly, so cleverly. 'Conscience! What is conscience! I make it up for myself. Why am I tormented by it? From habit. From the universal habit of mankind for seven thousand years. So let us give it up, and we shall be gods.' It was he who said that, it was he who said that!"

"Yes, but he is spiteful. He laughed at me. He was impudent, Alyosha," Ivan said, with a shudder of offense. "But he was unfair to me, unfair to me about lots of things. He told lies about me to my face. 'Oh, you are going to perform an act of heroic virtue: to confess you murdered your father, that the lackey murdered him at your instigation.'"

"That's what he says, he, and he knows it. 'You are going to perform an act of heroic virtue, and you don't believe in virtue; that's what tortures you and makes you angry, that's why you are so vindictive.' He said that to me about me and he knows what he says. . . ."

"Yes, he knows how to torment one. He's cruel," Ivan went on, unheeding. "I had an inkling from the first what he came for. 'Granting that you go through pride, still you had a hope that Smerdyakov might be convicted and sent to Siberia, and

Mitya would be acquitted, while you would only be punished with *moral* condemnation' ('Do you hear?' he laughed then)— 'and some people will praise you. But now Smerdyakov's dead, he has hanged himself, and who'll believe you alone? But yet you are going, you are going, you'll go all the same, you've decided to go. What are you going for now?' That's awful, Alyosha. I can't endure such questions. Who dare ask me such questions?" (IV, 11, x).

All the loopholes in Ivan's thoughts, all his sideward glances at another's words and another's consciousness, all his attempts to get around the other's words and to replace them in his soul with an affirmation of his own self, all the reservations of his conscience that serve to interrupt his every thought, his every word and experience, condense and thicken here into the completed replies of the devil. Ivan's words and the devil's replies do not differ in content but only in tone, only in accent. But this change of accent changes their entire ultimate meaning. The devil, as it were, transfers to the main clause what had been for Ivan merely a subordinate clause, uttered under his breath and without independent accent, and the content of the main clause he makes into an unaccented subordinate clause. Ivan's reservation concerning the main motive for his decision is transformed by the devil into the main motive, and the main motive becomes merely a reservation. What results is a combination of voices that is highly intense and maximally eventful, which at the same time is not dependent on any opposition in content or plot.

But of course this full dialogization of Ivan's consciousness is—as is always the case with Dostoevsky—prepared for in a leisurely fashion. The other's discourse gradually, stealthily penetrates the consciousness and speech of the hero: now in the form of a pause where one would not be appropriate in monologically confident speech; now in the form of someone else's accent breaking up the sentence; now in the form of an abnormally heightened, exaggerated, or anguished personal tone, and so on. From Ivan's first words and from his entire inner orientation in Zosima's cell, through his conversations with Alyosha, with his father, and especially with Smerdyakov before his departure to Chermashnya, and finally through his three meetings with Smerdyakov after the murder, this process of gradual dialogic dismantling of Ivan's consciousness stretches out, a process more pro-

found and ideologically complicated than was the case with Golyadkin, but structurally fully analogous to it.

Someone else's voice whispering into the ear of the hero his own
words with a displaced accent and the resulting unrepeatably unique
combination of varidirectional words and voices within a single word,
a single speech, the intersection of two consciousnesses in a single
consciousness—in one form or another, to one degree or another, in
one ideological direction or another—all this is present in every work
of Dostoevsky's.

The Petersburg Feuilletons

by Joseph Frank

Dostoevsky's chronic indebtedness in the 1840s not only forced him to write more rapidly than he would have liked, and to hurry the completion of work that should have matured; it also impelled him to keep a sharp eye on the literary marketplace, and to snap up any assignments that could bring a little extra cash. In the winter of 1847, we find him doing editorial work for an encyclopedia and complaining about the difficulty of correcting in galley proof an article about the Jesuits. Dostoevsky evidently had a special interest in the history and character of this Roman Catholic order, whose worldwide influence was later to become one of his persistent obsessions. Earlier, in the spring of the same year, he had picked up a more important assignment from the *St. Petersburg Gazette*. The writer who regularly supplied the feuilletons for this newspaper died unexpectedly; and the editor hastily filled the gap by appealing to some of the young St. Petersburg literati to furnish him with copy. Aleksey Pleshcheev wrote one for the issue of April 13, and it was perhaps through him that Dostoevsky learned of this journalistic opportunity. The next four feuilletons, signed F. D., were written by Dostoevsky himself.

These feuilletons completely vanished from sight after their ephemeral appearance, and were only unearthed and republished in the 1920s. Why Dostoevsky did not later himself reprint these four extremely interesting specimens of his early journalism is difficult to say; we shall offer a possible reason farther on. It could not have been, however, that the mature novelist was ashamed of having once turned his hand to a demeaning journalistic task. All the up-and-coming young talents of the Natural School—Grigorovich, Panaev, Turgenev,

"The Petersburg Feuilletons" by Joseph Frank. From *Dostoevsky: The Seeds of Revolt, 1821–1849*. Copyright © 1976 by Princeton University Press, Princeton, N. J. Reprinted in slightly abridged form by permission.

Goncharov, Sollogub, Pleshcheev—also wrote feuilletons, and Dostoevsky was simply joining a general literary trend. He had already written one such article for the ill-fated *Jester*, and had compared his own sprightliness and humor with Balzac's Lucien de Rubempré, who became the toast of Paris overnight after dashing off a brilliant piece that became the prototype of the new genre. Balzac's *Illusions perdues*, published in 1843, had glorified the feuilleton as a form created to capture all the glitter, excitement and variety of Parisian social-cultural life. Eagerly on the alert for the latest literary novelties, the younger Russian writers immediately adopted it as a vehicle for their own self-expression.

The invention of the feuilleton in France had been stimulated by a new, popular mass-circulation press which served as a medium of publicity and could influence the success or failure of books, plays, operas, and public spectacles of all kinds. Originally, the feuilleton had been simply a column of information about all such cultural novelites; but it quickly developed into the form of the modern book or theater review. Lucien de Rubempré's famous column was a scintillating account of a new play in which a young actress, his future mistress, was making her first important appearance. The feuilleton, however, in branching out to describe urban types and social life, also gave birth to the physiological sketch. Once the taste for such sketches had caught on, it occurred to Frédéric Soulié to unite them week by week with a loose narrative line; and this was the origin of the feuilleton-novel.

It is difficult to distinguish the feuilleton from the physiological sketch in any clear-cut fashion. One can say that the former is less marked by the ambition to portray the life of a particular social environment, and allows more freedom for the writer to roam wherever his fancy pleases and to display his personality. A lesser French practitioner, Nestor Roqueplan, spoke of "ce droit de bavardage" that, in his view, gave the feuilleton its special charm.[1] The writer of feuilletons ordinarily used this privilege to indulge in lyrical effusions and pseudo-personal "confessions"; and these created an atmosphere of intimacy between writer and reader that became a stylistic convention. Indeed, as we learn from Belinsky, the persona of the feuilletonist was

---

[1]Cited in V. L. Komarovich, "Peterburgskie feletony Dostoevskogo," in *Feletony sorokovykh godov*, ed. Iu. Oksman (Moscow–Leningrad, 1930), p. 93.

always understood to be highly conventional and stylized. The writer of a feuilleton, he says, is "a chatterer, apparently good-natured and sincere, but in truth often malicious and evil-tongued, someone who knows everything, sees everything, keeps quiet about a good deal but definitely manages to express everything, stings with epigrams and insinuations, and amuses with a lively and clever word as well as a childish joke."[2]

These words fit the personality assumed by the young Dostoevsky to the life. At first sight, his feuilletons may seem little more than unpretentious familiar essays, leaping from topic to topic solely according to the whimsical moods of the narrator. Depictions of Petersburg life and landscape, sketches of various social types, reflections and reminiscences, the stereotyped purveyance of the latest cultural tidings—all the standard ingredients are there, thrown together haphazardly to distract the casual reader. But the moment one reads a little less casually, it is evident that the feuilletons mean much more than they appear to say. With all their reticences and sly evasions, they do "definitely manage to express everything" (or at least a good deal) of what was preoccupying Dostoevsky—and many others like him—in the spring of 1847.

Nobody reading Dostoevsky's first feuilleton could have any doubt that its author was very much dissatisfied with the existing arrangement of social–political life in his fatherland. It is quite evident that he is smarting under the total lack of freedom in Russia to be informed about, and to discuss, matters of "public interest" for every thinking citizen. This point is made immediately in the sketch of two Petersburgers venturing into the street to welcome the arriving spring, and greeting each other after the long winter hiatus. The first question they invariably ask is "What's the news?"; and at this point the Petersburg chronicler notes a curious phenomenon. There is, he says, always "a piercing feeling of desolation in the sound of their voices, whatever the intonation with which they have begun their conversation." No explanation is offered for such a strangely despondent mood, which hardly suits the time of year; but Dostoevsky's reader, accustomed to the Aesopian language of Russian journalism,

[2]Cited in V. S. Nechaeva, *V. G. Belinskii*, 4 vols. (Leningrad, 1949–1962), vol. 4, p. 298.

would understand very well that the question was asked hopelessly because no answer of any interest could possibly be forthcoming: there was just no "news" of any kind worth talking about. Nonetheless, the question continues to be asked "as if some sort of propriety requires [Russians] also to participate in something involving society and to have public interests."

This vivid sketch is a good example of one of the techniques of insinuation that Dostoevsky uses—the device of what may be called the "unexplained enigma," to which the knowing reader supplies the proper solution. To make doubly sure that his readers get the point in this instance, Dostoevsky also uses hyperbolic irony to satirize the usual function of a feuilletonist—which was to supply "news" about public entertainment as a substitute for more substantial and potentially dangerous fare. "But I am a feuilletonist, gentlemen," exclaims the chronicler, "I must tell you about the latest news, the newest, most *thrilling*—it is fitting to use this time-honored epithet, no doubt invented in the hope that the Petersburg reader will tremble with joy at some sort of thrilling news, for example, that *Jenny Lind* has left for London." Each time that Dostoevsky refers to his conventional obligations as a feuilletonist to provide such "news," his tone is invariably one of withering scorn.[3]

Not only does Dostoevsky protest, in his first feuilleton, against the lack of a free press in Russia; he also alludes in the same fashion to the lack of free speech, the complete impossibility of any public discussion of vital social–political issues. "It is well-known," writes the chronicler, "that all Petersburg is nothing other than a collection of small circles, each of which has its statutes, its decorum, its laws, its logic, and its oracle." He wonders, with a knowing naiveté, why such "circles" are "so much a product of the [Russian] national character, which is still somewhat shy of public life and looks homeward." The answer provided is necessarily evasive, but could hardly have been misunderstood—life in a "circle" is "more natural, skill is not required, it is more peaceful. In a 'circle' you receive a bold answer to the question— *What's the news?*" In other words, one speaks more

---

[3]All citations from Dostoevsky's Petersburg feuilletons (1847) are from the Russian. See Dostoevskii, "Peterburgskaia letopis'," *Polnoe sobranie khudozhestvennykh proizvedenii*, ed. V. Tomashevskii and K. Khalabaev, 13 vols. (Moscow–Leningrad, 1926–1930), vol. XIII, pp. 8–32.

freely in a circle, one relaxes in relative security without having to worry about spies and informers.

Life in "circles" is thus a Russian device to carry on some sort of social-political life in the absence of civil freedoms enjoyed elsewhere; but it is, at best, only a feeble substitute for the real thing. One type of "circle"—the chronicler calls it "patriarchal"—exists, in any case, solely to provide a place where its members can talk cynically and amusedly, and conversation there never gets past "gossip or a yawn." There are, however, other "circles"—evidently those of the progressive intelligentsia—in which "a group of educated and well-intentioned pe·'ple . . . with inexplicable enthusiasm interpret various important matters" and come to general agreement "about several generally useful questions." But then, after the first upsurge of excitement, "the whole 'circle' falls into a kind of irritation, into a kind of unpleasant enfeeblement," and gradually sinks into a state of cynicism much like that of the "patriarchal" assemblage. There is no way for Russians to participate actively in the social-political affairs of their country; and this, as the chronicler intimates here for the first time, helps to explain a good deal about the Russian character.

It explains, for one thing, the kind of person who flourishes in "circles," and who is the bane of existence there for others. "You know this gentleman very well, gentlemen," the chronicler observes to his readers. "His name is legion. This is the gentleman with *a good heart*, and possessing nothing but *a good heart*." Actually, though he spends his time assuring all and sundry of his sterling moral qualities, this gentleman is a consummate egotist and perfectly oblivious of the rest of humanity. The comment of the chronicler about such a type already reveals Dostoevsky's sharp eye for—and intense dislike of—the "liberal" affectation of moral compassion that he would later pillory so brilliantly. Such a man, writes the chronicler, does not even suspect that "his hidden treasure, his good heart, can be ground and polished into a precious, sparkling, and genuine diamond" only when he begins to identify his interests "with those of society," only when he "shows sympathy for society as a whole."

Dostoevsky's portrait of the gentleman with "a good heart" is the first of a series of such derisive character sketches that take up most of the remainder of this feuilleton. Each deals with a personality who, behind a façade of virtue, conceals some defect of character or some form of vice. At this point Dostoevsky drops the technique of irony he has been using up to now—the technique of the *faux naif* so beloved of eighteenth century satirists, the *naif* whose incomprehension of what he sees enables the reader to see much more clearly—and shifts to that of simulated identification with what is being satirized. The Natural School had devoted itself to delineating much of Russian life precisely in terms of the contrast between a glittering surface of impeccable virtue and an underside of vicious corruption. What Dostoevsky now does is to *identify himself*, as chronicler, with the *opponents* of the Natural School, who were furiously protesting against its scandalous attempt to expose the injustices of Russian life. And while pretending to speak in the name and from the point of view of such critics, he cleverly makes his own contribution to the genre of social muckraking they were attacking by relying on innuendo and hyperbole to convey his real meaning.

"Good Lord!" the chronicler exclaims. "Where are the old villains of the old melodrama and novels, gentlemen? How pleasant it was when they were about in the world! It was pleasant because instantly, right at hand, was the most kindhearted of all men, who of course defended innocence and punished wickedness. That villain, that *tiranno ingrato*, was born a villain, ready-made in accordance with some secret and utterly incomprehensible predestination of fate. Everything in him was the personification of evil." In those happy days, there was no gap between appearance and reality; good and evil were clearly delimited, and no confusion between them was possible. But now, alas, "you are somehow suddenly faced with the fact that the most virtuous man, a man, besides, who is quite incapable of committing a crime, suddenly appears to be a perfect villain without even being aware of it himself." Even more, such a man lives and dies "honored and exalted" by all who knew him; quite often he is sincerely and tenderly mourned even "by his own victims."

As an example of this type of man, who is unforgivably now being slandered, the chronicler instances "my good friend Julian Mastakovich, a former well-wisher and even to some extent a benefactor of mine." Julian Mastakovich is a character in two of Dostoevsky's short stories; and he is here given a nonfictional existence, we may assume, because of the "confessional" convention of the form. Poor

Julian Mastakovich, a high bureaucratic official, is a man with a problem. He is about to marry, at the ripe age of fifty, a charming and perfectly unspoiled girl of seventeen; but he is troubled by the difficulty he may have in continuing to visit the apartment of a handsome widow, whom for the last two years he has been benevolently helping to conduct a lawsuit. The chronicler sympathizes with his dilemma, though he does not conceal his envy. How nice to have found such a charming young bride to console one's declining years!

Another example of the same type of eminently respectable person, who for some inexplicable reason has begun to be portrayed in the most unfavorable light, is culled by the chronicler from the pages of a recent story in the *Notes of the Fatherland*.[4] One episode, which Dostoevsky singles out for the attention of his readers, recounts the accidental breaking of a mirror at a children's party in the absence of the master of the house, a low-grade Moscow civil servant of unimpeachable respectability. "Ivan Kirilovich is a good man," the chronicler assures us; but he is also a petty family tyrant and a drunkard to boot, who tortures his ailing and long-suffering wife by his uncontrollable temper. The broken mirror predictably leads to a storm, and "a month later [the wife] dies of consumption . . . a kind of Dickensian charm fills the description of the last moments of the gentle, obscure life of that woman."

Biographers have of course seen in Ivan Kirilovich a reminiscence of Dostoevsky's father, especially since the chronicler remarks that the story "brought back many things to my mind! . . . I personally knew a man like Ivan Kirilovich. There are lots of them everywhere." Whether this assertion means any more than the similar reference to Julian Mastakovich is difficult to say; such claims of personal acquaintance in a feuilleton cannot be taken too literally. But even if we assume that Dostoevsky was struck by this story because he was reminded of his father, it is more important to note that he sees Ivan Kirilovich, not so much as an individual, but as a type. His father, that is, had now become fused in his sensibility with a whole class of similar

---

[4]This work has been identified as *Sboyev*, by A. Nestroyev. The name is a pseudonym for P. N. Kudryavtsev, a friend of Belinsky, who later became Professor of History at the University of Moscow. Belinsky commented on the same character and scene that Dostoevsky had also singled out. Belinsky, *Selected Philosophical Works* (Moscow, 1948), p. 477.

individuals, whose domestic cruelties were being exposed by the Natural School as a widespread social abuse. Dostoevsky's resentment against his father for having maltreated his mother—if we believe such resentment to have existed—was no longer a purely personal trauma festering in the depths of his subconscious; it has now become part of all the moral-social evils that were being attacked by the literary school to which he belonged.

In closing this first feuilleton, Dostoevsky appends some remarks on the past literary season which epitomize the procedure he has used throughout—oblique social criticism, combined with a disparagement of the traditional function of a Petersburg chronicler. "Gogol's book created a great deal of noise at the beginning of the winter," he remarks casually. "It's especially noteworthy that almost all newspapers and journals agreed about it, even those whose ideas continually contradict each other." The book referred to is Gogol's ill-starred *Selected Passages from My Correspondence with Friends*, which had been unanimously condemned for its glorification of all the existing institutions of Russia (including serfdom) as God-given and sacred. Dostoevsky thus indicates, by this concluding reference, the underlying moral–social evil of Russian life infecting all the rest; and he then shifts into a mockery of his obligation to be informative about the social season—a mockery whose words take on a special edge just after the reference to serfdom. "Sorry, I forgot the most important things . . . Ernst is giving still another concert; this occasion will be a benefit for the Home Aid Society for the Poor and the German Beneficial Society."

To a large extent, Dostoevsky's second feuilleton merely picks up and elaborates certain themes already begun in the first. It opens with a lengthy—far too lengthy—variation on the topic of the lack of "news" in Russian life and its deleterious effects on social behavior. One result is that a person who has "some kind of news in store, not yet known to anybody, and above all possessing the talent of narrating it agreeably," is someone of great importance in Petersburg. The most unlikely people—people who, under ordinary circumstances, would never get past the lackey at the door—are allowed to penetrate into closely guarded inner sanctums so long as they have "news." And the chronicler portrays the doglike servility of such personages, as well as

the condescending tolerance of those on whom they dance atten-
dance; each flatters the vanity of the other quite self-consciously, and
both are perfectly content. "Duplicity, concealment, masks—agreed,
its a nasty affair; but if at the present moment everybody appeared in
public as they really are, my God! it would be even worse."

This contrast between appearance and reality is then illustrated by
the chronicler in a very daring manner. For Dostoevsky now returns
to the theme he had already alluded to in mentioning Gogol's book—
the theme of serfdom; and this of course was a very ticklish matter.
To refer to such a subject directly was naturally impossible, and the
chronicler takes a very circuitous route to reach his destination. Once
again the technique adopted is that of ironical identification—this
time an identification, not with the opponents of the Natural School,
but with the kind of people who feel no need at all to gather in
"circles," and who seem perfectly satisfied with things as they are. "I
am sometimes even ready to burst into song from sheer joy," the
chronicler declares, "when entering some social gathering and seeing
such well-bred and respectable people sitting and discussing something decorously without at the same time losing a jot of their dignity."

For all his ecstasy, however, the chronicler admits that it is often
very difficult for him to grasp what is being discussed by such eminently seemly upper-class people. "Goodness only knows what they
talk about! Something, no doubt, quite inexplicably charming, for
they are all such charming and respectable men of the world, but it is
difficult to grasp all the same. . . . Occasionally you get the impression
that they were talking about some highly serious subjects, something
calling for thought; but afterward when you ask yourself what they
were talking about, you simply cannot find an answer: was it about
gloves, the state of agriculture, or about whether 'a woman's love is
lasting'? So that, I confess, sometimes I am overcome by a feeling of
melancholy." To help his reader understand the reason for such a
feeling, apparently so inappropriate in some delightful company, the
chronicler has recourse to an extended comparison—every word of
which, we may be sure, was carefully chosen.

Imagine, he says, that you hear the captivating music of a gay
fancy-dress ball sounding from some stately residence filled with light
and laughter and the bustle of society. You listen "elated, excited, a

desire for something has stirred in you, an aspiration. You seem to have heard life; and yet all you carry away with you is only a pale, colorless motif, an idea, a shadow, almost nothing. And you pass by as though distrusting something; you are hearing something else, you hear—sounding through the pale motif of our everyday life—another note, piercingly alive and sad, like Berlioz's ball at the Capulets.[5] Anguish and misgiving gnaw and tear at your heart *like the anguish that lies in the endless refrain of the despondent Russian song that rings out in such a native, familiar tone*" (italics added). Then follows this quotation from a poem:

Listen, . . . Others sounds are heard . . .
Sounds of despondent, desperate revelry.
Is it a highwayman singing there,
Or a maiden weeping in the sad hour of parting?
No, it is haymakers homeward bound. . . .

This passage is a superb illustration of Belinsky's point that a feuilletonist could "definitely manage to express everything" in the midst of what seems like inconsequential chatter. For Dostoevsky here is pointing his finger at the greatest moral-social blight on Russian society, and scornfully condemning those who nonetheless continue, with an untroubled conscience, to lead their dignified, civilized, self-satisfied lives. The juxtaposition of the fancy-dress ball with the peasant "revelers" speaks for itself; so does the "anguish and misgiving" that gnaw at the heart of the chronicler, and the "melancholy" that overcomes him while attending the festive gatherings of polite society. For the "reality" of Russian life is to be found, not in the social rituals of the ruling strata, but in the suffering and heartbreak of the enslaved peasantry.

Both of the topics so far broached in this second feuilleton are, it is clear, developments of themes which have already appeared in the one preceding. But there is also a third theme anticipating what is to come later—the theme of Petersburg as a symbol of Russian enlightenment and Russian assimilation of European progress. Descriptions of Petersburg, as we have mentioned, were part of the feuil-

---

[5]Berlioz conducted a number of concerts in St. Petersburg during the late winter of 1847, and included parts of his new Romeo and Juliet symphony in the program.

letonist's stock-in-trade; and Dostoevsky scatters them through his articles with a fairly liberal hand. Such urban landscapes are invariably in the gray and depressing tonality of the Natural School, which concentrated on the inclemencies of the Petersburg climate and the shabby squalor in whose midst its poorer inhabitants dwelled. The architectural glories of the Palmyra of the North (as earlier poets liked to call the city) are reduced to an image of "huge, damp walls . . . marbles, bas-reliefs, statues, columns which . . . shivered and chattered with the damp cold." What the chronicler picks out for notice is a tired and hungry cab horse, a funeral procession gloomily making its way through the streets with "strained, mournful faces" peeping from the carriages, passersby "looking pale green and stern, terribly angry with something." Even the Petersburg spring is compared to a sickly young girl, ailing and tubercular, whose cheeks suddenly flame into life and beauty for one moment only to fade the very next day.

At first glance, it might seem as if Dostoevsky would have nothing good to say for the city, which appears only as an inhuman and oppressive environment ruled by the crushing might of the Bronze Horseman and his descendants in the seats of power. But, like other westerners of the 1840s, Dostoevsky's attitude toward Petersburg was ambiguous: the city was not only the nerve center of tyranny and despotism, it was also, compared to Moscow, the symbol of Russia's desire to absorb Western progress and enlightenment; and it is in this latter guise that it shows up at the end of the second feuilleton. For here the chronicler compares Petersburg to the young, rather naughty son of an old-fashioned country gentleman who is himself quite content to vegetate in his comfortable, patriarchal existence. He wants his son, however, to "become a young European," even though he has heard about "enlightenment" only through rumor. But when the son throws himself into the process with noticeable enthusiasm, the old gentleman exhibits alarm at the foreign exterior and spendthrift ways of his offspring, "grumbles, becomes angry, [and] condemns both enlightenment and the West." Petersburg thus appears in a new guise and a much more favorable light; and Dostoevsky develops this theme at length in the next article.

Dostoevsky's third feuilleton stands somewhat apart from the others, and is much less intimately confidential and unbuttoned in manner. Abandoning the motley of the amuser and satirist, the chronicler dons the more dignified garb of the cultural commentator and makes his own modest contribution to the Western–Slavophil controversy then raging in Russian culture. Dostoevsky's little article can scarcely compete with the much weightier ones written by Belinsky and Herzen on the same subject at much the same time; but it is of great interest as the only semi-conceptual formulation of his ideas at this period. Some of these ideas are so much at variance with his later convictions that, if he ever went back to read this feuilleton, he must have regarded it with a shudder of distaste as a glaring example of the aberrations of his youth. Perhaps this is why he never resurrected his four pieces, and allowed them to remain buried in the files of the *St. Petersburg Gazette*.

The chronicler begins his reflections with a picture of the empty city vacated for the summer, and filled now only with workmen cleaning and rebuilding the winter-worn metropolis. "A fine, thick layer of white dust hangs in the torrid air," and the pedestrian "*flâneur* or spectator," is advised not to venture into the Nevsky Prospect "if he does not have the serious desire to resemble the Pierrot of the Roman carnival who is doused with flour." How, then, is a person who remains in the city to occupy his time? Well, he can, for example, look around at the architecture, "an important occupation, and even, truly, an educational one."

This thought recalls to the mind of the chronicler that, some time ago, he "had happened to read a French book entirely given over to contemporary conditions in Russia." What book is being referred to has never been satisfactorily established (my own candidate is the famous work of the Marquis de Custine, *La Russie en 1839*); but Dostoevsky culls from its pages some uncomplimentary remarks about Petersburg architecture. The chronicler recalls this acerbic French view as being that "there [was] nothing there particularly striking, *nothing national*, and the whole city [was] just a ridiculous caricature of several European capitals." On the other hand, the cultivated French tourist "is lavish in his praise of Moscow because of the Kremlin, utters a few florid, rhetorical phrases about it, and is gratified by how much nationality he finds in Moscow."

Waxing merry over this search by the foreign visitor for visible signs of the Russian soul, the chronicler ridicules his dislike of droshkys "because they diverge from the old, patriarchal wagonette, thus testifying to the manner in which everything indigenous and national in Russia disappears." But the chronicler's target turns out to be, not so much the visiting tourist himself, as those in Russia who adopt a similar point of view. For, he notes, such ideas "coincide with some—we shall not say Russian—but idle ideas of our own, conceived in the study." This is of course an allusion to the Slavophils, who are also delineated as those who search for Russian nationality in "a dead letter, an outworn idea, a heap of stones [the Kremlin] presumably recalling ancient Rus, and, finally, in a blind unconditional reversion to a slumbering native antiquity."

For the chronicler, this identification of Russian nationality with the Kremlin may have been true in the past; but it hardly exists any longer in the present. "It [the Kremlin] is an antiquarian rarity that you look at with special curiosity and with great reverence; but why it should be the height of nationality—that is beyond my understanding! There are some national monuments which outlive their time and cease to be national";—presumably the Kremlin belongs in this category. Even going so far as to deny that the Kremlin serves as a focal point for the religious-national feelings of the Russian people, he points out that they flock to other monasteries as well, and to foreign places of devotion such as Mt. Athos and Jerusalem. And do the Russian people, he asks, really know much more about their history than the names of Dimitry Donskoy, Ivan the Terrible, and Boris Godunov? Such arguments reveal to what extreme Dostoevsky was prepared to go in order to counter the Slavophil position.

Like a good Westerner, of course, he takes the opposite tack and celebrates the new capital over the old. It is no doubt true, the chronicler concedes, that Petersburg architecture is a chaos and a medley of styles, and that "much may furnish nourishment for caricature; but for all that, everything is life and movement." Petersburg is full of dust and plaster because it is still in the process of being built; "its future is still an idea; but this idea belongs to Peter the Great," and it is taking on flesh and blood and growing every day. Indeed, the medley of architectural styles in the city "all together recall the history of the European life of Petersburg and of all Russia." Petersburg is the living symbol of Peter's "great idea," and it supports and activates everything vital in the country—"industry, trade, science, literature, civilization, the principle and the organization of social life." Nor does this assimilation of Western culture, contrary to the fears of its opponents, involve any surrender to a foreign principle or way of life. "No, we do not see the disappearance of nationality in the contemporary effort, but rather the triumph of nationality, which, in my opinion, will not succumb so easily to European influence as many believe."

For all his pro-Westernism, we see that Dostoevsky is by no means willing to follow Maikov in rejecting nationality as a value. On the contrary, Dostoevsky's visceral nationalism is quite evident in the feuilleton, and sets up a perceptible tension between his ideas and his feelings. For while his main aim is to belabor the Slavophils, he does not miss the occasion to take a xenophobic sideswipe against foreigners who fail to understand Russia because "we stubbornly have refused up to now to be measured by the European standard." Frenchmen in particular refuse to recognize "anything not-French, either in art, literature or science, not even in the history of a people, and, most important, [they are] capable of flying into a rage because there exists some sort of other people with their own history, their idea, their national character and their development." This emphasis on Russian historical "uniqueness" is very close to Slavophilism, even though thrown out in the midst of an anti-Slavophil polemic. Herzen, with his usual aphoristic brilliance, wrote of the Slavophils in *My Past and Thoughts* that "like Janus, or the two-headed eagle, they and we [the Westerners] looked in different directions while one heart throbbed in us";[6] and this was already beginning to be true in the late 1840s.

Still, in 1847 Dostoevsky differs sharply from the later view he expressed of the relation between the people and the educated class. As we have just seen, Dostoevsky desired nothing more fervently than the liberation of the serfs and was deeply troubled by the suffering of the people. But, for all his nationalism, he had not yet accepted the Slavophil view of the Russian people as endowed with any extraordinary moral qualities and virtues. "What are the people?" asks the chronicler. "The people are ignorant and uneducated," and they look for leadership "to society, to the educated class." This is exactly the reverse of what Dostoevsky would say after Siberia, when he advised

[6]Alexander Herzen, *My Past and Thoughts*, trans. by Constance Garnett, revised by Humphrey Higgens, 4 vols. (New York, 1968), vol. 2, p. 549.

the educated class to look for guidance to the people. It is thus the intelligentsia who must lead the people along the path hewn out, with a giant hand, by Peter the Great, to the fulfillment of "his great idea."

Finishing off the third feuilleton with a general celebration of the intellectual and cultural activity of Petersburg in the past winter season, Dostoevsky continues the motif of the "great idea" embodied in the city and its key role as the crucible of Russian culture. As a footnote to this survey of the cultural scene, the chronicler praises the illustrations in a new edition of *Dead Souls* (also singled out for favorable comment by Valerian Maikov), and remarks that "in truth, it would be difficult to find a more auspicious time than the present for the appearance of a caricaturist-*artist*." The italicizing of this last word is quite significant. For to be an artist, in Dostoevsky's terminology, means precisely to transcend caricature in the direction of the "humanization" that Maikov had declared to be the source of aesthetic appeal. There can be little doubt that Dostoevsky was defining himself and his own artistic ambitions in lauding the illustrator who managed to hold a balance between these two conflicting tendencies.

If Dostoevsky's first three feuilletons are of great interest because of the information they supply about his ideas and attitudes in general, the fourth is of particular significance because it provides a partial self-commentary on his literary work. Here Dostoevsky returns to the important theme he had approached gingerly in his first feuilleton—the theme of how the oppressive conditions of Russian life influence the Russian character—and develops it in a very illuminating fashion. For it is these conditions, the chronicler now suggests, that create the type of characters we find portrayed in Dostoevsky's fiction of the same period.

Written in early June, this fourth feuilleton evokes the yearly exodus from the city of all those who, like the chronicler and his friends, are able to enjoy the pastoral delights of the countryside. But the chronicler immediately suggests that true relaxation and *dolce far niente* are not for the likes of himself and his readers (now presumed to be members of the intelligentsia). For, he says, Russians of this kind always carry with them the blighting pall of "analysis and comparison, a skeptical outlook, a secret thought, and always the obligation of some eternal, never-ending everyday task," that ubiquitous and inescapable "task" which haunted educated Russians trying to take a rural holiday in 1847.

This manifest incapacity of Russians—more exactly, a certain kind of Russian—to benefit emotionally from their sojourn in the bosom of nature, leads the chronicler to diagnose their situation a little more at length. Why should Russians have developed this "most unpleasant characteristic" of continual self-analysis and eternal dissatisfaction with life? The answer, he suggests, is that they "are tormented by a desire for external, spontaneous activity which they cannot satisfy." Indeed, this passion "for some sort of activity reaches a point of feverish and uncontrollable impatience; we all long for some serious occupation, many of us are full of evident desire to do good"; but all this pent-up emotion leads nowhere. "The trouble is that if anything has to be done we only become aware of it, as it were, from the outside. . . . Russians do things badly and sloppily because we do not really care how they are done." Why should they care, in other words, when their lives are completely in the hands of an all-powerful government which does not even allow them the right publicly to discuss its fiats?

As a result, Russian life does not cultivate any sense of inner discipline in the individual, or encourage a feeling of personal responsibility. And Dostoevsky then describes, in an extremely important passage, the psychological consequences of this unhappy situation. "When a man is dissatisfied, when he is unable to express himself and reveal what is best in him (not out of vanity, but because of the most natural necessity to become aware of, to embody and to fulfill his Ego in real life), he at once falls into some quite incredible situation; one, if I may say so, takes to the bottle in a big way; another becomes a gambler and cardsharp; another a quarrelsome bully; another, finally, goes off his head because of *ambition*,[7] at the same time completely despising ambition and even suffering because he has had to suffer over such nonsense as ambition." All this leads Dostoevsky to "an almost unfair, offensive *but seemingly very probable* conclusion," namely, that Russians "have little sense of personal dignity" and very little of what he calls "necessary egoism."

---

[7]The Russian word *ambitsia* does not have the same neutral meaning as its English synonym. In Russian, the word has the pejorative sense of self-love, pride, and arrogance.

Such a revaluation of egoism was very much in the foreground of Russian awareness in 1847; the combined influence of Fourier and Max Stirner had been working to transform this idea from the negative to the positive. It was in the summer of this year that Belinsky felt called upon to mull over the lessons of Stirner; and Herzen—whom Dostoevsky was reading with envy and admiration—had published his own conclusions a few months before Dostoevsky's feuilleton. "To eradicate egoism from a man's breast," Herzen wrote, "means to eradicate his vital principle, his leaven, the salt of his personality . . . I dare say that *a rational acknowledgment of self-will is the highest moral acknowledgment of human dignity and that all can aspire to it.*[8] Dostoevsky's remarks on "necessary egoism" spring from a similar conviction; and this favorable attitude toward personal self-assertion as a manifestation of "human dignity" furnishes an important clue (though by no means an exclusive one) to the interpretation of Dostoevsky's early work.

In the list of psychic malformations given above, we can easily recognize most of the character-types of Dostoevsky's fiction in the 1840s. Drunkards (old Pokrovsky, Devushkin in despair, Emelyan Ilyich in both *Poor Folk* and *An Honest Thief*); those who go mad out of "ambition" while despising the very idea (Golyadkin in *The Double*); those whose lack of "necessary egoism" leads to a pathological fear and neurotic insecurity (Mr. Prokharchin in the story by that name, Vasya Shumkov in *A Weak Heart*). The remarks in the feuilleton thus help to clarify the implicit social-psychological presuppositions of Dostoevsky's creations. Even though, as we shall see, these presuppositions were not understood by most of Dostoevsky's contemporaries—and perhaps he did not do enough to make their presence felt artistically—it is reasonable to assume that he conceived his characters as instances of the prevailing difficulty for Russians "to become aware of, to embody, and to fulfill [their] Ego in real life." But, it should be stressed, this does not mean that he absolves such characters from all individual responsibility for whatever lack of "personal dignity" they may exhibit.

Dostoevsky's fourth feuilleton thus gives us an illuminating glimpse into the ideological matrix of those works that remain within the

[8] A. I. Herzen. *Sochineniia*, 10 vols. (Moscow, 1955), vol. 2. pp. 382–383.

stylistic orbit of the Natural School. In addition, however, it also furnishes insight into a new vein of his production that begins in 1847—a vein which no longer focuses on a *chinovnik* of limited mental capacities but rather on a character-type of the intelligentsia: "the dreamer." The appearance of this type, like so much else in Dostoevsky, has usually been traced exclusively to the peculiarities of his psyche and seen in narrowly biographical terms; but it is impossible to accept this view as adequate. For one thing, impractical idealists in the grip of Romantic vagaries are by no means unknown in earlier Russian literature—Pushkin's Lensky (in *Eugene Onegin*) and Gogol's unhappy artist Piskarev (in *Nevsky Prospect*) both exemplify a similar cultural–spiritual dilemma. And, even more important, Dostoevsky's "dreamer" emerges exactly at the moment when a general campaign was being carried on against the dangers of *mechtatelnost* (dreaming, reverie) as a congenital malady of the Russian intelligentsia.

Everywhere one turns in Russian culture of the mid-1840s, one finds evidence of this campaign. High-flown Romantic ideals and attitudes are denounced as leading to a debilitating withdrawal from the world and the cultivation of a purely passive and self-satisfied attitude of exalted contemplation. Herzen published a series of slashing articles ridiculing the absurdity of Romantic affectations in the midst of "this bustling age, occupied with material improvement, social questions, science."[9] Belinsky inveighed against those who, modeling themselves on Schiller's ideal of "the beautiful soul," believed they could transcend the conflicts of ordinary life. Such people, he says, "know 'the sublime and the beautiful' only in books, and then not always; in life and reality they know neither the one nor the other."[10] The literary sensation of the early spring of 1847 had been Goncharov's *An Ordinary Story*, which contains a devastating portrait of a typical young provincial Romantic brought down to earth by contact with life in Petersburg, and by the admonitions of the chief "positive" character—a busy, disabused, cool, and hard-headed bureaucrat in charge of running a very efficient factory for the government.

Dostoevsky is merely echoing this widespread devaluation of Romantic *mechtatelnost* when, in a letter to Mikhail at the beginning of 1847, he remarks that while a rich and intense inner life is a spiritual

[9]Cited in A. G. Tseitlin, *I. A. Goncharov* (Moscow, 1950), p. 6.
[10]Ibid., p. 62.

good, those who live such a life too fervently are also in danger. For, he explains, "there is a terrible dissonance, a terrible disequilibrium, that comes to us from society. The *external* should be balanced with the *internal*. Otherwise, in the absence of external events, the internal acquires a much too threatening supremacy. Nerves and fantasy assume a very great place in one's existence."[11] This has often been taken as a self-confession; and there is no reason to deny that the young Dostoevsky who suffered from "hallucinations" may well have felt threatened by his own propensity to give way to "nerves and fantasy." It can scarcely be a hazard, though, that he expresses this fear only in 1847; nor should we overlook that the blame for the failure to find any appropriate external outlet is attributed to "society." Dostoevsky's own experience of psychic imbalance was certainly poured into his imaginative realization of "the dreamer"; but the significance that he assigns to the type in his feuilleton is inspired by the dominant social–cultural situation.

Dostoevsky's letter, indeed, jibes perfectly with the analysis of the dreamer that we find in his feuilleton. What is a dreamer? He is, we might say, the cultivated variety of the type of character produced by the frustrations of Russian life. Like the others, the dreamer too is "eager for activity, eager for spontaneous life, eager for reality"; but since this need cannot be satisfied, and because his character is "weak, womanly, soft," he is the kind of person who takes refuge in dreams and fantasies rather than in the more vulgar outlets of the less educated or the more virile. The cultured dreamer develops to an excessive degree the typical Russian practice of living completely in the world of "our illusions, our invented chimeras, our reveries, and all those extra remedies with which people nowadays try in any way to fill up all the dull emptiness of their everyday colorless life." It is in such natures that "little by little develops what is called reverie *(mechtatelnost)*, and a man finally becomes something not a man at all but some kind of strange neuter being—*a dreamer*." The marvelous portrait given of this type is too long to quote entire; but it is one of the gems of Russian prose. To paraphrase lamely, the dreamer is absent-minded and detached, temperamentally very unstable, solitary and self-absorbed, incapable of sustained effort even in his favorite occu-

[11]F. M. Dostoevskii, *Pis'ma*, ed. and annotated by A. S. Dolinin, 4 vols. (Moscow, 1928–1959), vol. I, p. 106, January–February, 1847.

pation of reading. Everything serves to nourish his capacity for living
in an artificial universe of his own creation—a world of imagination
and illusion far surpassing the real in attractiveness. "Sometimes entire nights pass imperceptibly in indescribable pleasures; often in a
few hours he [the dreamer] experiences the heavenly joys of love or of
a whole life, gigantic, unheard of, wonderful as a dream, grandiosely
beautiful."

The cultivation of such delights brings with it an increasing incapacity to tolerate reality ("the moments of sobering up are dreadful"),
and the dreamer becomes totally alienated from his real existence,
with all its anxieties and demands. "Little by little our prankster begins to shun crowds, to shun general interests, and gradually, imperceptibly, his talent for real life begins to dull. Finally, in his delusion,
he completely loses that moral sense which enables a man to ap-
preciate all the beauty of the actual. . . ." And the chronicler ends by
labeling such a life a tragedy, a sin, a caricature; but—"are we not all
more or less dreamers?" Whether or not he considers himself to be (or
to have been) a "dreamer," Dostoevsky makes clear that the time has
come for the intelligentsia to stop nourishing itself on such dreams
and to turn to the enormous tasks confronting them in Russian life.
Just two years later, he was to try to put such convictions into practice.

Dostoevsky is usually not thought of as a journalist at all, perhaps
because so many of the ideas he expresses are so distasteful to admir-
ers of his art. But he *was* a journalist all the same—and an immensely
successful and influential one during the 1870s, when his *Diary of a
Writer*, published in monthly installments, was the most widely read
broadsheet ever to have appeared in Russia. Even earlier, during the
1860s, he was an indefatigable contributor of polemical articles to the
two magazines he edited jointly with his brother (*Time* and *Epoch*).
This is not the place to discuss his work as a publicist any further; but
it is relevant to note that all his writing in this format bears the stamp
of the feuilleton style.

Dostoevsky evidently found that the easy, casual manner of the
feuilletonist fitted him like a glove; and one never finds him later,
even when presumably expounding ideas, writing anything that can
be considered ordinary expository prose. His stance is always personal
and intimate; his points are made not by logical persuasion but

through sketching character-types, dramatizing attitudes, narrating experiences and observations. To be sure, the whimsical tone of the feuilletonist of the 1840s, though never abandoned completely, is replaced by that of the serious and sometimes choleric social observer; but his use of irony and persiflage remains the same, and so does the identification with the reader who becomes an implicit partner in a dialogue. From this point of view, Dostoevsky's five-finger exercises in the 1840s mark the début of an essential aspect of his career.

Reading Between the Genres:
Dostoevsky's *Diary of a Writer* as Metafiction

by Gary Saul Morson

"Can one perceive as an image that which has no image?"—Ippolit Terentiev, in *The Idiot*.

Russian writers are constantly telling us what their works are not. "What is *War and Peace?*" asks Tolstoy. "It is not a novel, still less a *poema*, still less a historical chronicle. *War and Peace* is what the author wanted and was able to express in that form in which it was expressed. Such a declaration of the author's disregard for the conventional forms of a creative work in prose might have seemed presumptuous if it were not deliberate and if it lacked examples. The history of Russian literature from Pushkin's time not only presents many examples of such a departure from European form, but does not even give one example of the opposite. Beginning from Gogol's *Dead Souls* and up to Dostoevsky's *House of the Dead* in the modern period of Russian literature there is not a single creative work in prose, at all rising above mediocrity, which has quite fitted into the form of a novel, a *poema*, or a tale." If Tolstoy is essentially correct—and I believe he is—then a central problem of Russian literary criticism should be to determine the poetics of works that deliberately lie in the interstices between recognized "European" genres. The very titles of Russian works often point to the genres they lie between—they are *poemas* in prose and novels in verse—or insist that they follow no recognized rule at all:

"Reading Between the Genres: Dostoevsky's *Diary of a Writer* as Metafiction," by Gary Saul Morson. From *The Yale Review*, copyright © Yale University, vol. 68 (Winter 1970), pp. 224–234. Reprinted by permission of *The Yale Review* and the editor.

"notes" and "diaries" are not so much genres as anti-genres. To read Russian literature is to learn to read between the genres; we must ask (to paraphrase Ippolit Terentiev's question), what are the laws of works which profess to have no laws?

To extend the argument, we often doubt not only the kind of literature we are reading, but whether we are reading literature at all. In the middle of his fiction "Lucerne," Tolstoy interrupts his narrative to tell the reader that "this is not a fiction, but a positive fact, which can be verified by anyone who likes from the permanent residents at the Hotel Schweizerhof, after ascertaining from the papers who the foreigners were who were staying at the Schweizerhof on the 7th of July." Here Tolstoy is claiming more than "realism," he is claiming reality; rather than mere fidelity, he insists on literal (not simply literary) truth. Many of Tolstoy's direct addresses to the reader which so disturbed Percy Lubbock and others derive from his attempt to write what simultaneously is and is not literature, to speak between "is" and "as if." And here again Tolstoy is emblematic of his tradition as a whole; Russian literature is deliberately and self-consciously made up of forms which have usually been considered to straddle the boundaries of art—autobiographies, memoirs, notebooks, utopias. Not only Russian writers but Russian fictions are constantly denying art—and therefore themselves.

Like Rabelais's Abbey of Thélème, this order seems to be defined by simple negation of traditional models, by the quest for paradoxical and interstitial forms. The reader brought up on European novels and with a firm sense of the rules and possible variations of fiction is left to define what these new antirules can be. Or he can, of course, simply dismiss the best of the Russian tradition as so many loose and baggy monsters, and so avoid an essential problem for a student of Russian literature: the poetics of the boundary, the conventions of the threshold.

Perhaps no work raises these problems more clearly than Dostoevsky's *Diary of a Writer*. We know from external evidence that Dostoevsky intended his work as a new genre, with strict poetic laws of its own, and believed that after years of labor "the *Diary* has at last matured to the point where even the slightest change in its form is impossible." Yet when we look at the text we see nothing but the "image of imagelessness," an icon of chaos.

Whatever our definition of literature may be, this work will probably challenge it. Advertisements are included in the text, as are notices about subscription rates, missed issues, and the mechanics of publication and distribution. Writer, editor, and publisher—they are one person, but their roles conflict—all speak to us in the text about their difficulties in producing the text in which they speak about their difficulties, and appeal for understanding from their readers for being forced to write to readers who do not understand them. Chapter titles, which presumably should tell us what the articles they introduce contain, often tell us everything else, including why they cannot fulfill their normal function. They often seem to entitle only themselves; and when they do refer to the following article, they may be indecipherable, and approach the length of some of the shorter articles.

Above all, there is the vexing problem of the kind of material that the *Diary* contains. This work of literature includes a great deal of apparently nonliterary material. The reason that "The Dream of a Ridiculous Man" and "The Meek One" are usually excerpted from the *Diary* is, of course, that they are mostly polemical journalism; and a case against the *Diary* as a work of literature could rest on Wellek's and Warren's commonsense assertion that "we reject as poetry or label as mere rhetoric everything which persuades us to a definite outward action. Art imposes some kind of framework which takes the statement of the work out of the world of reality. Into our semantic analysis we thus can reintroduce some of the common conceptions of aesthetics: 'disinterested contemplation,' 'aesthetic distance,' 'framing.'" And any defense of the *Diary* as literature rather than laboratory would also have to explain the perplexing inclusion of the notebooks for stories in the same work as their finished text—and, for that matter, of stories which insist falsely that they are only notebooks for stories.

I propose to make this defense on the grounds of metafiction. The *Diary*'s formal paradoxes function as part of its broader strategy to *define* literature. It challenges our definitions in much the same way that the "anxious objects" of modern art or the anti-fictions of modern literature do: because it is a fiction *about* the nature of fiction-making. Rigorous artistic laws govern its apparent chaos, and the *Diary*'s formal paradoxes are as deliberate as those of its metafictional predecessors—*Tristram Shandy*, *Eugene Onegin*, and, above all, *Don*

Quixote (which it so often cites). A self-conscious anomaly, it violates the conventions of literature to make us aware of what those conventions are.

Thus the *Diary* does not exist on the boundaries of art: it dramatizes them. We must not read it as a writer's notebook, but as the imitation of such a notebook. We need only glance at the real notebooks for this published "notebook" to see the difference between real and scripted spontaneity; and we will also read in these real notebooks the *plans* for the apologies for supposedly spontaneous digressions. As the title suggests, this is not a diary but *The Diary of a Writer*—and that, to cite Pushkin's comment on the hybrid form of his metafiction *Onegin*, is "a devil of a difference." If we miss that diabolical difference, we will mistake author for persona, statement for performance; we will be like Smerdyakov, who objects to Gogol's Dikanka stories because they are "not true," or like the readers of *Notes from the House of the Dead* who, the diarist complains, mistook the narrator for the author and "are even now asserting that I was exiled for the murder of my wife."

Like all metafictions, the *Diary* does what it says; and what it says is that it may say anything. Its law, it tells us, is lawlessness. In the tradition of self-referential literature, the *Diary* contains numerous descriptions of itself—we recall Tristram's labyrinthine diagrams of his own work—in the form of notes, apologies, digressions, and, one step further, digressions about digressions (the debt to *Onegin* is obvious). Implicitly or explicitly, all of these self-referential notes refer back to the "announcement" in the January 1876 issue, which states the rules of this new work, the contract that obtains between writer and reader: "This will be a diary in the literal sense of the word, an account of the impressions I have really lived through each month, an account of what I have seen, heard, and read. Stories and tales may of course be included, but it will be preeminently about real events." All that I have seen, heard, and read; real events and also stories—it would be hard to say what these "rules" prohibit. This is a Thélèmite command—recall that the one rule of Rabelais's abbey is "Do as you wish."

The point of this note, of course, is that the subject of this self-referential fiction is the conventions of reading—in this case, reading this work. We learn our expectations by seeing them violated, we discover how much we rely on an implicit set of conventions by being forced to read without them. For all fiction, and each genre within fiction, depends on a contract that tells us how to take the statements that follow. Implicitly or explicitly, the work is preceded by what Gregory Bateson calls a *meta*communicative statement, a statement about how to take future statements. These are warnings of the type: "this is a joke," "take this as a metaphor," or "this is only a story." The very word "novel" or "tragedy" defines a set of expectations against which we are to read the text which follows. We must be able to understand this language about language, or, like Smerdyakov, and the readers of *Notes from the House of the Dead*, we will not be able to read at all. They do not, but we must see that all fiction, and each genre, is framed, as surely as a physical frame surrounds a picture, by a set of conventions which govern the realm that the frame encloses. (My use of the word "frame" refers not only to the passage from Wellek and Warren, but also—and more importantly—to Erving Goffman's recent study, *Frame Analysis: An Essay on the Organization of Experience*. Though neither Bateson nor Goffman is a literary theoretician, and they rarely discuss literature directly, both are indispensable for a study of metaliterature.)

The announcement to the opening issue of the monthly *Diary* pretends to state the conventions of this new genre, but in fact the only positive information it contains is the price of a subscription. To use Shklovsky's terms, the diarist "bares the device" of the "fictional contract"; this is not only a statement *about* the work, but a statement *in* the work. Like most metafiction, the *Diary* makes art out of the statement of the conventions of art, literature out of the promise of literature. We must ask, with Lord Byron, "Who will then explain the explanation?" Or in the language I prefer to use: the frame itself is framed.

If the heart of literature, as the formalists have taught us, is in its "literariness," then the heart of metaliterature is in its "metaliterariness." To understand the poetics and coherence of the *Diary*, we must concentrate on its metacommunicative statements, on its statements about itself. For the peculiar frame at the beginning of the *Diary* promises more than violated promises: it also promises more of such frames. These frames typically occur as transition passages, as joints between journalism and fiction, and call attention, usually by the topos of an apology, to the shift in conventions we must make in order to read what is not true, what is "only a story."

The frame to "The Boy at Christ's Christmas Party" refers directly to the "announcement" which opens the 1876 *Diary* (both of these frames occur within the same issue) as it apologizes, and then retracts its apology, for violating the promise to write "preeminently about real events." "And *why* did I make up such a story," the diarist archly asks at the close of his narrative, "one that conforms so little to an ordinary, reasonable diary, and still less to a writer's diary? And after I have promised to write preeminently about real events! But the point is that it still seems to me and I still keep fancying that all this could really happen—that is, what occurred in the basement and behind the woodpile; but as for Christ's Christmas Party, I really don't know what to tell you, could that have happened or not? But that is *why* I am a novelist, in order to invent things."

The story's opening frame also plays on the narrative's problematic status between fact and fiction. "But I am a novelist and it seems that I did make up one 'story' myself. Why do I write 'it seems' when I know for certain that I did make it up? But I keep fancying that it happened somewhere, at some time, precisely on Christmas Eve, in *some* huge city during a terrible frost." Not only does this frame comment on the boundaries of art, it exists on them. Beginning on a conjunction, it continues from the preceding article, whose final sentence insists that everything the diarist says is absolutely true; and it leads into a story whose narrator constantly reminds us of his role in "inventing" his fiction. The frame, in other words, self-consciously places itself between fact and artifact. This is the moment when we watch the diarist shifting from rhetoric of journalism to "the rhetoric of fiction." "Reality is transfigured, *passing through art*," wrote Dostoevsky in an early essay; the frames of the *Diary* are structured to dramatize the paradoxes of the moment of "passing through." Here is a time of maximal liminality, a moment when, in Dmitri Karamazov's words, "all shores meet, and all contradictions exist side by side." We are made to pause on the threshold, in a passage—I use the word in its literal as well as literary sense—between texts that ask to be read with the conventions of journalism and narratives which insist on those of fiction.

For what is most problematic about these passages is their own status. Do we take these metacommunicative statements as part of the story or are they really mere introductions? Is their denial of their own fictionality itself a well-wrought literary convention? At what point can we safely assume that the statements are no longer those of the diarist but of a fictional persona ("not me," as he says of the narrator of "Bobok"), when does he put on his mask? It is a question that has vexed anthologizers, who have handled the problem in radically different ways. On the one hand, the Soviets have included all of the preceding articles as part of the story, thus doubling its length; on the other, Constance Garnett leaves off the conjunction on which it begins and the last sentence of the closing frame in a desperate attempt to rip text from context and turn metafiction back into simple fiction.

The point is that the status of the frames is deliberately in question. Do their directives to read the story as fictive apply to themselves? I think they do, just as the "announcement" to the January issue of the *Diary* is an intrinsic part of the *Diary* (as the diarist's frequent play with it proves). The heart of metafiction is in its metacommentary; threshold art is defined by its thresholds. What these frames really frame is the process of framing.

The *Diary*, in other words, is structured as a pattern of violated expectations, and its apologies serve to reaffirm rules so that they may again be violated. The *Diary*'s wit derives from our knowledge of these conventions; there is no parody if we do not know what is being parodied. The *Diary* is not lawless, but systematically unlawful; it is not without structure, but intentionally anomalous. The distinction is vital. We can regard it as anomalous only if we come to understand the tradition it deliberately flouts; and that, in fact, is the point of flouting it. "When something is firmly classed as anomalous," observes Mary Douglas (in *Purity and Danger: An Analysis of Concepts of Pollution and Taboo*), "the outline of the set in which it is not a member is clarified." Rules can really be *honored* in the breach.

The reason the *Diary* includes advertisements, information about the mechanics of publication, and apologies to readers who have not received their issues in the very text is simply that they are not supposed to be there. These passages work in much the same way as the ironic "footnotes" to *Onegin* do. By including imitations of material that is normally not part of the text, Dostoevsky plays with the per-

plexing problem of the boundaries of art. We must not be like the
student I had who read the "editor's note" which concludes *Notes from
Underground* and complained that I had assigned an abridged edition.
These margins are not marginal. They frequently echo themes of the
text; we need only recall that irate misreaders and anonymous letter
writers are the protagonists of several of the *Diary*'s fictions. The
reader is presented with indeterminate boundaries of a work about
literary boundaries, the thresholds of a threshold. And once we have
begun to see the interconnections of these margins with the text, we
reach the point where we do not know how to "take" them for fear we
should "mis-take" them. We are made to experience the lack of, and
the need for, literary conventions and rules for reading; and so we
come to learn what those rules are.

We must learn to read between the genres. It is in this context, I
think, that we must understand a perplexing class of works which
reappear in—and perhaps define—the *Diary*. I am referring to pieces
which, like the *Diary* itself, seem to pause deliberately between fiction
and nonfiction, and which I therefore call semifictional. "The 'Certain
Person's' Half-Letter," "A Plan for a Satirical Story," "The Centenar-
ian," and a collection of other works all insist that they are not
finished stories, but only plans for stories, mere sketches. They present themselves, as the *Diary* presents itself, as notebooks, works in
progress—works which may, in fact, eventually be included in the
Diary itself.

But we must recognize this mode of narration as a well-wrought
artifice; and to do so, we need only remember that Ivan Karamazov
narrates the Grand Inquisitor legend in the same way. It is, he tells us,
only the prose draft of a "poem" he might have written; and he tells us
the whole story in the subjunctive: "that would have been one of the
finest passages of the poem"; "I meant to end it like this." Both Ivan
and the diarist tell their story and then protest that it is not written.
"In short, it seems to me that the type of an anonymous scolder is not
at all a poor theme for a story," the diarist apologizes after he has
presented the "plan" for the work. "Of course," he concedes, "here
Gogol would be needed." Both Ivan and the diarist have it both ways;
this story, they seem to say, is not a story. The closing frame of "The
Boy at Christ's Christmas Party" is simply the most obvious of many
such cases.

The semifictions thus dramatize the *Diary*'s own central paradoxical status as a published notebook, a "writer's diary" (the very phrases are oxymoronic). They insist on being read simultaneously with two opposing sets of expectations on the part of the reader, those of "journalism" and those of "fiction." The reader must pause to consider whether their statements claim literal or artistic "truth," whether they are being made in the real world or the world of "as if." Has Dostoevsky really received this document, or is he using the literary convention of the found manuscript? The *Diary* relies on our making errors, and includes irate letters from readers who do. And to extend the point, while some of these letters are from real readers, others are from fictitious ones (the narrator of "Bobok," for instance), and the ontological status of a third group is almost impossible to determine. To avoid making mistakes, we try to look for clues in the text, signs of conventionality; and this again becomes part of our enforced lesson on the experience of reading. It is certainly no accident that one of the *Diary*'s earliest articles, "Mummer," is a case study in detecting a forgery, a process that parallels our own attempt to detect fictionality. Indeed, many of the semifictional pieces are about the kind of framing problems they dramatize, situations where one can mistake performance for spontaneous action, fiction for nonfiction. Themselves duplicitous, these semifictions tell of conspiracies, forgeries, fabrications, hallucinations, seances. Here again, Don Quixote serves as a central symbol for the diarist. This other knight of the mournful countenance is the model of the perfect misreader, one who does not know that the fictions he reads are just that. The form of a diary—a work in which one looks at oneself—is perhaps the analogue to the mirror in *Don Quixote*: both are reflective, both disillusion, both teach us to look at how we look, and so to see the world aright. But we, the real readers, must learn the crucial difference between credibility and credulity, between belief and suspension of disbelief.

The semifictional pieces are, therefore, a threshold genre within threshold art. If the theme of the writer's diary is the creative process itself, then these pieces dramatize the moment when reality is "passing through" to art, when the plot is being plotted. They are the climax of the story of the creation of stories, and our sense of the drama of reading them is in being allowed to watch an artist in the usually private process of creation. We see him read the press in search of literary material, observe him limn the outlines of a story; then a semifictional piece presents its tentative embodiment in literary form; and, at last, a finished fiction may follow. For "The Meek One," the process occurs over many issues; the composition of "The Boy at Christ's Christmas Party" takes place within a single number of the *Diary*. As readers, we are placed in the ambiguous position of a private public, watchers of a process of struggle by which the author arrives at his polished result. It is the paradox implicit in reading another's diary, and the form takes to an extreme the place of an audience that John Stuart Mill says obtains in all poetry: it is not so much heard as overheard.

It should be evident that the semifictions cannot be excerpted from the *Diary* without losing their point—to dramatize the midpoint of the creative process. But the same reasoning applies to the final stories as well. Read in the *Diary*, they derive dramatic force from being the result of the creative process we have witnessed; the pleasure of these texts is in part our consciousness of the problems the diarist has resolved before our eyes. Placing the finished story next to its own notebooks turns the entire *Diary* into a dramatization of the process of creative "deformation" (in the Shklovskian sense of the word), of the bestrangement of raw material into art. When we read "The Boy at Christ's Christmas Party," we not only read it as a story; we also see the motifs and fragments which we have just seen in the articles immediately preceding the story reassembled in an artistic structure. We read vertically as well as horizontally. These stories are the last chapter of the story of the "quest for form." Art is made from the making of art, and what the reader experiences is the experience of reading.

Aristotelian Movement
and Design in Part Two
of *Notes from the Underground*

by Robert Louis Jackson

Cause and effect is like a wheel.

JAPANESE BUDDHIST PROVERB

"You know what a *transition* is in music," Dostoevsky wrote his brother Mikhail on April 13, 1864. That's exactly what we have here. In the first chapter we have what appears to be chatter," he writes with reference to part two of *Notes from the Underground* in its original tripartite division. "But suddenly this chatter resolves itself in the last two chapters in unexpected catastrophe." Of course, there is an organic, indeed causal connection between the seeming chatter and the unexpected catastrophe. The catastrophe is unexpected only for the reader; for the author it is as inevitable, from the dramatic and ideological points of view, as the catastrophe of Sophocles' Oedipus or Melville's Ahab.

The action of part two in *Notes from the Underground* takes place at least sixteen years before the philosophizing of part one; the Underground Man is writing his "notes" in the early 1860s. The whole romantic and philosophically idealistic atmosphere of the Russian 1840s, moreover, has determined in a literal way the features of the Underground Man as a social type. Such people as the author of the notes, Dostoevsky writes in his footnote–preface to *Notes from the Underground*, "not only can but even must exist in our society, if we take into consideration the circumstances which led to the formation of

"Aristotelian Movement and Design in Part Two of *Notes from the Underground*," by Robert Louis Jackson. From *The Art of Dostoevsky. Deliriums and Nocturnes*, pp. 171–88. Copyright © 1981 Princeton University Press. Reprinted by permission. The footnotes have been abridged.

our society." The Underground Man, he continues, "is one of the representatives of a generation still living. In this extract, entitled 'The Underground,' this person introduces himself, his outlook, and as it were seeks to explain those causes that have led, and were bound to lead to his appearance in our milieu." The writer of the notes has undergone an intellectual crisis since his experiences in the 1840s. Nonetheless, his psychological and philosophical self-exposition in part one reveal to us fundamental patterns of mind and behavior that made inevitable his tragic encounter with the prostitute Liza in the 1840s (the central episode in part two).

Dostoevsky's dominant message in *Notes from the Underground* (expressed directly in the penultimate chapter of part one in passages removed by the censor, and dramatically in the denouement of the Liza episode) is that only through Christian love and self-sacrifice—not through self-assertion, caprice, irrational rebellion, "twice two is five"—can man break the chain of an inwardly binding and blinding determinism. Only in this way can he escape from the underground and the deadly dominion of "twice two is four." Only in this way can he attain authentic freedom and the fullest expression of personality. The solution to man's problems is ethical, not numerical.

The self-defeating, destructive nature of irrational will philosophy, of underground "spite," is already evident in part one of *Notes from the Underground*, though the Underground Man's polemics with the rationalist–utilitarians, his tragic stance of revolt, tends to obscure the main figure in Dostoevsky's overall design. It is in part two, however, that the bankruptcy of irrational will philosophy is demonstrated with devastating force. The action here, taking place in the 1840s, forms an ironic commentary on the Underground Man's central notion that capricious behavior may preserve for us "what is most precious and important, namely, our personality and our individuality." The action begins precipitously on that fateful Thursday afternoon (II) when the Underground Man, unable to bear his solitude, decides to visit his old school friend Simonov; it includes the ill-fated dinner at the Hôtel de Paris, the mad ride to the brothel, the first encounter with Liza, the duel with Apollon at his flat, the second encounter with Liza, and, finally, after a moment of reversal and recognition, the catastrophe.

The movement toward catastrophe is singularly linear and Aristotelian: effect follows cause swiftly and relentlessly. Every attempt by the Underground Man to introduce the irrational into his life only locks him more firmly into an irreversible course that must end in catastrophe. Every attempt to affirm his independence and self-mastery only deepens his sense of psychological dependence and humiliation. In turn, his suffering arouses in him more frenzied attempts to win his freedom, that is, to achieve real self-mastery and self-determination. But his every bit of demonstrative self-expression, every flight of imagination or caprice, only further emphasizes the ineluctable character of the tragic action—his essential impotence in what appears to be, from his point of view, a closed, meaningless, and tyrannical universe.

The Underground Man's "bumping duel" with the officer on Nevsky Prospect (II, 1)—an episode that lies outside the main course of events in part two—is paradigmatic for the whole inner drama of the Underground Man. It exposes vividly to us the mechanism of the psychological experiment, always irrational in character, and the profound *un*freedom of the Underground Man in that experiment.

More than anything the Underground Man craves recognition, respect, a place in the universe. After periods of moral and spiritual stagnation he blindly goes out into the world seeking, as he puts it, "contradictions, contrasts." He is, in a manner of speaking, a gambler playing a game with reality; he is seeking identity or a sense of being in chance encounters with fate. But he himself is the little black ball. He goes into a tavern hoping to pick a quarrel and be thrown out of the window. But he is simply ignored. An officer at a billiard table— the game of billiards itself is symbolic—matter-of-factly moves him out of his way, simply does not notice him, treats him like "a fly." The Underground Man insists, "the quarrel . . . was in my hands"; he had only to protest and be thrown out of the window. But he tells us that he "thought the matter over and preferred . . . rancorously to efface myself." "Even at that time," the Underground Man observes at the beginning of his discussion of his episode, "I carried the underground in my soul." "I preferred," he says; but the exercise of choice is only apparent; it was for want of "moral courage," he observes, that he did not follow through his instinct to protest and suffer the consequences. What is certain, however, is that the quarrel was precisely *not* in his hands. Rather, he was caught up in a hopeless quarrel with reality; he was a victim of compulsive underground patterns of behavior.

The Underground Man's attempts at a bumping duel with the offending officer—and the final duel itself on Nevsky Prospect—form a sequel to the tavern scene. The officer, like all the other great powers of Nevsky Prospect, is a social embodiment of those laws of nature that have been humiliating the Underground Man, moving relentlessly down upon him. Here on Nevsky Prospect the Underground Man makes a despairing effort to assert his independence before the embodied force of history, to inject the irrational into the everyday rational order or status quo. Through caprice he seeks to break the chain of necessity that binds him, to rise from a humiliated nonentity to a self-respecting, free entity, to put himself, as he expresses it, on an equal "social footing" with his enemy.

Dostoevsky underscores the unfree character of the Underground Man's challenge to Nevsky Prospect: "I was simply *drawn* there at every possible opportunity," the Underground Man observes. After the incident with the officer, he says, "I felt drawn there more than ever." Then, after many failures to engineer a head-on collision with the army officer—" 'Why do you always have to step aside first,' I would ask myself over and over again in a state of crazy hysteria . . . 'there's no law about it, is there?' "—victory finally comes to him, "suddenly," "unexpectedly," accidentally:

> The night before I had definitely determined not to carry out my ruinous intentions and to forget all about it, and with this goal I went out for the last time onto Nevsky Prospect just in order to find out how I would forget all about it. Suddenly, three paces from my enemy, I unexpectedly made up my mind, shut my eyes and—we knocked solidly against each other shoulder to shoulder! I did not retreat an inch and passed him by absolutely on an equal footing! He didn't even look around and pretended that he did not notice; but he only pretended, I am certain of this (II, 1).

Of course, the Underground Man's sense of victory and self-mastery is no more substantial or real than the pawnbroker's sense of victory in his bedside duel in "A Gentle Creature." There is only an illusion of victory, one that in both "duels" is based on a mistaken notion of the adversary's state of mind.

The duel with the army officer on Nevsky Prospect (unlike the bedside duel) has a strong comic, or tragicomic tonality; it does not end in catastrophe. Yet it serves to illustrate the completely abstract, psychological, and essentially amoral character of the Underground Man's experiments. Indeed, it reveals the wholly compulsive and reactive character of his human relations. The army officer—who could be anybody, who indeed is only one of the "generals, officers of the guards, hussars, and ladies" before whom the Underground Man gives way on Nevsky Prospect—only exists to test the lacerated ego of the Underground Man. The latter moves zombielike, as though in the grip of some external force; he is drawn to the field of action as though by a magnet; he goes into action only after he has decided not to take action, and then he does so unexpectedly and almost blindly. In all of these psychological details, the Underground Man's bumping duel anticipates the manner in which Raskolnikov will be drawn into his experiment. The mental atmosphere of fatality and the role of accident after a deceptive moment of freedom from obsession are some of the elements shared by the two experiments.

The irony of the bumping duel episode (like the irony of Raskolnikov's experiment) is clear: there are no manifestations of freedom of will here. Far from being a master of his fate, the Underground Man in his very efforts to declare his independence from the laws of nature demonstrates his enslavement to them.

The drama that is played out on the tragicomic plane of Nevsky Prospect—a Gogolian world where everything has the conventional and abstract character of a stage, where "all is deception"—is then replayed as tragedy in the Petersburg underground in the series of interlocking psychological duels that begin with the Underground Man's visit to his friend Simonov. In place of Nevsky Prospect, a relatively harmless testing ground, we have not only the Underground Man's noxious set of friends and the thoroughly obnoxious Apollon but the prostitute Liza. When the Underground Man "bumps into" Liza at the end of his descent into the Petersburg underworld—a descent that is everywhere accompanied by imagery and reminders of death—he will spiritually destroy her, just as decisively as Raskolnikov will physically destroy the old pawnbroker in his quest for self-definition.

The Underground Man's power duels with his old schoolmate Zverkov, deeply rooted in his personal history, result in one catastrophic humiliation after another. He plunges into the adventure at the Hôtel de Paris against his better reasoning, and with a premonition of disaster. "Of course, the best thing would have been not to go altogether," he observes at the threshold of this new encounter with "reality." "But that was now more than ever impossible: once I begin to be drawn into something, then I find myself totally drawn into it, head first." "I could no longer master myself," he recalls, "and I was shaking with fever." Dostoevsky repeatedly emphasizes that the Underground Man is not in control of his own fate. It is with a feeling that "after all everything is lost anyway" that he rushes down the stairs of the Hôtel de Paris in pursuit of his enemies.

As he rides off to the brothel in a sledge, the Underground Man is tremendously active in his imagination: slapping, biting, shoving, and spitting at his enemies. But on closer inspection, we recognize that this is the frenzied action of a man who in his romantic dreams is himself being beaten and dragged about and who is in the complete control of his tormentors. Protest here is as impotent as the groans of a man with a toothache (in the Underground Man's example in part one), who is conscious only that he is "completely enslaved" by his teeth.

In the midst of his romanticizing the Underground Man suddenly feels "terribly ashamed, so ashamed that I stopped the sledge, got out of it, and stood in the snow in the middle of the road." But he leaps back into the sledge again, remarking, "It's predestined, it's fate!" These words fully define his unfreedom. As he rushes on he realizes that there is no force that can stop the course of events: "All is lost." The sense of impending doom manifests itself everywhere. "Solitary street lamps flickered gloomily in the snowy haze like torches at a funeral." Like Euripides's Hippolytus in his carriage, the Underground Man is rushing along out of control—or rather, in the control of the very laws of nature, the implacable logic of humiliation and self-humiliation, of which he is victim. "Twice two is four is not life, gentlemen, but the beginning of death," the Underground Man declares in part one. Not surprisingly, he casts himself early in the sledge scene in the role of a drowning man. When he arrives at the brothel and discovers that his old school friends have departed, he breathes a sigh of relief: "It was as though I had almost been saved from death."

References to death accumulate on this journey into the underground, defining a psychological syndrome in which the impulses to destruction and self-destruction are closely interwoven. The Petersburg underground, the lower depths of Petersburg that the Underground Man inhabits and knows so well, is itself a kingdom of death. The Underground Man repeatedly evokes this funereal atmosphere in his first encounter with Liza in the brothel. With reference to a coffin carried up from a basement brothel, for example, he says, "Some day you too will die, you know, and you'll die just like that one died." He goes on to detail the terrible degradation and death of prostitutes like Liza: "Your name will disappear from the face of the earth just as though you had never been born! Filth and swamp, filth and swamp, and you may knock vainly at your coffin lid at night when the dead arise, crying, 'Let me live a bit in the world, good people! I lived—but I had no life.' " At one point he dilates upon the joys of parenthood, but this sentimental scene is bracketed by the funeral world of Petersburg. The Underground Man's preachment to Liza is outwardly lofty, didactic, detached; inwardly, it is murderous; it is a deep laceration and self-laceration. He emerges from the brothel terribly upset: "It was as though some kind of crime were weighing on my spirit."

The episode in which the Underground Man confronts Apollon the servant is central in defining the true nature of the Underground Man's universe and his place in it. Here the servant is master—and master, servant. Apollon is not a symbol of the god of sunlight, but a kind of plebeian god of death, a rat exterminator who also reads psalms over the dead. He is the precise embodiment of those deadly laws of nature that have been humiliating the Underground Man all his life. "He is my tormentor," the Underground Man says of Apollon. The Underground Man constantly rebels against the suave and contained servant (for example, by withholding his wages), but he always capitulates to him in the end. So, too, in the encounter with Apollon after his visit to the brothel, the Underground Man vainly tries to best Apollon:

> "Listen"—I cried to him—"Here is your money, you see it; there it is . . . but you won't get it, you-will-not-get-it until you come respectfully with bowed head and ask my forgiveness. Do you hear!" "That will never be!" he answered with a kind of unnatural self-confidence. "It shall be!" I screamed. . . . "I can lodge a complaint against you at the police station" [Apollon

observes]. "Go and lodge your complaint!" I roared. "Go this very minute, this second! But all the same you are a tormentor, tormentor, tormentor!" But he only looked at me, then turned around and no longer listening to my screams went to his room with measured step (II, 8).

The Underground Man follows Apollon to his quarters and repeats his demand. Apollon bursts out laughing and remarks, "Really you must be off your head."

This whole scene (II, 6) echoes in a parodic form the notion of the Underground Man (I, 8) that nothing in the world would induce a man to give up his free will. Even if "chaos and darkness and curses" could be calculated, "well, man would deliberately go mad in order not to have reason and to have his own way," in order to prove that he was "a man not an organ-stop!" The Underground Man is indeed mad in this scene. But is a madness that attests more to the tragic bankruptcy of personality than to man's heroic defense of his independence. "The theme of this time is self-preservation," Max Horkheimer comments in his *Eclipse of Reason*, "while there is no self to preserve."[1] The words might well be applied to the Underground Man.

"I'll kill him, I'll kill him," the Underground Man shrieks with reference to Apollon. Madness and murder, of course, are closely linked in the tragic drama of Dostoevsky's antihero. The Underground Man threatens to kill Apollon in the presence of Liza who has just arrived on the scene. Even at this moment he senses the outcome of his humiliation at the hands of Apollon: "I dimly felt that she would pay dearly *for all this* . . . I was angry at myself, but . . . a terrible anger against her suddenly flared up in my heart; I could almost have killed her, it seemed." For the second time, the Underground Man takes out his humiliation on Liza. Indeed, on the moral-spiritual plane, he murders Liza. After his cruel tirade, in which he savagely exposes the motives of his behavior toward her, the Underground Man remarks: "She turned white as a handkerchief, wanted to say something, her lips worked painfully, but she collapsed in a chair as though she had been felled by an ax." This allusion to murder by ax is closely linked with the more famous ax murder in *Crime and Punishment*.

[1] Max Horkheimer, *The Eclipse of Reason* (New York, 1947), p. 128.

The Underground Man's frenzied assault on Liza in this scene is also a terrible self-laceration in which he exposes and tramples upon his nature. His violent self-exposure—"I am the most disgusting, most ridiculous, most petty, most stupid, most envious of all worms on earth"—arouses in Liza a feeling of pity and compassion: "She suddenly leapt up from her chair in a kind of irrepressible impulse and all drawn towards me but still feeling timid and not daring to go further, extended her arms to me. . . . It was here that my heart, too, gave way. Then she suddenly rushed to me, threw her arms around me and burst into tears. I too could not restrain myself and burst out sobbing as I never had before. . . . "

This moment, a kind of "recognition scene" following a classic peripety or reversal in the drama of the Underground Man, points the way out of the underground. In the embrace of the Underground Man and Liza, all walls of ego and pride are dissolved. It is a moment of revelation of higher truth, an epiphany, a pietà. The fundamental problem of freedom posed in *Notes from the Underground* is not resolved here; it is dissolved. It is not twice two is four, not twice two is five, but reciprocal love that is the way out of the underground.

The Underground Man ironically affixes as an epigraph to chapter ix, part two, of his notes the two final lines from Nikolai Nekrasov's famous poem, "When from the darkness of error" (*Kogda iz mraka zabluzhden'ia*, 1846): "And my house, fearlessly and freely / As mistress you can enter now." (He cites the same lines in chapter viii of part two.) The narrator in this sentimental poem addresses a prostitute whom he would save from her fate. For the epigraph to part two of his notes as a whole, the Underground Man takes the opening fourteen lines from the same poem:

> When, from the darkness of error
> I saved a fallen soul
> With a fervent word of conviction,
> And, laden with deep anguish,
> Wringing your hands you curses heaped
> Upon the vice that ensnared you;
>
> When you related to me the story
> Of everything that went before me,
> Lashing with memories

An unheeding conscience;
And suddenly, covering your face with your hands,
Full of shame and horror
You burst into tears,
Aroused, shaken,—
Etc. etc. etc.

In the light of the Underground Man's half-cynical preachment to Liza on the evils of her way of life and his invitation to her to visit him, Nekrasov's words are first perceived by the reader in the sarcastic vein of the Underground Man's "etc. etc. etc."—that is, as mockery of the romantic and sentimental ethos of the 1840s, an ironical comment on the tragedy of naive idealism. But the moment of reversal and recognition in chapter ix reveals Nekrasov's poem in another light. These lines, and in particular the unquoted stanza that immediately follows the verses cited in the epigraph, now point to the tragedy of the Underground Man as perceived by Liza, the one character in *Notes from the Underground* who embodies Dostoevsky's ethical message. The Underground Man's "etc. etc. etc." comes at a crucial point in Nekrasov's poem—just before the lines:

I shared your torments
I loved you passionately
And I swear that not for a moment did I offend
With the wretched thought of turning away.[2]

Dostoevsky's response to Nekrasov's poem was a complex one. The sentimental pathos of this poem was not alien to Dostoevsky. The theme of the "restoration of the fallen man," as Dostoevsky wrote in 1861, is "the basic idea of all art of the nineteenth century. . . . It is a Christian and supremely moral idea." There can be no question of any contempt on his part for the core ideal of Nekrasov's poem. Dostoevsky, who later placed Nekrasov as poet alongside of Pushkin and Lermontov, saw the weak and tragic side of this naive, noble enthusiasm of the 1840s, an enthusiasm that he himself had shared with Nekrasov. But he certainly did not relate to the poem in the sarcastic vein of the Underground Man. The "etc. etc. etc.," then,

---

[2]Nekrasov subsequently replaced this quatrain with the lines: "*Believe me: I listened with sympathy / Greedily I hung on every word . . . / I understood everything, child of misfortune! / I forgave everything and forgot everything.*"

comes from the Underground Man, not from Dostoevsky. The whole epigraph is part of the Underground Man's notes and cannot be regarded as an independent authorial comment.

Indeed, Dostoevsky brilliantly undercuts the Underground Man's sarcasm. In his final encounter with Liza the Underground Man finds himself in the role he had cast for her—a person in need of salvation. The reader perceives Nekrasov's poem in a new, tragic light: it is Liza who expresses the lofty idealistic ethos of Nekrasov's poem; it is Liza who invites the Underground Man—however naively—not into a bookish romantic realm, but into a contract of reciprocal love in the very depths of the Petersburg hell. It is the Underground Man, in contrast, who is full of shame and horror before himself, who, wringing his hands and savagely exposing himself, bursts into tears. At this point, the reader realizes that it is the Underground Man, not Dostoevsky, who has been savagely parodying Nekrasov and that he has now been trapped by his own parody. Dostoevsky did not abandon the idealistic ethos of the 1840s, but reinvested it with a tragic Christian content.

Nekrasov's poem, in the sarcastic interpretation of the Underground Man, thus cannot be viewed as Dostoevsky's epigraph to part two of *Notes from the Underground*. If there are (or were) any poems that might possibly be viewed as such an epigraph, they would be the poems by Apollon Maikov and Yakov P. Polonsky that Dostoevsky as editor of *Epokha* (the journal in which parts one and two of *Notes from the Underground* first appeared) juxtaposed with the opening pages of "The Underground" and "A Story Apropos of Falling Sleet."[3] On page 292 of *Epokha* (no. 4, 1864), opposite the title page of part two of the Underground Man's notes (with his epigraph), we find the following poem by Polonsky:

> All that tormented me—all has been long ago
> > Magnanimously forgiven
> > Or indifferently forgotten,
> And if my heart were not broken,
> Were not aching from weariness and wounds,—
> I would think: all is a dream, all an illusion, all a deception.
> Hopes have perished, tears have dried up—
> > Passions that sprang up like storms

[3] These poems appear only in the journal *Epokha*.

Have vanished like fog.
And you who in bestowing dreams upon me
Were a comfort to my sick soul—
You have been carried away, like a cloud of rising dew
Disappearing behind a mountain.

Polonsky's poem, poignant and elegaic, emerges in the context of part two of *Notes from the Underground* as a mournful comment on the idealism of the 1840s and the tragic drama of the Underground Man and Liza. Had Dostoevsky adopted the Underground Man's sarcastic attitude toward Nekrasov's poem and its romantic ethos, he would hardly have juxtaposed it with Polonsky's poem, a poem that shares the romantic pathos and emotional tone of Nekrasov's verse. Polonsky seems here to converse with Nekrasov: he speaks of lost hopes, of the illusory, dreamlike, deceptive character of the past; but he does so in pain, entirely without mockery. Here in Polonsky's poem, viewed as an epigraph to part two, we begin to approach Dostoevsky's most intimate response to Nekrasov and the idealism of the 1840s—a response that is echoed later in his moving tributes to Nekrasov and George Sand on the occasion of their deaths (*Diary of a Writer* in June 1876 and December 1877 issues).

The moment of illumination for the Underground Man is a transitory one. Immediately he is caught up again in a tragic dialectic of self-will and humiliation. The sexual encounter that follows his spiritual reconciliation with Liza turns out to be a fresh insult, a final testimony—openly acknowledged by the Underground Man—to his conception of love as the "right to tyrannize" and be "morally superior."

The last paragraph of *Notes from the Underground*, beginning with the words, "even now, after all these years, it is with a particularly *bad feeling* that I recall all this," almost has the character of a detached chorus. Here the disillusioned idealist looks back on his encounter with Liza through sixteen years of remorse and suffering with a crime on his conscience: "never, never shall I recall that moment indifferently." The words of the Underground Man are now devoid of pun or paradox. He distances himself from the events described and places his own tragedy in a general broadly cultural and social light. He defines himself as an antihero. His tone seems to approach the

calm objectivity of Dostoevsky's footnote-preface, or prologue, to
Notes from the Underground. A change in the Underground Man's consciousness has taken place in sixteen or more years. (Indeed, we cannot properly analyze the notes of the Underground Man without
taking into account the shift that has occurred in his thinking since the
1840s.) What he failed to achieve in life he has to a considerable
extent gained in his notes: perspective on himself and his dilemma, a
perception of himself as morally and socially bankrupt.

It was, in part, to seek "relief" from his "oppressive memory,"
perhaps even to "become good and honorable" through the "labor" of
writing, that the Underground Man put down his recollections. And,
indeed, something unexpected happened in the process of writing. "I
made a mistake, I think, in beginning to write," he remarks at the
conclusion of his notes. "At any rate, I have felt ashamed all the while
I was writing this story [*povest'*]; consequently this is no longer literature, but a corrective punishment." The Underground Man gives
ironical emphasis to the word "story": these are not entertaining or
escapist stories; they are unadorned reality; they are shameful
tragedy. This is not the reader's kind of literature (the Underground
Man's irony is plain). This is not a romantic story: the posturing hero
and his play-acting have been brutally exposed. "A novel must have a
hero, but here all the features of an antihero have been *deliberately*
gathered together, and, chiefly, all this will produce a most unpleasant impression because we are all divorced from life . . . so much so
that we sometimes feel a sort of disgust for the real 'living life' . . . and
we are all agreed that life in books is better." (The ironical narrative
voice of Dostoevsky merges with the voice of the Underground Man
in this final passage.) There is, indeed, nothing invented in the Underground Man's reminiscences. The sentimental-romantic "hero" of
the 1840s—in fact, the whole ethos of romanticism—has been presented in the bitter perspective of the disillusioned idealist. What the
Underground Man declares at the end of part one, after admitting
that he made up the concluding speech of his imaginary critics, could
serve as an epigraph to his reminiscences: "But it is really the only
thing I did invent."

The Underground Man's impulse to play with the material of his
life and his penchant for the phrase may be felt in the notes. But this
impulse to play, or "tell a story," to evade the true sense of his life, like

all of the Underground Man's capricious attempts to escape his underground fate, does not succeed. He cannot evade the truth. "I shall not attempt any order or system," the Underground Man remarks on the threshold of part two with characteristic bravado and caprice. "I shall put down whatever I remember." Yet his reminiscences, like his philosophical discourse, are no more free from order or system than he is free from the laws of nature.

We must not confuse the Underground Man's subjective rejection of system, order, evolution, or historicism with the objective conditions of his enslavement to order. His impulse to put down his notes cannot be separated from his recollection of the episode with Liza that has been oppressing him for "some time." It cannot be separated from his broader effort to understand himself and his whole tragedy—or in the words of Dostoevsky, to "explain those causes that have led, and were bound to lead to his appearance in our midst." The Underground Man, much like the pawnbroker in "A Gentle Creature," is caught up in a dialectic of guilt that relentlessly drives him toward the truth. Beneath the surface of his seemingly casual notes, as beneath the surface of the seemingly random adventures of the hero of the 1840s, we observe a strict "psychological sequence" (a phrase Dostoevsky uses to describe the undercurrent in the pawnbroker's ruminations), a tragic system and order.

' Within the action," Aristotle remarks in his *Poetics*, "there must be nothing irrational." And again, with respect to plot: "Everything irrational should, if possible, be excluded."[4] The irony of the action in part two of *Notes from the Underground*—and, indeed, in the whole life of the Underground Man—is that the Underground Man himself, contrary to all his intentions, brings about these model Aristotelian conditions in the drama of his life. He puts a fatal order into the episodic plot of his life; he creates his own tragic necessity out of the accidental matter of his everyday life and encounters. The purely literary expression of this fatal ordering of the episodic plot of his life can be found in the notes of the Underground Man—perhaps the most connected, sequential, and tragically coherent "notes" ever written in any language.

[4]See *Aristotle's Theory of Poetry and Fine Art,* trans. and with critical notes by S. H. Butcher, 4th ed. (New York, 1951), pp. 54, 97.

By the end of his reminiscences we realize what is already evident
from the Underground Man's exposition of his irrational will
philosophy in part one: that he has been caught in a master plot that is
historical, linear, and Aristotelian, a plot that he seeks, always vainly,
to foil. We see him, in short, as he sees Liza—as entangled in a chain
that grows tighter the more he seeks to escape from it:

> Though I may be degrading and defiling myself, still I'm not
> anybody's slave; it's here for a moment, and then off again, and
> you've seen the last of me. I shake it off and am a different man.
> But you are a slave from the very start. Yes, a slave! You give up
> everything, your whole freedom. And even if you should want to
> break these chains later on you won't be able to; they will only
> entangle you more and more tightly. That's the kind of cursed
> chain it is. I know that kind. And I'm not going to speak of
> anything else, for you wouldn't understand anyway, I dare say
> (II, 6).

The Underground Man is the embodiment of irrational behavior.
Yet the singularity of his underground is that in it absolute chance is
indistinguishable from absolute necessity. His play with chance only
masks a surrender to the organized force of a self-conceived fate. In
this we find the central message of Dostoevsky. Man, he believed,
renouncing faith in God—that is, faith in a coherent Christian
universe—must inevitably confront the world as blind fate. Never was
a Dostoevsky hero (unless it be Fyodor Karamazov) more railroaded
by fate, by the uncontrollable dynamics of his inner being, than the
Underground Man. As we see him in part two in his own representation of his life—a drama he understands very well—nothing remains
episodic. Every attempt to introduce the irrational into his life and to
bring an illusion of authentic freedom, choice, self-determination;
every attempt to play with the plot of his life only further underscores
his subjection to the power of blind destiny. There is a precipitous
movement toward catastrophe, a moment of reversal, and then disaster, followed by a choral response. Borrowing from Aristotle's *Poetics*,
we might say that the final reversal, or recognition, arose from the
internal structure of the plot, and that this reversal produced "pity
and fear," and that "actions producing these effects are those which,
by our definition, tragedy represents."[5]

[5]*Ibid.*, p. 41.

Yet *Notes from the Underground* is not Aristotelian tragedy any more than is *Crime and Punishment*, nor can Raskolnikov and least of all the Underground Man stand in for heroic Promethean types.[6] The Underground Man and Raskolnikov conceive of themselves as victims of fate; but their real tragedy, in Dostoevsky's explicitly Christian outlook, is their despair. W. H. Auden has written that at the end of a Greek tragedy we say, "What a pity it had to be this way"; while at the end of a Christian tragedy we say, "What a pity it had to be this way when it might have been otherwise."[7] Dostoevsky might have directed these final words to the tragedy of the Underground Man. But they would not have prevented him from introducing into his Christian universe the strict laws of ancient tragedy—odious laws, in his view—which become operative whenever man fails to discover in his inner life the governing principles of Christian freedom: love and self-sacrifice.

After his crucial definition of himself as an antihero and his critique of society the Underground Man concludes his notes. "But enough," he writes, "I do not want to write any more 'from the Underground. . . .' " "However, this is still not the end of the 'notes' of this paradoxicalist," Dostoevsky observes in a final passage detached from the body of the notes. "He could not restrain himself and went on writing." There is certainly no doubt that the Underground Man was capable of writing on and on. There is also no doubt that the notes of the Underground Man—what Dostoevsky has entitled *Notes from the Underground*—constitute a unified structure. The drama that unfolds in part two has a beginning, middle, and end. The author of this work, though not its protagonist, is Dostoevsky. His final comment—"But it seems to us, too, that one can also stop here"— suggests that the Underground Man's desire to call a halt to his writing represented an intuitive understanding of the inner dynamics of his own drama. Dostoevsky's comment signals, as a kind of authorial punctuation, that on the dramatic and ideological planes this final chapter of the Underground Man's notes to all intents and purposes is terminal.

[6]"Raskolnikov's story," writes Konstantin Mochulsky, "is a new embodiment of the myth of Prometheus' revolt and the tragic hero's destruction in a struggle with Fate." See Mochul'skii. *Zhizn' i tvorchestvo* (Paris, 1947), p. 255.

[7]W. H. Auden, "The Christian Tragic Hero," in *New York Times Book Review*, December 16, 1945.

Dostoevsky and Rousseau: The Morality of Confession Reconsidered

by Robin Feuer Miller

In Dostoevsky's work the truth will out in various ways, but it rarely finds unadorned release through the mode inherently concerned with the utterance of truth: the confession. (The definition of confession that will be operative in these pages is the following: a confession is a statement or written document of some length, which is narrated to someone else and usually reveals a dark secret or crime.) Dostoevsky consistently treated the confession as a problematic, double-edged form. As such, we may expect to see the confession functioning simultaneously as an expression of pride and an experiment in humility. Indeed, the terms become interchangeable. Pride masquerades as humility and vice versa. Confessions may seek to provoke, titillate, or lie; the narrator may expose, disguise, justify, or lacerate himself. But rarely does the confession consist of a simple, repentant declaration of wrongdoing or moral weakness. Dostoevsky's scrutiny and critique of the literary confession frequently assumed the form of a veiled polemic with Rousseau and with his *Confessions* (1781).

At times Dostoevsky even allowed the veil to drop and, through his characters, named his adversary. Dostoevsky, whose life-long argument with Rousseau resembled his relationship with Belinsky, reacted

This essay is dedicated to the memory of Rufus Mathewson.

"Rousseau and Dostoevsky: The Morality of Confession Reconsidered" by Robin Feuer Miller. From *Western Philosophical Systems in Russian Literature*, ed. Anthony A. Mlikotin (Los Angeles: University of Southern California Press, 1979), pp. 89–101. Reprinted with slight stylistic changes by permission of the author and publisher.

to Rousseau with simultaneous attraction and repulsion.[1] Moreover, Dostoevsky condemned Rousseau's philanthropy *(chelovekoliubie)* as well as his habit of confession. In the notes for *A Raw Youth* (1875–1876), for example, Dostoevsky wrote, "He hates Genevan ideas [an indirect, but clear allusion to Rousseau] (that is, philanthropy; that is, virtue without Christ) . . ." By equating philanthropy with "virtue without Christ," or, as Joseph Frank has put it, with "the application of Christian moral-social ideals to worldly existence,"[2] Dostoevsky made the notion of philanthropy a signpost for the political ideas he detested. Dostoevsky singled out two episodes from the *Confessions*—one in which Rousseau describes how he would wander the streets and haunt dark alleys where he could "expose [him]self to women from afar off" and the other in which he recounts his false accusation of a defenseless girl of the theft of a ribbon—as offering particularly rich opportunities for parodic variation in his own fiction. Nevertheless, despite Dostoevsky's sustained critique—through parody and polemic—of Rousseau's *Confessions*, he felt, throughout his entire career, a continued attraction to the confessional mode and always had a predilection for first person narratives both in his short stories and in his longer fiction.[3]

In *The Insulted and Injured* (1861) Valkovsky speculates about the notion of men confessing their worst acts: "If it were only possible (which, however, from the laws of human nature it never can be

[1]Yurii Lotman, "Russo: russkaia kul'tura XVIII-nachala XIX veka," *Zhan-Zhak Russo. Traktaty* (Leningrad, 1969), pp. 603–4. For a more complete set of my bibliographical references and citations, see the first printed version of "Rousseau and Dostoevsky: The Morality of Confession Reconsidered," *Western Philosophical Systems in Russian Literature*, Anthony M. Mlikotin, ed. (Los Angeles: University of Southern California Press, 1979), pp. 89–101, or *Dostoevsky and The Idiot: Author, Narrator and Reader* (Cambridge: Harvard University Press, 1981), pp. 175–82. For another, and excellent, reading of the relationship of *Notes from Underground* to Rousseau's *Confessions* see Barbara Howard, "The Rhetoric of Confession: Dostoevsky's *Notes from the Underground* and Rousseau's *Confessions*," *SEEJ*, vol. 25, no. 4, (winter 1981), pp. 16–33. All quotations from Rousseau are from his *Confessions*. I have indicated in parentheses the book and section from which I have quoted.

[2]Joseph Frank, *Dostoevsky: The Seeds of Revolt, 1821–1849* (Princeton: Princeton Univ. Press, 1976), p. 193.

[3]Leonid Grossman, "Stilistika Stavrogina," *Sobranie Sochinenii*, II (Moscow, 1928), 143–44.

possible), if it were possible for every one of us to describe all his own whole truth, but in such a way that one wouldn't hesitate to disclose not only what he is afraid to tell his best friends, but what, indeed, he is even, at times, afraid to confess to himself; then, the world would be filled with such a stench that we should all have to gasp for breath" (III, 10). (Later, in *Notes from Underground* [1864], the Underground Man boasts that the substance of his disclosure will consist of precisely these worst acts and truths that men are afraid to confess to themselves.) Nevertheless, Valkovsky creates the opportunity for making such a confession. He compares the thrill of confession, of suddenly removing the mask, to the thrill of indecent exposure. He describes a crazy Paris official who wandered about dressed only in his cloak: ". . . whenever he met anyone in a lonely place . . . he silently walked up to him, with the most serious and profoundly thoughtful air suddenly stepped before him, threw open his cloak and showed himself in all the . . . purity of his heart. That would last for a minute, then he would wrap himself up again, and silently . . . he would pass by the petrified spectator, as importantly and majestically as the ghost in *Hamlet*" (III, 10).

Valkovsky's metaphor of confession as indecent exposure finds its ultimate source in Rousseau's *Confessions* and thereby marks the beginning of Dostoevsky's long moral critique of this genre as defined by Rousseau. Early in the *Confessions* Rousseau wrote, "My disturbance of mind became so strong that, being unable to satisfy my desires, I excited them by the most extravagant behaviour. I haunted dark alleys and lonely spots where I could expose myself to women from afar off in the condition in which I should have liked to be in their company. What they saw was nothing obscene, I was far from thinking of that; it was ridiculous. The absurd pleasure I got from displaying myself before their eyes is quite indescribable" (I, 3). Dostoevsky has taken one of Rousseau's anecdotes and has made Valkovsky transform it into a symbol for confession in general.

Valkovsky had addressed his confession to the narrator, calling him throughout, "my poet." Just as Stavrogin is to do later, Valkovsky tries to make something literary out of his confession. He sprinkles his narrative with literary allusions: he invokes the Marquis de Sade and, by relating an anecdote about his affair with a seemingly virtuous woman, whom he compares to the abbess of a medieval convent, a secret and profligate sinner, Valkovsky suggests that he has read such Gothic novels as Matthew Lewis's *The Monk* (1795) and Charles Maturin's *Melmoth the Wanderer* (1820), novels which enjoyed significant popular success in Russia. Despite Valkovsky's attempts to elevate his confession to the status of art, however, it remains a form of vanity, of contemptuous, indecent exposure that depends upon the existence of an audience to outrage. One cannot expose oneself indecently in private—or before God. The narrator perceives Valkovsky's corrupt use of the confessional genre, "I agree that you could not have expressed your spite and your contempt for me and for all of us better than by your frankness to me. You were not only not apprehensive that your frankness might compromise you before me, but you are not even ashamed before me. You have certainly resembled that madman in the cloak" (III, 10).

The Underground Man, on the other hand, actually repeats Rousseau's solitary indulgences, but he does not consciously create a metaphor for confession out of these experiences. "I indulged in debauchery alone, at nights, in secret, fearfully, filthily, with a shame which never left me. . . . even then I already carried the underground in my soul. I was terribly afraid lest anyone should see me, recognize me. I visited various dark places" (II, 1).

Even in *The Possessed* (1873) the life style of the young Stavrogin— the Prince Harry with his Falstaff Lebyadkin—may partially derive from this same anecdote of Rousseau, although Stavrogin's roots in Dostoevsky's own underground characters are certainly dominant. Stavrogin shares Rousseau's fascination with "extravagant behavior" and "absurd" pleasures. In the notes for *The Possessed*, "Nechaev," who becomes Pyotr Verkhovensky in the novel, makes a characteristically cynical passing reference to Rousseau which offers a nice example of the way in which Dostoevsky permits his less savory characters to express his own views in outrageous form: "Useful also are drunkenness, and pederasty, masturbation, as in Rousseau. All this tends to bring things down to a median level."

Toward the end of his career, in *A Raw Youth* (1875–76), Dostoevsky returned again to the theme of Rousseauian "exposure." One evening Arkady and a student approach a respectable woman on a deserted street, and, "preserving unruffled countenances as though it were the natural thing to do," they enter into a description of "various filth and obscenities, which the filthiest imagination of the filthiest debauchee could hardly have conceived." Arkady confesses, "I repeated this diversion for eight days ... At first I thought it original ∴.. I once told the student that Jean-Jacques Rousseau describes in his 'Confessions,' that he, as a youth, loved quietly to display himself from behind a corner, to uncover the usually covered parts of his body and lie in wait in this condition for passing women" (III, 6). After more than fifteen years, Dostoevsky has made explicit reference to this particular episode from the *Confessions*. But by now, through its reworkings in *The Insulted and Injured* and *Notes from Underground* the source for this passage belongs as much to Dostoevsky himself as it does to Rousseau.

But it is in the notes for *A Raw Youth* that Dostoevsky again makes an explicit comparison between the act of confession and indecent exposure as he had had Valkovsky do a decade and a half earlier. This time, however, Rousseau is named and he figures in both terms of the comparison: Dostoevsky equates Rousseau's solitary vices with his "literary" ones. "Just as Rousseau found enjoyment in exposing himself, so did he find voluptuous pleasure in exposing himself to young people—even corrupting them by his complete frankness *(otkrovennost')*." Yury Lotman has observed that for Dostoevsky "sincerity" often became in his fiction synonymous with self-love, and the enjoyment of confession—a baring of the soul—became equivalent to the enjoyment of self-contemplation, of egoism, of voluptuousness, and, frequently, of crime.[4]

In *Notes from Underground* Dostoevsky allows his Underground Man an acute perception of the confession as a contradictory, easily misused form. But Dostoevsky does not permit him to escape his addiction to the confessional mode. The Underground Man reasons that a confession such as his cannot occur without some notion of an audience. Like any other mode of narration, it must be directed toward someone in order to exist at all, even if that audience never really gets to read it. He writes to his imagined audience, "Why, in fact, do I call you 'gentlemen,' Why do I address myself to you as though you were really my readers? Such confessions as I intend to make are not printed or given to others to read" (I, 11). He writes that he wants to

[4]Lotman, "Russo ... ," p. 604.

try to confess the whole truth, but even as he acknowledges this, he must deny the possibility of success.

The certain failure of his venture lies in the nature of the confessional genre itself: it is impossible simply to express a thing directly and explicitly without distorting it. By narrating a confession, the one who confesses inevitably becomes involved in questions of narrative technique, style, presentation of self, and the effect of his words on his imagined (or actual) audience. The Underground Man is tortured by this knowledge. He writes, "I will observe by the way: Heine maintains that true autobiographies are almost impossible, and that man himself is bound to lie about himself. In his opinion, Rousseau, for example, certainly lied to himself in his *Confession*, and even intentionally lied, out of vanity. I am certain that Heine is right; I understand very well how sometimes one may, solely from vanity, attribute whole crimes to oneself, and I can even very well conceive what sort of vanity that may be" (I, 11).

Though the Underground Man represents a repository of the values and beliefs against which Dostoevsky was struggling, Dostoevsky has given him the same precious understanding with which he later endowed Myshkin in *The Idiot*; both characters see that an attempt to portray oneself or one's ideas directly inevitably leads to some degree of distortion. Myshkin, however, in his role as a confessor (the recipient of confessions) seeks to accept all the various motives inherent in any confession, and to forgive those that are vain or dishonest. Like the one who actually confesses, the reader or recipient of the confession treads on dangerous ground and may be as quickly distracted from the purported thrust of the confession as is the narrator of the confession. For, as a spectator or reader or listener, the person who hears or overhears the confession also finds himself inevitably considering such issues as modes of presentation, psychological motivations, and a host of other concerns that perhaps should be, but are not, extraneous to the simple act of communication.

The Underground Man unwittingly lays bare his own vanity and irresistible need to distort. He agrees with Heine's view of Rousseau in the *Confessions* and tries to set himself apart from Rousseau's stance. He justifies his own confession by observing, "But Heine had formed an opinion about a man who confessed before the public. I write only for myself" (I, 11). Nevertheless, in narrating his confession only for himself, he has found it necessary to postulate an audience; his narration cannot exist without imagined readers.

Always the first to realize his own inconsistency, the Underground Man sets out to justify why, then, he has had to invent readers:

> ... and I announce once and for all that if I write as if I were addressing readers, that it is only for show, because it is easier for me to write that way. It is a form, only an empty form; I shall never have readers. . . . But here, for example, someone will catch at the word and ask me: if you really don't count on readers, then why are you now making such compacts with yourself, and on paper too. . . . Why are you explaining? Why are you apologizing?—Well, there it is,—I answer. There is a whole psychology here, however. Perhaps it is that I am simply a coward. And perhaps, it is that I purposely imagine an audience before me in order that I may conduct myself in a more dignified way while I write. There are perhaps a thousand reasons (I, II).

Yet to be more "dignified" means, in some sense, to justify one's acts, to attribute a worthiness to oneself. The Underground Man goes on to justify the act of writing:

> But again: for what reason, why do I in particular want to write? If it is not for the sake of the public, then shouldn't I simply recall everything in my own mind without putting it on paper? Quite so, but on paper it comes out, somehow, more imposing. There is something more inspiring in it; it will be a greater judgment upon myself; it will augment my style. Besides— perhaps I will actually receive relief from writing things down. . . . Finally, I am bored. . . . Writing will actually be a sort of work. They say that a man becomes good and honest through work. Well, there is at least a chance (I, 11).

Despite his verbal machinations, the Underground Man has not escaped the same failings he has just attributed to Rousseau: confession through vanity and self-justification and the inevitable need for the narrator of a confession to lie. He has put his confession in writing for the vain reason that it will be more "imposing." As with Valkovsky and Stavrogin, the literariness of his work is essential. He feels it to be important as a way of "augmenting his style." The very act of confession functions as a cathartic atonement; indulgence in the confessional form helps compensate for the content of the confession. He hopes to obtain relief through writing: the act of writing may itself make him a better man. But all his explanations and analyses about the nature of confessions and of their readers cannot bring him closer to the philosophical purpose of a genuine confession—to complete honesty, humility, or repentance.

In *The Idiot* (1868) the confessions told at Nastasya Filippovna's nameday party contain the same bracing mix of vanity, self-justifications, and lies as did the confessions of Valkovsky or the Underground Man. Once again Dostoevsky engages in a direct polemic with Rousseau and his *Confessions*. But this time he abandons his reworkings of the "indecent exposure" episode in favor of another episode from Rousseau's work.

Ferdyshchenko, who serves as a herald of disorder and of brutally-arrived-at truths, presides over the uneasy group of guests at Nastasya Filippovna's nameday as a mater of ceremonies.[5] He is accepted as a court jester—albeit one without wit—with special privileges to blurt out the truth. Ferdyshchenko proposes the *petit-jeu* in which each person must confess his worst action. It is no surprise that under Ferdyshchenko's aegis the confessional form will be heartily misused. When Ganya notes that everyone will be certain to lie, Ferdyschenko answers, "yes, and the entertaining thing is just how a man will lie." Moreover, for all his self-avowed lack of "wit," Ferdyshchenko perceives a crucial fact which any narrator must take into account: audiences would rather witness the fall of a hero than the fall of any ordinary man. "Well, gentlemen, of course I must set a noble example, but what I regret most at this moment is that I am so worthless and am in no way remarkable. . . . Well, what in fact is of interest in the fact that Ferdyshchenko committed a nasty deed?" (I, 13).

The confession becomes a mode of titillation for bored guests who want "cheering up." Their desire for originality has decayed into a

[5]Mikhail Bakhtin has written of the "carnivalized" worlds of "Bobok" and of *The Idiot*, where "People appear for a moment outside the normal situations of life, as on the carnival square or in the nether world, and a different—more genuine—sense of themselves and of their relationships to one another is revealed." He designates to Ferdyshchenko the role of a "petty mystery-play devil" whose suggestions for the evening's entertainment help "to create the carnival-square atmosphere" (Bakhtin, *Problems of Dostoevsky's Poetics*, trans. R. W. Rotsel (Ann Arbor, Ardis, 1973), p. 120).

hunger for anything provocative. Even Nastasya Filippovna has been infected. She agrees to Ferdyshchenko's proposal on the grounds that it's "terribly original." Thus, the confessions narrated by Ferdyshchenko, General Epanchin, and Totsky begin in an atmosphere of cynicism and hunger for the sensational. As Totsky notes, "Truth is possible here [in this game] only by accident, through a certain kind of boasting of the worst kind, which is unthinkable and completely indecent here [at the party]" (I, 13).

In his narrative Ferdyshchenko confesses to having pocketed a three-rouble note left on his hostess' work table. He then showed much kindness to the house maid who was falsely accused of the deed; he tried to persuade her to admit to the theft, assuring her that she could count on the leniency of her mistress. "I felt an extraordinary pleasure, particularly from the fact that I was preaching while the note lay in my pocket" (I, 14). He spent the money that evening on a bottle of wine. When the audience responds with disgust, Ferdyshchenko shows his malevolent, but accurate understanding of what is typically most appreciated and expected by the audience of a confessional narrative, "Bah! You want to hear the worst act of a man and you demand that there be something shining in it. The worst acts are always filthy. . . ." (I, 14).

As a narrator he refuses to give the audience what they want, although he involuntarily seeks their approval. His contempt for the confessional genre does not exempt him from wishing that its effect would be pleasant all the same. The narrator takes wry note of Ferdyshchenko's enraged loss of composure when he observes his audience's disgust, "Strange as it may be, it is very likely that he expected a completely different success from his story" (I, 14). Ferdyshchenko has cynically toyed with his audience's expectations, but he cannot divorce himself from his need to be accepted. Although Ferdyshchenko did not openly refer to Rousseau as the Underground Man had done, his anecdote has been largely inspired by one of the principal episodes in the *Confessions*. (Typically, Dostoevsky probably also used his own previous work as a source here. Ferdyshchenko's pleasure at his successful framing of the servant girl and his delight, at the same time, in pretending to preach to her with dignity and kindness resemble Luzhin's failed attempt to frame Sonya in *Crime and Punishment* [1866].)

In this early episode Rousseau describes a crime that had tormented him for forty years: he once stole a pink and silver ribbon.[6] When it was discovered on him, he falsely accused the young cook of the household, Marion, saying she had given it to him. Ferdyshchenko's similar false accusation of the maid-servant has left him singularly free from remorse (indeed it gave him "extraordinary pleasure") while it is remorse for this deed which has activated Rousseau's need to write his confessions. Rousseau writes, "The burden, therefore, has rested till this day on my conscience without any relief; and I can affirm that the desire to some extent to rid myself of it has greatly contributed to my resolution of writing these Confessions" (I, 2). (The Underground Man, for all his alleged rejection of Rousseau, had admitted the same motive—the motive of finding "relief"—for his own confession.)

But Rousseau's analysis of his deed reveals a certain self-satisfaction and unnerving self-confidence. He does not admit the possibility of a lie:

> "I have been absolutely frank in the account I have just given, and no one will accuse me, I am certain, of palliating the heinousness of my offence. But I should not fulfill the aim of this book if I did not at the same time reveal my inner feelings and hesitated to put up such excuses for myself as I honestly could. Never was deliberate wickedness further from my intention at that cruel moment" (I, 2).

In fact, by the end of his account he seems to have become positively proud of his crime. "So the memory tortures me less on account of the crime itself than because of its possible evil consequences. I have derived some benefit from the terrible impression left with me by the sole offence I have committed. For it has secured me for the rest of my life against any act that might prove criminal in its results. I think also that my loathing of untruth derives to a large extent from my having told that one wicked lie. . . . I have little fear of carrying the sin on my conscience at death" (I, 2). Here is a unique brand of spiritual vanity not even dreamed of by Valkovsky or the Underground Man,

---

[6]For a particularly compelling interpretation about the underlying motives for Rousseau's deed, see Paul deMan, "The Purloined Ribbon," *Glyph*, no. 1, vol. I, 1977, pp. 28-50.

or even by Ferdyshchenko. Rousseau exonerates himself with unshake-
able impunity. His *Confessions* provide the model for this genre
throughout the nineteenth century.

The resemblance of Ferdyshchenko's anecdote to this crucial
episode in the *Confessions* thus alerts the reader to the presence of a
serious parody and critique of the confessional form. During the
course of Nastasya Filippovna's party, everyone, from the narrator-
chronicler and the reader to the characters themselves, shares a
knowledge that the typical confession is often a morally bankrupt
form.

General Epanchin, the next participant in the *petit-jeu*, relates an
incident that occurred thirty-five years earlier when he was a poor
second lieutenant. Late one afternoon he cursed an old woman, his
former landlady, for appropriating his soup bowl as payment for a
broken pot. She sat facing him with no response. Later, he learned
that she had been dying at the very time he'd been swearing at her. To
assuage his guilt, fifteen years ago he had provided for two ill old
women; he is even considering the establishment of a permanent
endowment at the public hospital.

Ferdyshchenko, now no longer a narrator but a member of the
audience, responds, "And instead of your nastiest deed, your Excel-
lency, you have told one of the good deeds of your life; you have
cheated Ferdyshchenko!" (I, 14). Certainly the general's intention
(whether successful or not) in his confession of a "worst deed" has
secretly been to narrate a "best deed." (Yet the general, contrary to his
intent, has perhaps unknowingly narrated his worst deed after all: he
has related a personal evil deed that he sought to erase by an act of
impersonal good—by establishing "a permanent endowment by providing a capital fund." Throughout the novel the "author" Dostoevsky
explores the ways in which goodness travels through the world; he
establishes a consistent opposition between effective acts of personal
goodness and the ineffective, even harmful results of institutionalized
beneficience—philanthropy [*chelovekoliubie*].)

General Epanchin's confession resembles that same episode from
Rousseau's *Confessions* of which Ferdyschchenko made use. But where
Ferdyshchenko's anecdote reflected the content of Rousseau's tale
about the stolen ribbon while systematically detaching itself from
Rousseau's emotional stance of repentance and eventual self-

justification, here the general mimics Rousseau's attitude toward the deed, his stance of guilty, but lofty sincerity. The general notes that though the action occurred long ago (thirty-five years, as compared to Rousseau's forty), he cannot recall it without experiencing a pang, ". . . the more time goes by, the more I think of it. . . . Without doubt, I am guilty, and, although I have already regarded my deed for a long time with the passing of years and with the change in my nature as being the deed of a stranger, I nevertheless feel sorry" (I, 14). Rousseau had expressed a similar sentiment: "I took away lasting memories of a crime and the unbearable weight of a remorse which, even after forty years, still burdens my conscience. In fact, the bitter memory of it, far from fading, grows more painful with the years" (I, 2). Of course the general's easy "after-dinner" attitude toward his crime does not have the ring of sincerity that Rousseau's lament does: instead his words both recreate and ridicule the structure of Rousseau's confession.

Moreover, both men, Rousseau and General Epanchin, end by being the ones to bestow forgiveness upon themselves. Rousseau assures himself that "really my crime amounted to no more than weakness" (I, 2). General Epanchin takes these self-assurances even further, "So that, I repeat, it seems strange to me, all the more that if I am guilty, I am not completely guilty. . . ." (I, 14). He manages finally to blame the old woman for letting herself die at that unfortunate moment. Furthermore, each confidently proclaims that the evil deed has yielded a measure of good. We have already encountered Rousseau's insistence that his "sole offense" had "secured for him for the rest of his life against any act that might prove criminal in its results. . . . Poor Marion finds so many avengers in this world that, however great my offence against her may have been, I have little fear of carrying the sin on my conscience at death" (I, 2). In like spirit, General Epanchin describes his subsequent acts of philanthropy. Through his parodic reworkings of these two episodes from Rousseau—the incidents of "indecent exposure" and the stolen ribbon—Dostoevsky has exposed the literary confession as reflecting alternatively a desire to shock one's audience or to justify oneself before it.

Totsky is the last participant in the *petit-jeu*. His account of his worst action arouses interest in the reader and the other characters because they all know one of his worst deeds already; indeed, the results of his violation of Nastasya Filippovna have generated the plot of most of the novel so far. His confession, however, does not have direct roots in Rousseau's *Confessions* but instead derives its style and content from an unabashed blend of Lermontov and Dumas *fils* (especially his novel *La Dame aux Camelias*). Nevertheless, like Valkovsky, the Underground Man, and Stavrogin, Totsky seeks a kind of moral exoneration through the fact that the event and its retelling resemble the aesthetic contours of fictional art. For all these characters, a life that has come to resemble literature is at the same time absolved from serious moral accountability. At the end of his narrative, Totsky himself admits that "it came out decidedly like a novel" (I, 14). For Totsky, there can be no worse deed because, for him, immorality does not exist. Thus, in his hands the confessional genre becomes, simply, absurd. Totsky cares only for beauty, taste, and originality; it is impossible for him to make a genuine confession.

In Stavrogin's "Confession" in *The Possessed* (1873) we may discover further echoes of Rousseau's false accusation of the servant maid Marion. The crucial chapter, "At Tikhon's," which contains Stavrogin's confession, was not originally published with the novel because Katkov, the editor of *Russkii Vestnik* felt it was too controversial. This chapter has survived in two versions: the galley proofs of the December 1871 issue of *Russkii Vestnik* with Dostoevsky's corrections and an unfinished copy made later by Anna Grigorievna Dostoevskaya from an unknown manuscript.[7] In this chapter and particularly in Stavrogin's statement itself, Dostoevsky relentlessly explores the moral implications and voluptuous motivations potentially inherent in false accusation (albeit a passively enacted accusation). The more indirect modes of parody and ridicule have been abandoned. Stavrogin allows the child Matryosha to be flogged for the supposed theft of his penknife. But Stavrogin, while adopting Rousseau's stance of complete honesty, does not adopt Rousseau's tones of regret or self-

[7]For a discussion of the complicated history of this chapter in both its versions, see F. M. Dostoevskii, *Polnoe sobranie sochinenii v tridtsati tomakh*, XII (Leningrad, 1975), pp. 237–53. I have enclosed in brackets any sentences from Anna Dostoevsky's copy. Her version contains essential variations from the earlier one. The Russian editors of the recent complete collection of Dostoevsky's works consider her version to have the status of an independent redaction, although they have presented the earlier version as the main one.

justification. ["I immediately felt that I had done something base, and at the same time I felt a certain pleasure, because suddenly a sensation burned through me like an iron, and I began to indulge in it.] ... Reaching the point of absolute fire in myself, I could at the same time completely control it, even stop it at the highest point, only I rarely wanted to stop" ("At Tikhon's," II).

This anecdote, a confession of moral voluptuousness, recalls aspects of both the episodes from Rousseau's *Confessions* under discussion here—Rousseau's episode of indecent exposure and his false accusation of Marion—and creates a frightening synthesis of them. The pleasure which Stavrogin experiences in his sadistic torment of Matryosha resembles the pleasure felt by Rousseau in his lonely rambles as well as recalling the other characters in Dostoevsky's works who sought out both occasions for voluptuous exposure and occasions to confess their "indecent" acts. "I want everyone to look at me," writes Stavrogin toward the end of his statement. Rousseau's encounter with Marion spurred him on to write his *Confessions* and to seek the good. Stavrogin's encounter with Matryosha, whom he initially allows to be thrashed for taking his penknife (although he sees it lying on the bed), also "inspired" his confession, but his relations with her end only after he has precipitated and witnessed her suicide. Indeed, the degree to which Dostoevsky polemicized with and parodied the Rousseau of *The Confessions* in "At Tikhon's" cannot be overestimated, and Grossman has aptly observed that Stavrogin "without doubt repeats the psychological experience *(opyt)* of Rousseau, just as Dostoevsky reproduces the style of his brilliant confession *(pokaianie)*."[8]

Moreover, Stavrogin actually names Rousseau. The passage quoted above continues: "I am convinced that I could live my whole life like a monk, despite the bestial voluptuousness with which I have been endowed and which I have always provoked. Abandoning myself with unusual immoderation until the age of sixteen to the vice which Jean-Jacques Rousseau confessed to, in my seventeenth year I stopped at that very moment when I decided to. I am always master of myself when I want to be. And so ... I do not want to plead irresponsibility for my crimes because of my environment or because of illness" ("At Tikhon's," II). Yet even as Stavrogin describes his self-control over "the vice which Jean-Jacques Rousseau confessed to," his actual con-

[8]Grossman, "Stilistika ... ," p. 146.

fession, as Tikhon realizes, is inspired by spite and hatred. Tikhon understands that Stavrogin is not ashamed "to confess" but is "ashamed of repentance." Stavrogin's confession itself constitutes a further act of the moral voluptuousness to which he is addicted, for it debases the aim of a genuine confession: to express regret and seek repentance.

For Stavrogin (as for Valkovsky) the choice of his audience is all-important. He says to Tikhon, "Listen, I'll tell you the whole truth: I want you to forgive me, and along with you a second and a third, but all the others—absolutely let them hate me" ("At Tikhon's," II). (Rousseau also chose his audience carefully: "My purpose is to display to my kind a portrait in every way true to nature . . ." [II, 1]) As Tikhon knows, that which most terrifies Stavrogin is the possibility of being laughed at, of being considered ridiculous. Tikhon's understanding of this fear of being thought ridiculous once again evokes the presence of Rousseau who observed, "It is the ridiculous and the shameful, not one's criminal actions, that it is hardest to confess."[9] (I, 2) Stavrogin bitterly accuses Tikhon, "You find the figure I cut, when I kissed the foot of the dirty little girl, ridiculous . . . I understand" ("At Tikhon's," II). Tikhon realizes that Stavrogin wants his crime to be thought impressive, horrible. If, instead, others were to find it disgraceful or shameful or "inelegant," Stavrogin could not bear it.

Stavrogin's confession, which he has presented to Tikhon on already printed sheets, was judged by both the narrator-chronicler and by Tikhon himself as a literary document. They each become literary critics rather than spontaneous listeners or readers. The narrator comments on the numerous "spelling mistakes" and irregular style in the document. Tikhon describes Stavrogin's tendency to intensify his style and offer details "merely to astound the reader," and eventually offers Stavrogin a formal criticism of his "work": "Even in the very form behind this great penitence *(pokaianie)*, is contained something [that to the world is] ridiculous, [seemingly false . . . not to mention the form which is not firm, vague, and, as if from the weakness of fear, undignified. . . .]" ("At Tikhon's," II). The written confession necessarily forces its readers to judge it as a literary document, thus it can never function simply as the communication of a deed. Instead, it

[9]The Russian editors cite Tikhon's indirect allusion to Rousseau as well, XII, p. 321.

deflects both author and audience away from reacting to straightforward statements and involves them in secondary considerations of style, form, and even spelling.

Dostoevsky rarely mentioned Rousseau in his writings, but his involvement with Rousseau's *Confessions* was particularly intense.[10] For Dostoevsky, a character's use of the confessional mode was always problematic. On the one hand, ideally, a confession could register and convey the condition of the inner man, but, on the other, in reality, the very act of making a confession—the attempt to portray one's own inner being—could easily falsify or change the essential idea the author of the confession was initially seeking to express.

Ironically, both Belinsky and Strakhov, two ideologically opposed critics, compared Dostoevsky to Rousseau, although Dostoevsky himself so often took issue with him. Belinsky wrote in 1846: "I am now reading *The Confessions*—in all my life, few books have acted on me as powerfully as this one," but subsequently he remarked, "I have a great loathing for this man. He so resembles Dostoevsky." Nearly forty years later, in 1883, Strakhov wrote to Tolstoy, "I cannot consider Dostoevsky either a good or a happy man. He was spiteful, envious, dissolute, and spent all his life in a state of agitation that made him appear pitiful and would have made him appear ridiculous if he had not at the same time been so spiteful and so intelligent. Like Rousseau, however, he considered himself the best and the happiest of men." Strakhov's comments would have especially embittered Dostoevsky, for it was precisely Rousseau's habit of self-justification that Dostoevsky held up to scrutiny time and time again.

One cannot imagine Dostoevsky saying openly, without having assumed the guise of a fictional persona, as Rousseau does: "So let the numberless legion of my fellow men gather round me, and hear my confessions. Let them groan at my depravities, and blush for my misdeeds. But let each one of them reveal his heart at the foot of Thy Throne with equal sincerity, and may any man who dares, say, 'I was a better man than he' " (I, 1). Without some kind of irony, qualification, or distance Rousseau's faith in his own sincerity is unnerving. Dostoevsky, whom one may tentatively, gingerly equate with Myshkin in this respect—although it is, of course, always dangerous to make such

[10]For a general discussion of the role of Rousseau in Dostoevsky's works, see Dostoevskii, *Pis'ma*, ed. A. S. Dolinin, II (Moscow, 1930), pp. 510–511.

equations between authors and characters—always acknowledged his "double thoughts"; he never, to use Lionel Trilling's phrase about Rousseau, claimed an "uncompromising . . . pre-eminence in sincerity."[11]

In Dostoevsky's canon, then, the literary-bookish-written confession most often tends to lie, to seek self-justification, or to aim at shocking the audience. But Dostoevsky does concede that the choice of an audience is important, and successful, genuine confessions do occur—witness Raskolnikov with Sonya, or "the mysterious visitor" with the elder Zosima, or even the hapless Keller with Myshkin. But in each case, the confession of one's transgression before a good soul is only a first step, as Raskolnikov and the mysterious visitor learn. The successful confession retains a sacrament, a sacred communication. Rousseau's *Confession*, a confession made to his peers, opens itself up to charges of self-interest or self-justification. Dostoevsky reconsidered this mode—the romantic and literary commonplace of the confession—he exposed and parodied it. But he ended by restoring the confession to its original form, that of a confession by man before God and before the collective manifestation of Him that resides in the people. Dostoevsky's characters partake fully of the romantic-realistic climate surrounding them: they are obsessed with fulfilling their own destinies, with developing their own individuality. But Dostoevsky imposed stern moral terms upon this participation. Genuine confessions, when they occur, do not further the development of any of these self-oriented drives. Instead, the genuine confession always serves to reunite man with other men and with the whole universe; motives of self-justification or explanation, and especially questions of literary style, become forever irrelevant.

[11]Lionel Trilling, *Sincerity and Authenticity: The Charles Eliot Norton Lectures, 1969–70* (Cambridge, Mass.: Harvard University Press, 1972), p. 58.

Raskolnikov's City
and the Napoleonic Plan

by Adele Lindenmeyr

Having lived in Petersburg's Haymarket area in the 1840s and 1860s, Dostoevsky observed at close hand the strains and dislocation created by unplanned urban growth. In a little noted passage in *Crime and Punishment* recounting Raskolnikov's thoughts just before the murder (I, 6), Dostoevsky connects these urban problems to Raskolnikov's thoughts and subsequent actions. Raskolnikov imagines a reconstruction of Petersburg aimed especially at improving the crowded, wretched conditions of Haymarket. This passage yields insights into the character of Raskolnikov and the thematics of the novel. In it, the city takes two forms, both of which have a powerful psychological influence on Raskolnikov: the squalid reality of Haymarket and the ideal of his imagining, modeled after Napoleon III's reconstruction of Paris. Both cities, real and ideal, support Raskolnikov's motive and justification for the murder. For Dostoevsky, however, the reality of Haymarket undermines Raskolnikov's utilitarian, Napoleonic scheme of reconstruction and, by extension, his intellectual rationale for the murder.

Dostoevsky set the great majority of his works in Petersburg and made extensive use of the character types and scenes of that city. Commentators such as Leonid Grossman have pointed out the close attention he paid to urban reality and the resulting authenticity of his works for contemporary readers. Donald Fanger has argued that Dostoevsky's recreation of mid-nineteenth-century Petersburg serves suc-

"Raskolnikov's City and the Napoleonic Plan" by Adele Lindenmeyr. From *The Slavic Review*, vol. 35 (March 1976), no. 1, pp. 37–47. Reprinted with slight changes by permission of the editor.

ceeding generations of readers as "realistic ballast, his way of anchoring the feverish improbabilities of the action of his books in real life."[1]

The Petersburg that Dostoevsky most often portrays bears a distinct geographical and socioeconomic identity. Fashionable districts seldom appear in his writings. The classical architecture of Petersburg, Dostoevsky remarks in "Little Pictures" in the *Diary of a Writer* for 1873, "is extremely characteristic and original and what always struck me was that it expresses all its characterlessness and lack of individuality throughout its existence." The Haymarket *(Sennaia Ploshchad')* area, however, and similar quarters of the city fascinated him. His daughter describes how in the 1840s he roamed "the darkest and most deserted streets of Petersburg. He talked to himself as he walked, gesticulating, and causing passers-by to turn and look at him."[2] He often chose as the setting for a story the middle- and lower-class parts of the Admiralty district around Voznesensky Prospect and Haymarket, which in the mid-nineteenth century had little in common with the classical buildings and squares of the administrative and fashionable parts of the district. The Haymarket neighborhood, where in the 1860s Dostoevsky lived on the corner of Carpenter's Lane and Little Tradesmen Street, is especially prominent in *Crime and Punishment.*

What exactly was the urban reality of this part of mid-nineteenth-century Petersburg? Rapid, unregulated expansion in the 1860s was changing Peter I's carefully planned city and creating serious problems unbefitting the capital of a huge and powerful empire. With the emancipation of the serfs in 1861, peasants migrated in ever greater numbers to the capital to seek jobs in the city's growing industries and services. This influx and the economic and social changes brought on by the growth of manufacturing strained Petersburg's already inadequate facilities—water supply, health and sanitation services (there were cholera epidemics in the city in 1848 and 1866), and housing. The consequences for the population were manifest: disease, unemployment, crime, prostitution, and drunkenness were widely discussed in the contemporary press of the capital.

Petersburg's most notorious slum was the area around Haymarket. The market itself was one of the oldest, largest and busiest centers of

[1]Donald Fanger, *Dostoevsky and Romantic Realism* (Chicago, 1967), p. 134.
[2]Aimée Dostoyevsky, *Fyodor Dostoyevsky, A Study* (London, 1921), p. 49.

small-scale retail trade in the city. Its transient population and filth made it an ideal breeding ground for infectious disease.[3] Every available corner of the overcrowded, ill-equipped tenements surrounding the market was let out at high rents; with 247 people per house the Haymarket neighborhood had the highest population density in the city.[4] A local landmark nicknamed the "Vyazemsky Monastery" was a great block of slums owned by Prince Vyazemsky, which served as the location of the "Crystal Palace" tavern in *Crime and Punishment*. As a center of trade for the capital and the surrounding region, Haymarket abounded with cheap eating houses and taverns. Raskolnikov's own small street, Carpenter's Lane, housed eighteen taverns.[5] The overcrowding, disease, drunkenness, and immorality of Haymarket finally drew government attention in 1865, when an official commission was established to investigate conditions there.[6]

This, then, was the Petersburg that Dostoevsky knew well and chose to depict in *Crime and Punishment*. Haymarket serves as background to the thoughts and actions of Raskolnikov. These two components of the novel, Raskolnikov and the city, are closely linked. The people and conditions of Haymarket are often introduced through Raskolnikov's consciousness. For example, the novel opens with Raskolnikov's reaction upon descending from his room onto Carpenter's Lane on a July day:

> The heat on the street was terrible, and the closeness, crowds, lime everywhere, scaffolding, bricks, dust and that particular summer stench so well-known to every Petersburger who did not have the possibility of renting a summer house—all this together shook the young man's nerves, already unsettled without it. (I, 1)[7]

This part of Petersburg, to which Dostoevsky immediately gives a

---

[3]Akademiia nauk SSSR, Institut istorii, *Ocherki istorii Leningrada*, vol. 2 (Moscow-Leningrad, 1957), p. 147.

[4]Reginald E. Zelnik, *Labor and Society in Tsarist Russia: The Factory Workers of St. Petersburg, 1855–1870* (Stanford, 1971), p. 242; see also James Bater, *St. Petersburg: Industrialization and Change* (London, 1976).

[5]E. Sarukhanian, *Dostoevskii v Peterburge* (Leningrad, 1970), p. 164.

[6]Zelnik, p. 58.

[7]F. M. Dostoevskii, *Polnoe sobranie sochinenii v tridtsati tomakh*, vol. 6 (Leningrad, 1973). All further quotations from *Crime and Punishment* refer to this edition.

tangible atmospheric, social, and economic identity, has a powerful attraction for Raskolnikov. The magnificent panorama of the capital city along the Neva River left Raskolnikov, like Dostoevsky, "with an inexplicable coldness" (II, 2). Even though Haymarket's stifling atmosphere and drunken crowds revolt him, Raskolnikov is drawn to it many times throughout the novel ("By force of habit, following the usual course of his previous walks, he headed straight for Haymarket. . . ." (II, 6). There Raskolnikov comes face to face with the debilitating consequences of nineteenth-century urban reality—the exploitation of women and children, the drunkenness and destitution. In one of Haymarket's many taverns, for example, he hears Marmeladov's autobiography. These observations support the self-willed and utilitarian aspects of the theory developed in his article. In fact, Dostoevsky uses the reality of Petersburg not only as background but also to influence Raskolnikov's thoughts and actions and to develop his theme.

One passage in part I, chapter 6 of the novel illustrates Dostoevsky's sensitivity to the city and his incorporation of it into the themes and polemics of his writing. This passage records Raskolnikov's thoughts as he is walking to the pawnbroker's house to commit the crime. It begins with Raskolnikov, distracted from thoughts of the impending murder, lost in certain "extraneous thoughts":

> Before, when he happened to picture all this in his imagination, he sometimes thought that he would be very much afraid. But he was not very afraid now, he was even completely unafraid. He was even occupied at this moment by certain extraneous thoughts, though not for long. Passing by the Yusupov Garden he even began to consider the construction of tall fountains and how well they would freshen the air in all the squares. Gradually he came to the conclusion that if the Summer Garden were extended to the whole Mars Field and even joined with the garden of the Mikhailovsky Palace, it would be a beautiful and most useful thing for the city (I, 6).

These "extraneous thoughts," reminiscent of Raskolnikov's other dreams, derive from contemporary problems in the planning of Petersburg. Architecture greatly interested Dostoevsky. As a student at Petersburg's Main Engineering School in the Mikhailovsky Castle, he had studied the history of architecture enthusiastically, and this interest continued throughout his life. Dostoevsky, then, was no doubt familiar with the history of architecture and city planning in Petersburg. Raskolnikov's own ambitious scheme recalls the monumental scale and conception of Petersburg architecture and planning inaugurated by Peter I. But even the Admiralty district, the political and social center of the capital and the empire as well as the location of Haymarket, revealed the failure of this grand tradition. Although the district was the focus of much planning and construction in the eighteenth and early nineteenth centuries, most of these projects were aimed at creating a magnificent ensemble of palaces, government complexes, and vast squares for military drill and parades, modeled after Western European capitals. Meanwhile, architects and planners ignored the spontaneous, haphazard growth of the living and working areas of the city such as Haymarket, with the resulting inadequacy of services and serious social dislocation.

The lack of waterways and parks is one example of the failure to respond to problems exacerbated by urban expansion. Canals, ponds, fountains, and gardens were important not only aesthetically but also practically. Situated on the Neva delta, Petersburg was vulnerable to flooding. Waterways were essential to lessen the impact of flooding and to drain the marshy land to make it habitable. Currents of cool air created by fountains would help alleviate the heat of the Petersburg summer with which Dostoevsky opens his novel. Fountains and canals would also help in combatting the frequent fires (there was an especially serious outbreak of fires in 1862, which sparked a polemic between Dostoevsky and Chernyshevsky on politically motivated arson) and augment the city's water supply; in the 1860s water had to be brought to houses from the rivers and canals by water-carriers. Overcrowded housing made parks and landscaping for public recreation particularly necessary.

Dostoevsky is referring directly to these needs and the failure to meet them in the passage quoted above. Petersburg's waterways, like the Catherine Canal which Raskolnikov crosses on his way to the pawnbroker's house, were dangerously polluted. Despite the cholera epidemic and fires of the 1860s, little had been done to upgrade the capital's water supply. Raskolnikov's proposal to build tall fountains to "freshen the air in all the squares" echoed contemporary debates. Along with the problems of crime and drunkenness, the local press drew attention to the city's inadequate water supply; in July 1865 three Petersburg newspapers, *Peterburgskii Listok, Invalid,* and *Golos,* called for the building of more fountains in the city.[8] Central Petersburg also lacked parks. The only park built in the Admiralty district in the first half of the nineteenth century was K. I. Rossi's ensemble of the Mikhailovsky Palace and Garden of 1819-25. Built for Alexander I's brother Mikhail, the Garden was closed to the public in the 1860s. The Yusupov Garden, which Raskolnikov passes on the way to the pawnbroker's house, had been privately owned until 1863, when the city acquired it and turned it into a public park. Hardly more than an arid field with a small pond and a fountain, the new park nonetheless drew crowds of Haymarket's lower-class inhabitants in summer. Raskolnikov's plan to extend the Summer Garden to the Mars Field and the garden of the Mikhailovsky Palace would have created one great park for the Admiralty district—a "beautiful and most useful thing for the city."

The boldest attempt to meet both the aesthetic demands of a capital city and the physical needs intensified by changing urban conditions was to be found not in Russia but France during the Second Empire. The rebuilding of Paris by Napoleon III and his Prefect of the Seine, Georges Haussmann, was the most prominent example of farsighted city planning in its day, and provided Dostoevsky with the model for Raskolnikov's plan to rebuild Petersburg.

Napoleon III fancied himself a landscape architect and city planner. His uncle Napoleon Bonaparte had made plans to rebuild Paris during his reign; his nephew, anxious to establish legitimacy by his link with his illustrious predecessor, revived the project and pursued it enthusiastically. In 1852, at the start of the Second Empire, Paris was an overgrown medieval city with crowded and disease-ridden slums, dark, winding streets, primitive water and sewer systems, and treeless boulevards—conditions similar to those of Haymarket. In less than twenty years Napoleon and Haussmann had straightened and widened streets, cleared slums, constructed public buildings and

---

[8]Editors' note in Dostoevskii, *Prestuplenie i nakazanie,* "Literaturnye pamiatniki" edition, eds. L. D. Opul'skaia and G. F. Kogan (Moscow, 1970), p. 741, and in *Polnoe sobranie sochinenii,* vol. 7 (Leningrad, 1973), p. 333.

parks, and redesigned the water and sewer systems, thus creating the modern city of Paris.[9]

Particular attention was paid to the creation of parks and open spaces. Napoleon III instructed Haussmann to establish "pocket parks" wherever building construction presented the opportunity. He believed that neighborhood parks would beautify the city, improve public health, and elevate working-class morality. Twenty-two such parks, planted with trees and flowers and furnished with benches and fountains, were eventually created. More famous were the major municipal parks established by Napoleon and Haussmann—the Bois de Boulogne, the Bois de Vincennes, and three large parks within the city. The Emperor personally supervised the transformation of the Bois de Boulogne from a barren promenade into a vast area for public recreation with lakes, winding paths, cafés, a grotto, waterfalls, and a racetrack. Napoleon also directed the creation of a similar park for the crowded districts of eastern Paris, the Bois de Vincennes. By 1870, Paris had 4,500 acres of municipal parks, compared to the 47 acres of twenty years before. As David Pinkney has concluded:

> First among practical planners and builders Napoleon and Haussmann thought not only of the vistas and facades of a "parade city," but also of the needs of traffic, of water supply and sewers, of slum clearance and open spaces. Here they were concerned as no planners before them with social utility and . . . they made to Paris and to city planning sociological contributions of the first order.[10]

Dostoevsky no doubt knew of Napoleon's ambitious project. Educated Russians in the 1860s followed events in the West closely. Like most other periodicals of the time, Dostoevsky's own journals, *Vremia* and *Epokha*, devoted regular columns and articles to reports and interpretations of European and American news. The perspective of the commentaries in *Vremia* and *Epokha* reflected Dostoevsky's attitude then toward reform and the issue of Russia and the West—although some positive aspects of European society were noted, the

[9]See David H. Pinkney, *Napoleon III and the Rebuilding of Paris* (Princeton, 1972).
[10]*Ibid.*, p. 221.

overall evaluation was critical—and cautioned against importing European ideas into Russia.[11] The May 1862 issue of *Vremia*, for example, contained a scathing attack on the adventurism of Napoleon III's regime:

> There are no obstacles on the path of the harmonious development of the internal and external strengths of the state, prosperity, well-being, etc. Is there some deficit of several hundred million?—nothing to it; posterity will pay the interest on it. Send a corps of troops across the ocean?—nothing to it; posterity will pay the interest on the war costs and the glory will be pure profit. Rebuild the city?—nothing to it; posterity will answer for everything. Now the city of Paris is taking out a new loan of 125 million francs for new works for the public welfare.... For these "public welfare" things an additional 139 million has been put into the budget.... But what do these millions signify now, when posterity will pay the interest on them, thanks to the loan system![12]

Just after this article appeared, Dostoevsky visited Europe for the first time; he traveled there again in the summers of 1863 and 1865. In letters home he expressed a qualified admiration for Paris. He wrote his brother Nikolai, a civil engineer, on August 28, 1863:

> I liked the appearance of Paris this time, that is the architecture. The Louvre is an important thing and that whole quay right up to Notre Dame is an amazing thing. It is a pity, Kolya, that you, having qualified as an architect, have not gone abroad. An architect cannot not go abroad. No plan will give the true impression.

To his sister-in-law Varvara Konstant on September 1, however, he complained:

> I do not like Paris, although it is terribly magnificent. There is much to see, but when you look around, a terrible weariness comes over you.

Discussing Paris in *Winter Remarks on Summer Impressions* (1863), Dos-

[11]For discussion of Dostoevsky's journalism see V. S. Nechaeva, *Zhurnal M. M. i F. M. Dostoevskikh "Vremia," 1861–1863* (Moscow, 1972) and idem, *Zhurnal M. M. i F. M. Dostoevskikh "Epokha," 1864–1865* (Moscow, 1975).

[12]"Politicheskoe obozrenie," *Vremia*, May 1862, p. 6.

toevsky adopts a sarcastic tone reminiscent of the *Vremia* article. His admiration of certain aspects of Parisian architecture does not lessen his general contempt for the Second Empire, especially its bourgeoisie:

> *Bribri* [a bourgeois French husband] is extremely naive at times. For example, while walking about the fountains he will start to explain to *ma biche* [his wife] why fountains spurt upwards, he explains to her the laws of nature, he expresses national pride to her in the beauty of the Bois de Boulogne, the play of *les grandes eaux* at Versailles, the success of Emperor Napoleon and *gloire militaire*, he revels in her curiosity and contentment, and is very satisfied.[13]

In early 1865, a few months before Dostoevsky began *Crime and Punishment*, the publication of Napoleon III's *History of Julius Caesar (Histoire de César)* created a sensation in Europe and Russia. The preface proclaimed Napoleon's doctrine on the role and significance of exceptional people:

> When extraordinary deeds testify to a high genius what can be more repulsive to common sense than to attribute to this genius all the passions and all the thoughts of an ordinary man? What can be more false than not to recognize the superiority of these exceptional beings who appear in history from time to time like shining beacons, dispelling the darkness of their epoch and lighting up the future?

The leading newspapers in Russia's two capitals, *Sankt-Peterburgskie Vedomosti* and *Moskovskie Vedomosti*, published translations of Napoleon's preface in February; reviews and debates soon filled other periodicals.[14]

Dostoevsky drew upon Napoleon III, especially his justification of Caesar, Napoleon Bonaparte, and himself in his book, for the character of Raskolnikov and his theory of the exceptional man, standing above ordinary laws and morality. The third notebook for *Crime and Punishment* confirms this influence in the note: "Porfiry, NB. 'Tell me, is the article in *Vedomosti* yours? Did you study it or write it [*ili uchit'sia*,

[13]*Polnoe sobranie sochinenii*, vol. 5 (Leningrad, 1973), pp. 93–94.
[14]F. I. Evnin, "Roman *Prestuplenie i nakazanie*," *Tvorchestvo F. M. Dostoevskogo*, ed. N. Stepanov (Moscow, 1959), p. 154.

ili pisat']?' "[15] Dostoevsky also incorporated Napoleon III's reconstruction of Paris into the novel as the source of Raskolnikov's plan to rebuild Petersburg, and thus linked Napoleon and Raskolnikov again. While on his way to commit the murder, which his theory justifies, Raskolnikov develops the theory further. Emulating Napoleon III, he devises a plan for a city both beautiful and useful. His plan for rebuilding Petersburg is based on the assumption that a rational, superior man can control and change his environment. Thus the plan and the crime are directly related: they share the same ideological foundation and draw upon the example of Napoleon.

Raskolnikov can rationalize both the murder and his plan to rebuild Petersburg in the same terms, for they serve similar ends. The crime is conceived as a means to improve the lives of himself, his family, even the whole of mankind, while his plan for a reconstructed Petersburg has as its object the improvement of the lives of Haymarket's inhabitants. One probable result of his plan, for example, would be to channel currents of cooler, fresher air around Haymarket by building fountains around the city, much in the same way that Napoleon built his pocket parks. Such fountains could serve other useful ends, such as supplying water for consumption and fire-fighting, as well as beautifying the city. Raskolnikov's plan would also provide Haymarket's inhabitants with a large park like Napoleon's great municipal parks, a need which the Yusupov Garden failed to meet. Since Haymarket, with its strange power of attraction, is the center of Petersburg for Raskolnikov, he not surprisingly devises a plan that satisfies some of the needs of this most wretched part of the city.

Raskolnikov's scheme to rebuild Petersburg, based on the same principles of utilitarianism and superior will that underlie the crime, should have buttressed his conviction that the murder is justifiable. But his train of thought suddenly shifts, and the passage continues:

> Suddenly here he became interested in just why, in all big cities, people lived and settled not solely by necessity, but by some particular inclination, in just those parts of the city where there was dirt and stench and all kinds of squalor. Then he was reminded of his own walks around Haymarket, and for a moment

[15]I. I. Glivenko, ed., *Iz arkhiva F. M. Dostoevskogo: "Prestuplenie i nakazanie,"* *Neizdannye materialy* (Moscow-Leningrad, 1931), p. 196.

he awoke [*ochnulsia*]. "What nonsense," he thought. "No, better not to think of anything at all!"

"So, truly, those being led to execution fix their thoughts on every object which they meet on the way," flashed through his mind, but only flashed like lightning; he himself extinguished this thought as soon as possible. . . . (I, 6).

The inhabitants of Petersburg and "all big cities" seem indifferent to the kind of rational improvements in their surroundings that Raskolnikov has just been planning for them. Their indifference and their irrational "inclination" to live in the squalid parts of the city seem to undermine his plan to rebuild it. Raskolnikov then recalls how he himself has been drawn many times to Haymarket for no particular reason. Indeed, the crime he is about to commit is the result not of rational will but of just such an accidental walk. The previous day, after dreaming of peasants killing a mare, Raskolnikov renounced his plan for the murder; but instead of going directly home, he was drawn again to Haymarket, where Lizaveta's overheard remarks provided him with the opportunity to commit the crime. The next words—"and for a moment he awoke"—are elliptical. What they may represent is Raskolnikov's momentary realization that he is no Napoleon, and that if his Napoleonic, utilitarian scheme for rebuilding the city is undermined by the behavior of Haymarket's inhabitants and his own irrational actions, then his Napoleonic, utilitarian rationale for the murder may be in question as well.

By now, however, Raskolnikov has almost reached the pawnbroker's house, and his momentary awakening gives way to the dominant Napoleonic motive. He emphatically rejects the entire train of thought, especially the implications that question his original justification for the crime; " 'What nonsense,' he thought. 'No, better not to think of anything at all.' "

In this interpretation Raskolnikov's thoughts just prior to the murder underscore the importance of the Napoleon figure and principle in his thinking, and the influence upon him of contemporary developments in Western Europe—in this case, Napoleon's reconstruction of Paris. He emerges as a young man representative of his decade, when educated Russians paid close attention to ideas and changes in Europe, and Russia itself was undergoing fundamental reforms. The attraction of Europe for Raskolnikov is a basic element of his character and thought. It leads him to various mistaken ideas, among them the rebuilding of Petersburg as well as the theory justifying the murder.

Moreover, this passage affirms the important role of the city in Dostoevsky's novelistic technique, even more important than previous commentators have suggested. The city serves as more than background. Dostoevsky was highly sensitive to the two forms a city could take: the grim reality of nineteenth-century urban conditions, like those of Haymarket, but also the city as an abstraction, like the Petersburg of Peter I or the Paris of Napoleon III. He uses the dialectic of these two forms of the city in the early passage in *Crime and Punishment* analyzed here. As an abstraction, the city reinforces Raskolnikov's theory of superior will and utilitarian action. But Raskolnikov also perceives the irrational reality of Petersburg, which complicates his theory and purpose—even leading him to a fleeting realization of his error. In Raskolnikov, Dostoevsky shows how the city, working as ideal and reality, has a direct psychological impact upon ideas and actions.

Dostoevsky:
The Idea of *The Gambler*

By D. S. Savage

In June 1866, while still at work on *Crime and Punishment*, then appearing serially in the *Russkii Vestnik*, Dostoevsky wrote to his friend A. P. Milyukov a letter in which there occurs the following paragraph:

> The novel for Stellovsky I haven't yet begun, but certainly shall begin. I have a plan for a most decent little novel; there will even be shadows of actual characters in it. The thought of Stellovsky torments and disturbs me; it pursues me even in dreams.

Dostoevsky's disquiet was due to the thought of the heavy penalties which under the terms of the contract the sharp publisher Stellovsky would be able to exact if the novel were not written and delivered by 1 November of that year. How the novel came to be written and Dostoevsky saved from Stellovsky's clutches through the engagement of the stenographer who afterwards became his second wife is well known. This "most decent little novel," eventually dictated within the space of twenty-six days, was that minor masterpiece, the most brilliantly executed of Dostoevsky's lesser works, *The Gambler*.

The story which was to be dictated with such facility to Anna Grigorievna Snitkin had already been projected three years previously. It is mentioned in a letter of September 1863 addressed to N. N. Strakhov. Dostoevsky was then in the midst of his troubled *affaire* with the tempestuous Apollinaria Suslova among the resorts and watering-places of Europe. This circumstance, together with Dostoevsky's known addiction to the gaming table, has led to the widespread and tenacious assumption that the book is directly autobio-

"Dostoevsky: The Idea of *The Gambler*" by D. S. Savage. *The Sewanee Review*, vol. LVIII (1950), pp. 281–98. Reprinted with slight stylistic changes by permission of the editor.

graphical in character—a misunderstanding which has thrown many a reader's vision of the story quite out of focus. "No reader of *The Gambler*," asserts E. H. Carr in his *Dostoevsky* (1931), "will doubt its autobiographical character," and he goes on to provide the *dramatis personae* with actual counterparts:—"Its much humiliated hero is the Dostoevsky of 1863: its heroine (her name, too, is Polina) is an idealized Suslova: the Frenchman De Grieux is a caricature of her Spanish lover," and so on. A revealing sentence in J. A. T. Lloyd's 1946 biography demonstrates the unquestioning continuation of this identification. "Just at this time," he lets slip of the events of 1867, "there seems to be no evidence of demands for money *from the heroine of the Gambler* [italics mine] though she had undoubtedly resumed her correspondence with the novelist"—a confusion of the actual and the fictional which is not unique in Dostoevsky criticism.

The sort of misapprehension to which this leads, or which it serves to perpetuate, is conveniently displayed in C. J. Hogarth's Introduction to his translation of *The Gambler* in the popular Everyman series. "The wretched victim of the gaming craze," he writes, "moves to his ruin amid the haunts of the rich and the fashionable or quasi-fashionable. The woman who could have saved him, but does not (apparently she is too intent upon putting him to the test to be able to foresee what would happen should he, when tested, be found wanting), is a curiously indefinite figure. She experiments with her lover, she eggs him on to gamble, she flouts and derides his affection for her, she avoids him, she does everything but speak the word in season which might have arrested his foot on the downward road which he is treading. Then she betakes herself to the other end of Europe, and from that safe distance sends him a message when it is too late to repair what she has permitted to happen. At the close of the story the unhappy gambler is seen striving to make a last choice between the gaming table and the woman whom he has long adored; and the curtain falls upon the enigmatical sentence: 'Tomorrow all this shall end!' "

According to this view, Dostoevsky's principal concern is with the portrayal of that well-worn type of romantic fiction, the *femme fatale*. Such, too, is precisely the accredited notion of Suslova, of whom Dostoevsky himself wrote: "Her egotism and self-love are colossal. She demands everything from others, and exempts herself from the

slightest obligation to others." If we are to believe E. H. Carr, "It was
she [Suslova] who showed him [Dostoevsky] how intimately hate may
be interwoven with love. She had revealed to him the appetite for
cruelty and the appetite for suffering, the sadistic and the masochistic,
as alternating manifestations of the sexual impulse." In Suslova's published diary there is recorded a comment of Dostoevsky on their relations. He said: "You cannot forgive me for the fact that you once gave
yourself to me, and you are taking your revenge for that: that is a
feminine trait." And Carr comments: "Such remained Dostoevsky's
diagnosis of the psychology of his mistress; and in subsequent novels,
beginning with *The Gambler*, he more than once portrays the woman
who gives a moment of exquisite happiness to her lover and then,
unable to forgive her own weakness, avenges it on him and on herself."

And yet there is in reality not the least justification for this naïve
identification of characters. Dostoevsky's creative processes did not
operate in quite that simple manner, and though he certainly drew
upon personal experience for the material of the story and for some of
the traits of his characters, as every novelist is bound to do, behind *The
Gambler* is no mere scandalous revelation of a personal history but, as
is usual with Dostoevsky's work, a dominating and shaping imaginative *idea*, to which everything in the action is related.

In the letter to Strakhov already mentioned, Dostoevsky says nothing about *femmes fatales* and the sado-masochistic feelings supposed to
be bound up with the sexual impulse. "My story," he writes (italics
mine), *"will depict a typical figure."*

> You know of course that last summer there was a great deal of
> talk in our journals about the absentee Russian. This will all be
> reflected in my story. And the present state of our interior or-
> ganizations will also (as well as I can do it, of course) be woven
> into the narrative. I depict a man of most simple nature, a man
> who, while developed in many respects, is yet in every way in-
> complete, who has lost all faith, yet at the same time does not
> dare to be a sceptic, who revolts against all authority and yet at
> the same time fears it. He comforts himself with the thought that
> in Russia there is nothing that he can do, and therefore con-
> demns in the harshest manner those who would summon the
> absentee Russian back to Russia. . . . The real idea, though, lies

in him having wasted all his substance, energies, and talents on roulette. He is a gambler, but no common gambler, just as the "miserly knight" of Pushkin is no common miser. . . . He is in his way a poet, yet he is ashamed of such poetry, for he feels profoundly its vulgarity, even though the *longing for touch-and-go* ennobles him in his own eyes. The whole story is concerned with his playing roulette for full three years. . . . The story may be very good indeed.

This outline will serve authoritatively to correct the distortions of the usual view; but it fails to indicate the depth of the underlying idea and the subtlety of its working out which were to appear in the finished novel.

The basis for the interpretation of Polina as the willful egotist lies principally in her conversation with Aleksey in the first chapter and the further conversation of Chapter Five when in response to his incoherent and slavish total offer of his life she bids him play a pointless trick upon a passing German baron and his wife. Aleksey, as tutor, has just rejoined the General's household at Roulettenburg, to find Polina, the General's stepdaughter, apparently dallying with two rival suitors, De Grieux, a mannered and insolent Frenchman who is financially interested in the General's affairs, and a decent, quiet English manufacturer, Mr. Astley. The General's *entourage* is awaiting expectantly the news of the death of his wealthy old aunt when, with the proving of the will, everything will be settled to everyone's satisfaction: De Grieux will receive back the money to obtain which the General has mortgaged his estates to him; the two children (whose inheritance their father has dissipated, and whose interests their half-sister Polina is watching over) will be made once more materially secure, and the expensive courtesan Mlle. Blanche will find it possible to marry the doting old man. At their first meeting Aleksey cross-questions Polina as to the situation at large, passing on to speak in a particularly blunt and open way of her relations with his supposed rivals. She admits that Mr. Astley who, as Aleksey says, "is shy and given to falling in love," is in love with her, but hotly denies that De Grieux has begun to pay his addresses, although she predicts cynically that he will certainly do so as soon as he is assured that she has come into something by the will. Her attitude to De Grieux is throughout that of disenchanted contempt and aversion. Aleksey advises coarsely:

"If I were in your place I should certainly marry the Englishman."

"Why?" asked Polina.

"The Frenchman is better-looking, but he is nastier; and the Englishman, besides being honest, is ten times as rich," I snapped out.

"Yes, but on the other hand, the Frenchman is a *marquis* and clever," she answered, in the most composed manner.

"But is it true?" I went on, in the same way.

"It certainly is."

Polina greatly disliked my questions, and I saw that she was trying to make me angry by her tone and the strangeness of her answers. I said as much to her at once.

"Well, it really amuses me to see you in such a rage. You must pay for the very fact of my allowing you to ask such questions and make such suppositions."

"I certainly consider myself entitled to ask you any sort of question," I answered calmly, "just because I am prepared to pay any price you like for it, and I set no value at all on my life now."

Polina laughed.

"You told me last time at the Schlangenberg, that you were prepared, at a word from me, to throw yourself head foremost from the rock, and it is a thousand feet high, I believe. Some day I shall utter that word, solely in order to see how you will pay the price, and trust me, I won't give way. You are hateful to me, just because I've allowed you to take such liberties, and even more hateful because you are so necessary to me. But so long as you are necessary to me, I must take care of you."

She began getting up. She spoke with irritation. Of late she had always ended every conversation with me in anger and irritation, real anger. (I)

At their second interview, Aleksey speaks with his usual freedom to Polina, and to her reproof replies:

"You know that I consider myself at liberty to say anything to you and sometimes ask you very candid questions. I repeat I'm your slave and one does not mind what one says to a slave and cannot take offence at anything he says."

"And I can't endure that 'slave' theory of yours."

"Observe that I don't speak of my slavery because I want to be your slave. I simply speak of it as a fact which doesn't depend on me in the least." (V)

The conversation then turns to roulette, and on the reason for Aleksey's need of money. He has already declared his conviction that roulette is his "only escape and salvation," and he now asserts under question that his object is "Nothing else but that with money I should become to you a different man, not a slave." He then divagates to his passion for Polina. "Why and how I love you I don't know. Perhaps you are not at all nice really, you know. Fancy! I don't know whether you are good or not, even to look at. You certainly have not a good heart: your mind may very well be ignoble." But to her retort, "Perhaps that's how it is you reckon on buying me with money, because you don't believe in my sense of honor," he responds with indignant, though incoherent, protestations.

Those who too readily accept the view of Polina which appears to be presented in these passages have been misled by Dostoevsky's device of giving the narration, not to a sympathetic character, as is customary and expected, nor to a detached observer, but to the villain of the piece, the ruined man. Not only does this at once purchase the reader's unwitting sympathy for him, but it provides an implicit comment on the partiality of human judgments by presenting all the facts necessary for the correct evaluation of the situation, but in such a way that the reader is obliged to piece them together for himself.

> She is fine though; she is: I believe she's fine. She drives other men off their heads, too, She's tall and graceful, only very slender. It seems to me you could tie her in a knot or bend her double. Her foot is long and narrow—tormenting. Tormenting is just what it is. Her hair has a reddish tint. Her eyes are regular cat's eyes, but how proudly and disdainfully she can look with them. . . . (VI)

Encountering such a picture of Polina, the temptress, the casual reader forgets that he is looking at her through the fevered mind of Aleksey, and that to others in the book—to the old Aunt or to the quiet Englishman—her qualities make a wholly different impression.

What, then, is the secret of the curious relationship which exists between the two? "Polina was always an enigma to me," ponders Aleksey in the eighth chapter, "such an enigma that now for instance . . . I was suddenly struck while I was speaking by the fact that there was scarcely anything positive and definite I could say about our relations. Everything was, on the contrary, strange, unstable, and, in fact, quite unique." Just before the crisis of their relationship, when the General's hopes of an inheritance have been demolished and Polina receives the insulting letter from the retreating De Grieux who is off to arrange for the sale of the General's mortgaged estates, Aleksey reflects for the first time on the beginnings of this unique and unstable state of affairs.

> Even if she did not care for me in the least, she should not, I thought, have trampled on my feelings like that and have received my declarations so contemptuously. She knew that I really loved her: she admitted me, she allowed me to speak like that! It is true that it had begun rather strangely. Some time before, long ago, in fact, two months before, I began to notice that she wanted to make me her friend, her *confidant*, and indeed was in a way testing me. But somehow this did not come off then; instead of that there remained the strange relations that existed between us; that is how it was I began to speak to her like that. But if my love repelled her, why did she not directly forbid me to speak of it? (XIII)

In the midst of the general crisis Aleksey pens a note to Polina, asking her whether she needs his life or not, whether he can be of use "*in any way whatever,*" and begging her to dispose of him as she thinks fit. Polina comes to his bedroom, shows him De Grieux's letter, and asks for counsel in the matter of the General's IOU for fifty thousand francs which the Frenchman has insolently returned as an insurance against what he fears may be Polina's sentimental claims upon him. In his excitement he bids her to wait for him while he rushes to the Casino: there he gambles frantically for some hours, wins an incredible sum, and returns to pile the money on the table before an overwrought and hysterical Polina.

> At last she ceased laughing and frowned; she looked at me sternly from under her brows.
> "I won't take your money," she declared contemptuously.
> "How? What's this?" I cried, "Polina, why?"
> "I won't take money for nothing."
> "I offer it you as a friend; I offer you my life."
> She looked at me with a long, penetrating look, as though she would pierce me through with it.
> "You give too much," she said with a laugh; "De Grieux's mistress is not worth fifty thousand francs."

"Polina, how can you talk to me like that!" I cried, reproach-
fully. "Am I a De Grieux?"

"I hate you! Yes ... yes! ... I love you no more than De
Grieux," she cried, her eyes suddenly flashing.

Then she suddenly covered her face with her hands and went
into hysterics. I rushed to her.

I realized that something had happened to her while I was
away. She seemed quite out of her mind.

"Buy me! Do you want to? Do you want to? For fifty thousand
francs, like De Grieux?" broke from her with convulsive sobs.
(XV)

Polina spends the night with him, alternating in her delirium between anxiety mixed with distrust and passionate tenderness for
Aleksey. Waking in the morning, however, she demands with hatred
and anger her fifty thousand francs, swings the money hard against
his face and runs from the room. Following, Aleksey is unable to find
her, but meeting Mr. Astley he learns from him that Polina is in his
care; that she is ill, and more over, that if she dies, he will answer to
the Englishman for her death. He then bids the gambler to run off to
Paris with his winnings, as "all Russians who have money go to Paris";
and, in fact, Aleksey is immediately afterwards ensnared by Mlle.
Blanche (who is present throughout as a counterpoise to Polina), and
taken off by her to Paris, where she quickly squanders his fortune and
sets him on the downward spiral of his career as an inveterate gambler
and lost soul.

It is not, however, until the final chapter that the true character of
Polina's feelings for Aleksey are openly stated—two years, that is,
after the main events of the story, when the ruined Aleksey meets Mr.
Astley near the Casino at Homburg and, discussing those events with
him, expatiates upon the attraction of Frenchmen for young Russian
women, hinting that, with such as De Grieux for rival, neither he nor
Mr. Astley "have made any way at all." The loyal Englishman is provoked to indignant speech.

"That's disgusting nonsense ... because ... because ... let
me tell you!" Mr. Astley, with flashing eyes, pronounced in a
quivering voice, "let me tell you, you ungrateful, unworthy, shallow and unhappy man, that I am come to Homburg expressly at

her wish, to see you, to have a long and open conversation with you and to tell her everything—what you are feeling, thinking, hoping, . . . what you remember!"

"Is it possible? Is it possible?" I cried, and tears rushed in streams from my eyes.

I could not restrain them. I believe it was the first time it happened in my life.

"Yes, unhappy man, she loved you, and I can tell you that, because you are—a lost man! What is more, if I were to tell you that she loves you to this day—you would stay here just the same! Yes, you have destroyed yourself. You had some abilities, a lively disposition, and were not a bad fellow; you might have even been of service to your country, which is in such need of men, but—you will remain here, and your life is over. I don't blame you. To my mind all Russians are like that, or disposed to be like that. If it is not roulette it is something similar. The exceptions are very rare. You are not the first who does not understand the meaning of work (I am not talking of your peasantry). Roulette is a game pre-eminently for the Russians." (XVII)

But in reality Polina's true feelings for Aleksey are evident in all her actions. All that is "unaccountable" in her behavior can be accounted for in the light of her love for him as it meets and wrestles with his total lack of love for her—or for anyone.

"I depict a man . . . who has lost all faith, yet at the same time does not dare to be a sceptic, who revolts against all authority and yet at the same time fears it. . . . The real idea, though, lies in his having wasted all his substance, energies, and talents on roulette," Whatever roulette means to Aleksey, it is closely related to his feelings for Polina.

Roulette will decide his whole life. "I knew for certain," he writes concerning his first entry into the Casino, "and had made up my mind long before, that I should not leave Roulettenburg unchanged, that some radical and fundamental change would take place in my destiny; so it must be and so it would be. Ridiculous as it may be that I should expect so much for myself from roulette, yet I consider even more ridiculous the conventional opinion accepted by all that it is stupid and absurd to expect anything from gambling."

On his initial visit the scene strikes him as "so dirty, somehow, morally horrid and dirty"; but he adds, "I notice one thing; that of late it has become horribly repugnant to me to test my thoughts and actions by any moral standard whatever. I was guided by something different."

That "something different" is an abandonment to Fate, or to Chance. Implicit in Dostoevsky's treatment from the beginning is the idea that to the man who, having lost God, is in process of losing himself, free and responsible choice has been obviated, so that he is left facing a universe which is subject down to the minutest details to an irreversible deterministic law. To this law, or Fate, which is by definition mechanistically rational and calculable, nothing can be opposed except blind, irrational Chance. For such a one, the fascination of the gaming table is that of the alternation of the calculable with the incalculable. Watching the spinning roulette wheel the gambler is, as it were, at the metaphysical source of being, and what he sees in front of him is nothing other than a symbolic model of the cosmic mechanism. The seduction which draws his soul is that of an ultimate irrational and groundless freedom which, containing equally within itself every possibility, is devoid of the power to actualize any of these possibilities and can give birth only to an ineluctable necessity.

> It seemed to me that calculation meant very little, and had by no means the importance attributed to it by some players. They sit with papers before them scrawled over in pencil, note the strokes, reckon, deduce the chances, calculate, finally stake and—lose exactly as we simple mortals who play without calculations. On the other hand . . . though there is no system, there really is a sort of order in the sequence of casual chances—and that, of course, is very strange. . . .
>
> As for me, I lost every farthing very quickly. I staked straight off twenty friedrichs d'or on even and won, staked again and again won, and went on like that two or three times. I imagine I must have had about four hundred friedrichs d'or in my hands in about five minutes. At that point I ought to have gone away, but *a strange sensation rose up in me, a sort of defiance of fate, a desire to challenge it, to put out my tongue at it.* I laid down the largest stake allowed—four thousand gulden—and lost it. Then, getting hot, I pulled out all I had left, staked it on the same number, and lost again, after which I walked away from the table as though I were stunned. I could not even grasp what had happened to me. (IV)

On the occasion when he rushes madly to the Casino to win the fifty thousand francs needed by Polina to return to De Grieux, the notion

of winning appears to him as "something fated, inevitable, predestined—as something bound to be and bound to happen ... not
as a chance among others which might or might not come to pass, but
as something which was absolutely bound to happen." All the same,
toward the end of his venture, when he has already won far more
than the requisite sum, he is driven by "strange perversity" to stake on
the color, red, which had already turned up seven times running. "I
wanted to impress the spectators by taking a mad risk, and—oh, the
strange sensation—I remember distinctly that, quite apart from the
promptings of vanity, I was possessed by an intense craving for risk.
Perhaps passing through so many sensations my soul was not satisfied
but only irritated by them and craved still more sensation—and
stronger and stronger ones—till utterly exhausted."

Ostensibly his aim in gambling is to amass money with which he
proposes to win Polina's respect. But in running off to win the fifty
thousand francs, he is driven afterwards to admit, "my love had re-
treated, so to speak, into the background." Having won a fortune, he
finds it useless, and abandoning Polina to Mr. Astley he exchanges
her quite fittingly for the woman who can be bought and listlessly
allows her to throw it away.

It is Fate (as despair) and Chance (expressed as the irrational)
which govern his life not only within but outside the Casino precincts.
Ensnared by the lascivious and avaricious Mlle. Blanche, he reflects,
"If it's to be Paris, let it be Paris, it seems it was fated at my birth,"
although the fate is merely a projection of his inner despair and with
an inner change, a coming to himself, Polina would at once be his.
And his "mad" exploit with the Baron is nothing more than the inter-
jection of the ungrounded irrationality of pure *possibility* into the rational order of daily life. "I can't make up my mind what happened to
me, whether I really was in a state of frenzy, or whether it was a
momentary aberration and I behaved disgracefully till I was pulled
up. At times it seemed to me that my mind was giving way. And at
times it seems to me that I have not outgrown childhood and
schoolboyishness, and that it was simply a crude schoolboy's
prank. .... She had told me to take off my hat, but I had bowed and
behaved like an impudent schoolboy on my own account. Goodness
knows what impelled me to! *I felt as though I were plunging into space.*"

Gamblers know what it is to "plunge"; to gamble *is*, indeed, "to
plunge." The sensation of plunging is that of vertigo. When Aleksey,

beginning to gamble on the night of the crisis, loses two thousand
florins and then a further eighty friedrichs d'or: is seized with fury
and blindly stakes his remaining two hundred florins, "haphazard, at
random, without thinking," there is "an instant of suspense like,
perhaps, the feeling experienced by Madame Blanchard when she
flew from a balloon in Paris to the earth." Clearly it is avidness for this
vertiginous sensation—a sensation of nothingness—which impels him
to his offer on the Schlangenberg: it is the identical sensation of
plunging into space which overcomes him when he walks forward to the
ungrounded irrationality of his gratuitous affront to the Baron.
Turned on itself, this sensationalism is suicidal: turned on another it is
murderous. "Do you know that I shall kill you one day?" Aleksey
asks the wrathful Polina. "I shall kill you not because I shall cease to
love you or be jealous, I shall simply kill you because I have an impulse to devour you."

> "Do you know, too, that it is dangerous for us to walk together? I
> often have an irresistible longing to beat you, to disfigure you, to
> strangle you. And what do you think—won't it come to that? You
> are driving me into brain fever. Do you suppose I am afraid of a
> scandal? Your anger—why, what is your anger to me? I love you
> without hope, and I know that after this I shall love you a
> thousand times more than ever. If ever I do kill you I shall have
> to kill myself, too. Oh, well, I shall put off killing myself as long
> as possible, so as to go on feeling this insufferable pain of being
> without you. Do you know something incredible? I love you
> more every day, and yet that is almost impossible. And how can I
> help being a fatalist? . . ." (V)

Dostoevsky's psychological insight here has nothing to do with the
crude notion of "the appetite for cruelty and the appetite for suffering, the sadistic and the masochistic, as alternating manifestations of
the sexual impulse." He perceives clearly that the "sexual impulse"
cannot be considered as a force in itself, that it is related to the primary spiritual condition of the participants in the sexual relationship,
which is thus not physically but metaphysically determined. When a
limitless egotism, acknowledging no authority and therefore deprived
of meaning and value, is brought into an erotic relationship, there
result the convulsive lacerations described by Dostoevsky—the writh-
ings of the distintegrating self in the throes of the knowledge of its
own nothingness.

"I set no value at all on my life now," says Aleksey to Polina in their first discussion, and yet it is this valueless life which he is offering her. The offer is itself an insult, and the insult is doubled by the consequent inability of a life which sets no value on itself to attribute value to another—it is because Aleksey despises his own being that he despises Polina and does in fact suppose, as she accuses, that he can buy her, or her respect, with money. In the relationship as determined by Aleksey they meet, not as persons, but as unbounded egos capable of nothing between total domination and absorption of the other, or total and suicidal submission. Polina's "unaccountable" behavior, then, perfectly expresses the dilemma in which she finds herself placed, and is the only alternative to complete severance of relations or to complicity in mutual destruction. It results, that is, from her striving toward a relationship of love which is conceivable only when each party ceases to be an ego and becomes a personality in an inward relation to the authority of truth (through faith in God).

The question of authority is implicit in the conversation concerning Aleksey's offer to throw himself from the Schlangenberg at her bidding—the supposed measure of his limitless devotion. But what is she to do with this unbounded power over him which he wishes to thrust into her unwilling hands, how is she to bear the burden of this absolute, unconditional authority over the life of another?

> "What use would it be for me to order you to jump off the Schlangenberg?" she said in a dry and peculiarly insulting manner. "It would be absolutely useless to me."
> "Splendid," I cried; "you said that splendid 'useless' on purpose to overwhelm me. I see through you. Useless, you say? But pleasure is always of use, and savage, unbounded power—if only over a fly—is a pleasure in its way, too. Man is a despot by nature, and loves to be a torturer. You like it awfully." (V)

The authority with which he wishes to overwhelm Polina—the total, despotic power which can result only in the personal extinction of its object (an extinction in which the subject too is involved) is the authority which he refuses to invest in God. Polina must become God in relation to him or he must become God in relation to Polina—and God is the fatal demiurge of the cosmic Necessity. That the question of authority can be posed in another way, that of an inward relation to truth, which at once brings into operation the obligation of personal

decision and moral choice and thus the realization, out of the abyss of
freedom, of one possibility rather than another—this does not enter
his mind. And yet it is only such inward polarity and obedience which
can transform him from an unbounded, ravenous, and chaotic ego to
a bounded personality, and make possible a relationship of love in
which the tyranny of subject over object is replaced by the mutual
intercourse of subject with subject. In asking him, instead of the sacrifice of his life, "such pranks as the one with the Baron," a substitu-
tion which arouses such fury in Aleksey, Polina is attempting to divert
the impulse of absolute destruction to a relatively harmless course.
But she does not succeed in establishing relations with the nothingness which is Aleksey; instead, she is made seriously ill. And yet even
after two years, withdrawn, at a distance, she is waiting in the hope
that he may regain himself and come to her of his own volition.

The manner of his presentation effectually disguises the inner
likeness of Aleksey to the hero of *Notes from Underground* written but
three years previously. The Underground Man, too, is obsessed with
the tyranny of a universal rational determinism which may be opposed only by a gratuitous assertion of the irrational, the absurd; he
too, unable to act—("Where are the primary causes on which I am to
build? Where are my foundations? Where am I to get them
from?")—rots away in idleness. He also conceives love as domination,
and his relations with the prostitute, Liza, are closely akin to those of
Aleksey with Polina. The Underground Man confesses:

> . . . it may be added that it was strange I should not love her, or
> at any rate, appreciate her love. Why is it strange? In the first
> place, by then I was incapable of love, for, I repeat, with me
> loving meant tyrannizing and showing my moral superiority. I
> have never in my life been able to imagine any other sort of love,
> and have nowadays come to the point of sometimes thinking that
> love really consists in the right—freely given by the beloved
> object—to tyrannize over her. Even in my underground dreams
> I did not imagine love except as a struggle. I began it always with
> hatred and ended it with moral subjugation, and afterwards I
> never knew what to do with the subjugated object. And what is
> there to wonder at in that, since I had succeeded in so corrupt-
> ing myself, since I was so out of touch with 'real life', as to have
> actually thought of reproaching her, and putting her to shame
> for having come to me to hear 'fine sentiments'; and did not

even guess that she had come not to hear fine sentiments, but to love me, because to a woman all reformation—all salvation from any sort of ruin, and all moral renewal—is included in love and can only show itself in that form. (II, 10)

The metaphysical impotence of Aleksey which afflicts him by reason of his *unbelief*, thus points backward to the Underground Man. More, it points forward to the condition of Stavrogin in *The Devils*. The incident of Stavrogin's biting the Governor's ear in the early chapters of that novel is a reduplication of Aleksey's unmotivated insult to the Baron, and its *disconcerting* effect is the same. In Stavrogin Dostoevsky was to explore the interior dialectic to unbelief to the last limit; but the conclusion, "from me nothing has come but negation . . . everything has always been petty and spiritless . . ." is anticipated in the smaller, meaner, "in every way incomplete" figure of the lost hero of *The Gambler*, that "most decent little novel" of 1866.

The Gaps in Christology:
The Idiot

by Michael Holquist

Crime and Punishment ends with the words: "But that is the beginning of a new story, the story of the gradual renewal of a man . . . of his slow progress from one world to another, of how he learned to know hitherto undreamt of reality. All that might be the subject of a new story, but our present story has come to an end." Now it is well known that Dostoevsky's next novel, *The Idiot*, was to revolve around a genuinely good," a "truly beautiful" man. The main character was to be an exemplary Christian: indeed, something like a Christ figure.[1] But Myshkin's story is not that new tale about a transfigured Raskolnikov alluded to in the conclusion of *Crime and Punishment*. That novel's dominant motif is the Lazarus story, with its emphasis on rebirth, rising from the dead, whereas the central metaphors of *The Idiot* are execution and apocalypse, not a sudden beginning of life but rather its too abrupt *end*.

The narrative structure of *Crime and Punishment* derives from Dostoevsky's variations on and fusion of two pre-existing plot types, the detective story and the wisdom tale, each presupposing its distinctive temporality: what we have called horizontal time in the first case, and vertical in the second. Much of the novel's meaning derives from its contrast between the linear, merely human, cause-and-effect time for which the detective story is a structural metaphor, on the one hand, and the mysterious stasis of a transcendent world, on the other, for

"The Gaps in Christology: *The Idiot*" by Michael Holquist. From *Dostoevsky and the Novel*. Copyright © 1977 by Princeton University Press, Princeton, N.J. Reprinted by permission of Princeton University Press.

[1]For Dostoevsky's own account of his intention to depict "a wholly beautiful individual," see his letters to Maikov (January 12, 1868) and S. A. Ivanova (January 13, 1868).

which the wisdom tale stands in as narrative marker. The resolution in the epilogue is dramatized as a movement between the two kinds of time. Raskolnikov's conversion experience is bodied forth as an abrupt shift to another narrative strategy, the significance of which is to recapitulate the drama of Christian redemption. The implication is that from now on for Raskolnikov there will be a balance between the two temporalities as he refers each moment of the rest of the linear progress that will be his life back to that one second of epiphany whose meaning will not change, that will insure his future against mere flux.

It is just such a moment that all the characters in *The Idiot* will seek, but that none of them will succeed in finding. Christian redemptive history in *Crime and Punishment* is used optimistically: the fusion of divine and human time is what Dostoevsky features in *Crime and Punishment*. However, the *split* between these two times constitutes the center of his next novel: indeed in all the rest of his novels *Heilsgeschichte* is treated less as a promise than as a paradox.

In contrast to *Crime and Punishment*, the lower layer in the palimpsest of *The Idiot*'s narrative structure is a single preexisting plot type. But it is one that contains in itself both temporalities present in the earlier novel. The plot of *The Idiot* is a series of narrative turns on the structure of Christ's execution and its relation to time before and after his death on the cross. Several executions are described in the novel, and the relationship of this symbol cluster to the crucifixion is made clear in the key role played by the younger Holbein's painting of Christ's corpse (1521).[2] The execution aspect of Christ's death is emphasized in reactions to the painting: "Some people may lose their faith looking at that picture," Rogozhin says (II, 4), because it shows a body so broken, so dead, that no resurrection seems possible from it. Ippolit, himself under sentence of premature death from tuberculosis, will say of Holbein (III, 4), "Here one cannot help being struck with the idea that if death is so horrible and if the laws of

----

[2]Dostoevsky had seen the painting in the Basle Museum in 1867, at the time he was feverishly attempting to get a conceptual grip on his new novel. His wife describes his excitement when first he caught sight of it, standing on a chair better to see it even though he could ill afford the fine that Anna Grigorievna was sure such a rash act would result in. See *Dnevnik A. G. Dostoevskoi: 1867 goda* (Moskva, Novaia Moskva, 1923), p. 366.

nature are so powerful, then how can they be overcome? How can they be overcome when even He did not conquer them . . . ?"

It is for this reason that executions figure so prominently in *The Idiot*. In each of the four books that constitute the novel a strategic place is assigned to descriptions or discussions of preordained death: Legros' death by guillotine in Lyons (I, 2; I, 5); a firing squad execution, halted at the last moment (I, 5); Dubarry's beheading (II, 2); speculation on the irony of execution as punishment for Ippolit, were he to commit murder since he is soon to die of his disease anyway (III, 5; III, 6); references to the fourteen-hour agony of the nobleman Glebov, condemned by Peter I to impalement on a stake in Red Square (IV, 5); and to the decapitation of Sir Thomas More (IV, 6). The possibility that Christ's moment of execution was final, that it did not result in resurrection and thus did not insure the sequence of *imitatio Christi* for other men—as it seemed to do for Raskolnikov, for instance—is the primary metaphysical dilemma of *The Idiot*.

It is also the major structural metaphor for the failure of Myshkin's sojourn in Russia, that spark of lucidity which interrupts his long years of darkness in the Swiss asylum, the brief six months whose events make up the novel's major plot. An inspired moment that subsequently fails to change anything, that fails to usher in an expected new order, is not only the dominant pattern of Myshkin's career, but of the other major characters' lives as well: Ganya's attempted engagement to Nastasya Filipovna; Ippolit's attempted suicide; Nastasya Filipovna's several attempts to break with her past; Aglaya's attempt to marry the Prince, her conversion to Catholicism, etc.

Thus the significance of the Christ story in *The Idiot* goes beyond mere characterological parallels between the saintly progress of Jesus and Myshkin, parallels that, in any case, have been remarked often enough.[3] Far more important are the differences between Myshkin and Christ, the way Dostoevsky exploits the root contradictions of Christian historiography as symbols for basic conflicts in the lives of his characters. A Christ whose appearance did *not* unseat the realities that had previously shaped history is invoked as a metaphor for the

---

[3] For a reading that takes this approach to an illuminating extreme, see: Romano Guardini, "Dostoevsky's *Idiot*: A Symbol of Christ," tr. Francis X. Quinn, *Cross Currents*, VI (Fall, 1956), pp. 359–82.

sameness of lives lived on the other side of epiphanies that failed to change them. Just as blood and avarice, powerlust and violence, ruled human history before Christ, so do they appear to do so *after* his coming, and it is the possibility of this failure that is the highest expression of all those other epiphanies—those given and those sought for—in the novel that in the end leave the brute seriality of events uninterrupted.

It is not particularly surprising that Dostoevsky should turn to Christology. But the particular way in which he deploys it in *The Idiot* needs further clarification. In his ideologically charged journalism he extends Christian salvation history to interpretations of particular nineteenth-century political events. He simply assumes that the possibility for the future redemption of the world coincides with a political boundary, and then goes on to use this doctrine as a jingoistic defense of Tsarist foreign policy. That is, he makes a direct parallel between two abstractions: the messiah and Russia. But in the fiction—and we shall have more to say on this—he relates the experience of Christ to the lives of individuals, and the novels' necessary emphasis on concreteness, detail, idiosyncrasy make such unmediated analogies impossible. The result, in the novels, is a radical analysis of *Heilsgeschichte*: not salvation in the future, but as the conceptual framework for how time itself works in Christian attitudes toward history. The paradox that Prince Myshkin—Dostoevsky's Christ figure—is an *idiot* is better understood if we remember that Christ's interlude on earth is also, in Christian historiography, a paradox.

Since Christ's coming did not usher in the millennium for all men, no matter what it did for the inner lives of *individual* men, his messianic prophecy created problems in the years after his death that continue to plague believers and nonbelievers alike. Among others, consider the claim Christians make "for a Galilean prophet's activity, ending with execution under a Roman governor who ruled Judaea under Tiberius, [a claim that] contradicts the modern historian's principle of historical writing."[4] The historian conceives time as linear, using B.C. and A.D. as mere conventions for dating all events, without assuming (or at least without instrumenting in his work) the unique-

[4]Oscar Cullman, *Christ and Time: The Primitive Christian Conception of Time and History*, tr. Floyd V. Filson (Philadelphia, Westminster Press, MCML), p. 20.

ness of the Incarnation: whereas for believers, that event effected a qualitative change at a given moment in history in the nature of *time itself*, so that things after it could never be the same again.

As the late French theologian Jean Daniélou, S.J., explains it: "The opposition is fundamental between the [historians' linear] conception and the Christian belief in a unique, irrevocable value belonging to the historical Incarnation. In the *Epistle to the Hebrews*, Christ is said to have entered 'once' . . . into the holy place, that is, when he ascended into God's heaven: something was there irrevocably gained. Nothing can ever again divide human nature from the Divinity; there is no possibility of a relapse; mankind is essentially saved. . . . The words 'past' and 'present' have here their full meaning."[5]

A basic peculiarity of the Christian attitude toward time, then, is that in it, "the center of interest is neither at the beginning, as it was for the Greeks, nor at the end as it is in evolutionary theories, but in the middle."[6] Christ is conceived as an eruption of eternal order into the temporal sequence. The momentary simultaneity of these two strata of time, which Christ made possible, resulted in a cutoff between the "horizontal" segments of time we designate B.C. and A.D. Consequently, Christian thinkers very early on had to meet the objection that while Christ's coming may have altered the state of mankind's spiritual life, no change was apparent in the historical world.[7] It is this seemingly contradictory aspect of Christology that occupies Dostoevsky in *The Idiot*, where it is treated as the dilemma of unique persons, a problem sustained at the level of individual psychology

[5]*The Lord of History: Reflections on the Inner Meaning of History*, tr. Nigel Abercrombie (Cleveland and New York, Meriden Books, 1968), p. 2. See as well: R. M. Grant, *The Earliest Lives of Jesus* (London, S.P.L.K., 1961), pp. 80–106.

[6]Daniélou, *The Lord of History* . . ., p. 7.

[7]It was to counter questions of this sort—questions that were exacerbated by Alaric's sack of Rome in 410—that Augustine systematized Christian historical doctrine in *The City of God*. He did not deny the apparent cutoff between Christ's coming and historical effect. Indeed, he made it the basis of his argument: the cutoff was there because of an even more essential division between *Civitas Dei* and *Civitas Terena*. For a treatment of Augustine that focuses on the meaning of this split for later historiography see: Erich Kahler, *The Meaning of History* (New York, George Braziller, 1964). See also Theodore E. Mommsen, "St. Augustine and the Christian Idea of Progress," *The Journal of the History of Ideas*, XII (June 1951), 346–74.

rather than of systematic theology. That is, he re-enacts the life-death-and-transfiguration of Christ, *as if Christ were not the messiah, but as if he were an individual.* What in the Bible is a series of acts interpreted according to their exterior, universal meaning, is rehearsed by Dostoevsky as the actions of particular men, whose meaning is inner, particular.

In its thrust against generalization *The Idiot* most clearly defines itself as a novel. The power of the Christ story is in its promise not just to one man, to me, but to *all* men; the emphasis may be on individual salvation, but the means of redemption have been systematized. In its generalizing tendency the Christ story is mythic and therefore stands at the opposite pole to the novel, which is grounded in the specific, the particular. This is what Lévi-Strauss means when he says of myth that it "is the most fundamental form of inauthenticity," where authenticity is understood "as the concrete nature of the knowledge people have of each other . . . contrary to what might seem to be the case there is nothing more abstract than myths."[8] The novel, on the other hand, is preeminently *anti*-systematic. Its discourse more than any other is open to contingency, the particular and unique.

Lukacs has defined "the inner form of the novel" as "the process of [a] problematic individual's journeying toward himself,"[9] as a genre in which individuality is understood as the action of one "who must create an entire world through his experience,"[10] out of himself, since he exists in a world where nothing is given by an exterior system. If, in *The Idiot*, the Christ story is present less as a characterological parallel for Myshkin than as a key to an important aspect of the novel's inner structure (in this case, the pattern of failed epiphanies that characterizes the whole), the same may be said of the frequent allusions that are made to Don Quixote in *The Idiot* (Aglaya hides Myshkin's letter in a copy of Cervantes' novel [II, i]; the Epanchins, Kolya and Radomsky discuss likenesses between the Prince and "the

[8]Georges Charbonnier, *Conversations with Claude Lévi-Strauss*, tr. John and Doreen Weightman (London, Jonathan Cape, 1969 [although the talks were given originally in 1959]), p. 55.

[9]George Lukacs, *The Theory of the Novel*, tr. Anna Bostock (Cambridge, Mass., M.I.T. Press, 1971 [originally published in 1920]), p. 80.

[10]*Ibid.*, p. 83.

poor Knight" [II, vi]; associations between Pushkin's "Poor Knight" fragment and Myshkin are made [II, viii]). At one level, surely, there is no doubt that similarities between Cervantes' hero and Prince Myshkin are being pointed to: their shared idealism, their championing of questionable "ladies," even their madness, although Dostoevsky gives this parallel a twist: while the Knight finally recovers at the end of *Don Quixote*, the Prince relapses into his former insanity. Myshkin is a failed double, almost a parody, of Don Quixote, much as he is a parody of Christ. But the presence of *Don Quixote* in *The Idiot* is more meaningful at a deeper level, as it dramatizes the thematic importance within *The Idiot* of that book's status as a novel. *Its genre is germane to its theme of Novel-ness.*

It has been written of *Don Quixote* that this "first great novel of world literature stands at the beginning of the time when the Christian God began to forsake the world; when man became lonely and could find meaning and substance only *in his own soul*, whose home was nowhere. . . ."[11] Cervantes' book is a novel in the degree to which it catalogues individuality more exhaustively than had ever been done before. It is no accident that it constantly undercuts the old chivalric romances, since its formal essence as a novel is opposed to the two formal tendencies of those romances that militate against individuality: their formulaic plots, making all stories the same; and their role-determined characterization (completely noble, completely vile), making all protagonists the same. The generic message of *Don Quixote* was that a new form had been found that was open to previously inexpressible idiosyncrasy.

Much as that novel dramatized the particularity of its universe through ironic contrasts with the system of Chivalry, so does *The Idiot* emphasize the contingency of its world by no less radically countering Christology. Christ's life as a *system* of salvation becomes a generality that can have only partial applicability in the lives of individuals whom novels depict in such relentless particularity.[12] Insofar as Christ is

---

[11]*Ibid.*, p. 103. Emphasis added.

[12]The Christ who appears in the Grand Inquisitor chapter of *The Brothers Karamazov* does so as a character in a legend, one of the many narrative forms that novel encapsulates. For a survey of other attempts to portray the Christ, see: Theodore Ziolkowski, *Fictional Transfigurations of Jesus* (Princeton, N.J., Princeton U.P., 1972).

conceived as a function of soteriology, he cannot figure in a novel, since he thus partakes of an absolute, and the novel, as D. H. Lawrence learned through his own painful experience in wrestling with the genre, is "incapable of the absolute ... in a novel there is always a tom-cat, a black tom-cat that pounces on the white dove of the Word...."[13]

That cat's name is contingency, and it counts among its victims not only the Word, but those who would speak It and only It. That is why Don Quixote haunts all subsequent novels: just as the Knight of La Mancha seeks to subordinate his life to the demands of Chivalry, so, in most later works, do the major characters thirst for a code, an absolute that will release them from their own contingency, even if the system is no more than a biography capable of knitting together the discrete moments of their lives into a continuous identity.[14]

It is this insistence on time as change, as that which problematizes unified identity in the novel, which led Lukacs to focus on temporality in his search for the genre's essence. For Lukacs the novel is the epic form of an age from which the Gods have fled. Such a view is particularly helpful, then, in understanding why corrosive time is so powerful a constitutive element of *The Idiot*: "... the bond with the transcendental home has been severed.... Only in the novel, whose very matter is seeking and failing to find the essence, is time posited together with form...."[15] It could in fact be said that Dostoevsky's plots, the characteristic form of Dostoevskian time, are set up to do nothing else so relentlessly as to dramatize the absence of essence in chronology, the separation of moment and sequence. Thus the basic urge in Dostoevsky toward the novel as his dominant mode of expression, since the time Lukacs invokes is one of becoming, of identity in flux: "The greatest discrepancy between idea and reality is time, the process of time as duration. The most profound and most humiliating

---

[13]Quoted in Frank Kermode, *D. H. Lawrence* (N.Y., Viking, 1973), p. 27. Kermode adds about his subject, in words that apply with equal force to Dostoevsky, "It was in the novels that he wrestled with these transcendent systems. The novels do not have a design upon us; their design is upon the unqualified, unsuspected dogmas of the treatises and letters, which must be made to submit to life."

[14]The novel is in its essence radically anti-utopian; perhaps that is why all novels are, ultimately, *Bildungsromane*.

[15]Lukacs, *The Theory of the Novel*, p. 122.

impotence of subjectivity consists . . . in the fact that it cannot resist the sluggish, yet constant progress of time; that it must slip down, slowly yet inexorably from the peaks it has laboriously scaled. . . ."[16]

The novel insists on the existence of the part by exhaustively demonstrating the inability of any whole to contain it completely. A creek may have a mean depth of only six inches, yet still contain isolated holes that are, say, ten feet deep. The novel always tells the story of that man who drowned in a stream with a mean depth of six inches. It always opts for the exception to the rules, whether they derive from the code of chivalry, from the code of society (as in most nineteenth-century English or French novels), or, as in the case of *The Idiot*, from the code of Christian salvation.

We are now able to speculate further as to why Dostoevsky chose (even before he had written it) as a title for this novel *The Idiot*: he does so to emphasize the subjectivity of his Christ figure. "Idiot" goes back through Latin *idiota* to the Greek word meaning private person (that aspect of a man *separate* from any collective identity) or layman, a man without professional knowledge (innocent of any *system* of knowing); the root for the word means "private," "own," "peculiar." Myshkin, then, as idiot, stands in for the isolated individual. In other words, he is *alone*, a would-be Christ figure who is denied the systematic time of *Heilsgeschichte*, a messiah who is a layman. He cannot have as an inhabitant of the novel-world that whole-part relationship that defines Christology, in which Jesus is a particular manifestation of the universal. Jesus' meaning is contained in the *telos* built into his biography; his life is lived toward resurrection, back toward his extra human, supra-individualistic state. The problem, on the other hand, for Myshkin is that he is only a subjectivity: his task is precisely to *find a telos*, to *achieve* a universality that can endow his particularity with meaning. Christ, by contrast, always exhibits the attributes of his role: he is the same yesterday today and forever, not only in his Godhood, but, for a believer, in his biography as a man as well. A Jesus who might, for example, be spiteful on occasion is unthinkable; he is always the same: supremely good. Thus he cannot serve as hero of a novel, the genre that more than any other flaunts variety in character, the rapidly shifting changes that dominate individual lives. Myshkin is saintly one

---

[16]*Ibid.*, pp. 120–21.

moment, silly the next; now he is certain, now confused—and what is more, he *knows* there is no unity in his life.

When Keller, who has come to the Prince to unburden his soul, to confess and purge himself, admits that he has come *as well* to borrow 150 roubles, Myshkin recognizes this sincere desire for purity that is immediately undercut by a *no less* sincere desire to exploit others as a trait that defines the human condition. "You might have been telling me about myself just now . . . indeed . . . everyone is like that . . . for it is terribly difficult to fight against these double thoughts [*dvoinye mysli*]" (II, 11). Double thoughts make unified sensibility, a non-dualistic identity particularly difficult to achieve. Myshkin may succeed in experiencing at one given moment a sense of wholeness, but the next moment will rob him of it. His attempt to live a unified existence is constantly exposed by the novel's relentless insistence on the multiplicity of identities that are merely human, merely personal.

Since the problem of identity is to find a common term for conflicting moments of plenitude and pettiness, self becomes a function of time, time that keeps going on, that will not stop, and that therefore continues to raise new contradiction, new knowledge of self, that must in its turn be integrated into a unity. A major expression of the dilemma is found in Myshkin's illness, epilepsy. There is a moment before the fit actually seizes him, "when suddenly amidst sadness, spiritual darkness and depression, his brain seemed to catch fire for brief moments. . . . His mind and heart were flooded by dazzling light. . . ." Myshkin senses not only that such a moment constitutes "the highest mode of existence" but that the special awareness such a moment grants him is awareness precisely of—self: ". . . the most direct sensation of one's own existence [remember that epilepsy is the sign of his idiocy] to the most intense degree" (II, 5).

But such a moment is followed, of course, by the onset of the fit. Although Myshkin says that he would give the rest of his life for the sake of his ecstatic second, suggesting parallels with the Faustian temptation to say "*Verweile, doch, du bist so schön,*" he knows that such an option is denied him. He is constantly thrust back into a lower state, dramatized as convulsion. Using the parable of Mahomet's (another epileptic's) water pitcher to illustrate the most important aspect of what he feels at the onset of a fit, he adds, ". . . At that

moment the extraordinary saying that *there shall be time no longer* becomes, somehow comprehensible." These words, taken of course
from the Apocalypse of John, emphasize that the power of the moment expresses itself as timelessness. After it has passed, when the
Prince lies grovelling on the ground in a helpless fit, when the falling
sickness fells him, he collapses not only into epilepsy, but falls back
into time again. Like Adam, he is cast out of Eden's *eternal now* into the
flux of the world's becoming, or like Christ, who leaves the eternity of
his Godhood to fall into time as a mere man. The disease thus provides a metaphor for both aspects of the novel's key problematic: a
feeling of wholeness that is then undercut, and the enormity of the
distance between the two states, the unbridgeable space that constitutes the pain of time. The constant collapse of privileged moment
gives a special meaning to that other central metaphor of the book,
the Apocalypse of St. John. It is present in Dostoevsky's text not
because of the flaming end it prophesies. The horror consists rather
in the discovery that there *are* no ends that give meaning, just as there
are no beginnings. The terror is not that the Barbarians will come, but
that they will not.

The cutoff that exists between moments that refuse to resolve
themselves into a sequence is dramatized in *The Idiot* at different levels
of narrative and in varying ratios of contradiction. The task in each
stratum of plot and range of dissimilarity is to find terms appropriate
to *particular* experiences, but that also, simultaneously, correspond to
a general series. The problem is perhaps most familiar to historians,
who must constantly answer the question: what is the proper perspective for explaining the relationships between events that are—in
themselves—discrete, events that will seem, without such a view, unre-
lated? "Unfortunately, no law of history enjoins that only those years
whose dates end with the figures '01' coincide with the critical points
of human evolution. Whence there derive some curious distortions of
meaning ... we appear to assign an arbitrarily chosen and strictly
pendulum-like rhythm to realities to which such a regularity pattern is
entirely alien."[17]

The problem in the history of individual lives in *The Idiot* is that no
essence can be found that will suffice to give shape to sequences that

---

[17]Marc Bloch, *The Historian's Craft*, tr. Peter Putnam (N.Y., Vintage Books,
1953), p. 182–83.

are therefore mere chronologies. Lives cannot be "periodized" because there is no point of view outside them to sanction the division of biographical eras.

The difficulty of finding a common term that will serve to connect otherwise discrete moments—conceived as an existential rather than historiographical dilemma—we have seen dramatized in the central metaphor of Myshkin's epilepsy: his inability to join health and illness, the moment of ecstacy that precedes his fits with the awful minutes he spends writhing on the ground in the grip of the epileptic attack itself. The unconsciousness he experiences between the onset of such fits and their aftermath is an epistemological as well as physical blackout, a symbol of his failure to find an identity that will connect the two experiences. There is no metaphysical copulative in the physical syntax of Myshkin's epilepsy.

The same pattern is present in the broken linearities that define biographical tasks for the other characters in *The Idiot.* The split between the "before" and "after" that Nastasya Filipovna cannot connect is marked by her seduction. At the age of seven her father goes mad and she becomes the ward of Totsky, although he does not make any great changes in her life until, returning from a long sojourn abroad, he notices she has become "a lovely child . . . playful, charming, and intelligent, who promised to become an extraordinarily beautiful young woman" (I, 4). At this point Totsky puts the girl in the hands of a Swiss governess who teaches her French. While Swiss governesses were extremely common at this time, the hint of Rousseau should not be missed, especially as the emphasis on a pedagogy oriented toward the simple, the natural, the Edenic, is taken up in the next step of Nastasya Filipovna's career as she is moved (after four years of such training) to another of Totsky's properties "in a more remote province," where she lives in a small wood house attended only by an old housekeeper and a maid. The house is filled with all the things to delight a young girl, and, in fact, the estate it is located on is called "as if on purpose *Otradnoe*," a word that may be translated as joy or consolation, but that has as well, Edenic overtones.[18] It is while she is

___

[18]In fact, in some English versions it is translated as Eden, as in Margarshack, *The Idiot* (Penguin Books, 1955), p. 65. It should be added that *Otradnoe* was a fairly common name for country estates in nineteenth-century Russia. In *War and Peace*, for instance, the provincial seat of the Rostov family is also called *Otradnoe*.

in this paradise that "Mr. Totsky himself put in an appearance. . . . Since then he seemed to have grown particularly fond of that remote little village in the heart of the steppes" (I, 4). The interval that Dostoevsky here marks with ". . ." is a typographical moment between Nastasya Filipovna's Edenic tick and the fallen tock of the remainder of her life. The full meaning of that break becomes apparent only when, as Totsky plans to marry a society woman, Nastasya Filipovna leaves the country and confronts her seducer in Petersburg: "Quite a different woman was sitting before him, a woman who was not at all like the girl he had known and had left in the village of Otradnoe only the previous July" (I, 4).

The Edenic parallel is pointed up later in the same chapter when it is said of Totsky, who is fearful that Nastasya Filipovna will not go along with his scheme to marry her off to Ganya Ivolgin, that he "did not quite believe her, even now, and was for a long time afraid that there might be a snake lurking beneath the flowers." This projection is one of the several inversions that mark relations between parents and children in *The Idiot*. The snake image is complicated further when it is recalled that the poem Nastasya Filipovna reads Rogozhin about Henry IV and Gregory VII is Heine's 1843 *Heinrich* (one of the significantly named series, *Zeitgedichte*). In the poem, as the Emperor kneels before the Pope, he dreams of revenge, "an axe that will smite the serpent of my sufferings."[19] The association is doubled here: not only is an association of Rogozhin (and his knife) with Henry (and his axe) made, but Nastasya Filipovna's association with a long lost *Otradnoe* is present as well. The two major themes of their relationship— passion conceived as a power struggle, and the religious overtones of being a "fallen woman" (is she the cause of her own down'fall, herself the serpent in her own Garden of Eden?), are both present in the Heine poem.

The rest of the five years remaining to Nastasya Filipovna after she leaves *Otradnoe* are spent not only in revenge, but in a frantic effort as well to recapture edenic time, to start afresh; failing to do so, she condemns herself to death, gives herself up to Rogozhin's knife. The search for a new point of origin that will efface her fall is best ob-

[19]The source for the quotation has been cited in: V. E. Kholshevnikov, "O literaturnykh tsitatakh u Dostoevskogo," *Vestnik leningradskogo universiteta*, 1960, No. 8 (Seriia istorii, iazyka, i literatury), Vyp. 2, p. 136.

served in the scandal scene that concludes the novel's first book. It occurs significantly on her name-day (she will gain the name of her true self), celebrated, of course, as her birthday (she will be born again). When Myshkin proposes to her she cries, "Oh, life is only beginning for me now!" And then abjuring the sequence inherent in a future shared with the Prince, she accepts Rogozhin, again stressing that she will start afresh. "I've spent ten years [since her seduction] behind prison bars and now it is my turn to be happy!" The scene ends as she dashes off into the night, having sloughed off her house and servants like the skin of another self, as she screams she will become a washerwoman or streetwalker (I, 16). Of course she, like Myshkin, finds that her moment of decision does *not* serve to change the logic of the life she has sought to break out of (her prison, as she says).

There are many other parallels between her biography and that of the Prince, which is why Dostoevsky so laboriously points up at each of their meetings the sense they share of having known each other *before* their first encounter. Both are orphans of ancient families, both have spent time in the country (he in Switzerland, she with a Swiss governess, both in a Rousseauistic state of innocence), and both regret being drawn into society. We learn of the Prince, as he stands amid the schemes that circle about him, that he has "an uncontrollable desire to leave everything here and go back to where he had come from, to some far-away solitary place. . . . He had a feeling that if he stayed here even a few days longer he would irrevocably be drawn into this world, and that this world would become his world thereafter" (II, 11). Myshkin is, in other words, afraid of falling into worldliness, and of course this is what happens as he becomes the center, the effective *cause*, of the intrigues that swirl in the rest of the novel, a condition for which his epilepsy—as a falling sickness—is the book's major metaphor.

Nastasya Filipovna's closeness to the Prince is underlined by her status as a "fallen woman," as, from the faraway place of her innocence and childhood, she plunges deeper and deeper into the world. She sees herself as a "fallen angel" (IV, 8) and constantly looks back to the past, an existential nostalgia that Dostoevsky emphasizes by constantly associating her with history. In the novel's most sustained and detailed account of her relations with Rogozhin (II, 3, 4) she tells the story of Henry IV's struggle with Pope Gregory VII ("You, sir haven't studied universal history, have you?"); there is also frequent mention of S. M. Solovyov's (the father of Dostoevsky's friend, the philosopher V. M. Solovyov) history, that Nastasya Filipovna has given Rogozhin to read. The significance of this choice consists first of all in its full title: *The History of Russia from the Most Ancient Times*. This is *her* iconic book just as *Don Quixote* is Myshkin's; it seeks to go back to the most primal origins, as she does. It also points to the crux of her problem, the difficulty of erecting continuous identity; just as Russia is orphan of the nations, so Nastasya Filipovna cannot find valid antecedents, as becomes clear in Dostoevsky's play with the history book and murder weapon.

As Rogozhin concludes his account of what happened to Nastasya Filipovna after she runs away from her name-day party with him, Myshkin picks up a knife lying on the table before him (II, 3). Twice Rogozhin takes it away from him, and yet the Prince picks it up a third time:

> Rogozhin seized it angrily, put it in the book, and threw the book [Solovyov's *History*] onto another table.
> "Do you cut the pages with it?" asked the Prince, but rather absent-mindedly as though still too preoccupied with his thoughts.
> "Yes, the pages . . ."
> "It's a garden knife [*sadovii nozh*], isn't it?"
> "Yes, it's a garden knife. Can't one cut pages with a garden knife?"

Rogozhin will kill her with this garden knife; but its first sheath is a history book—unfinished by Rogozhin (he has not cut all its pages). Thus it is that Nastasya Filipovna's death will come from the interrupted history of Russia. Long before the end of her life, *its* history had been interrupted by Totsky's seduction. Her constant attempts to "begin life anew" constitute a pattern of jerky biographical gestures that will not fall into a connected series, a history. She never succeeds in recapturing *otradnoe*, and so the two parts of her life are as marked off from each other as the opened versus the as-yet-uncut pages of the copy of Solovyov she gives Rogozhin. The reason for so radical a split in her biography is that she attaches a transcendent significance to her existence before the seduction: like the open pages of the book, it was full of meaning. On the other hand, the years after the seduction are as meaningless as the still uncut, still unread pages of that book. The inability to overcome this gap drives her on to ever more hysterical attempts to wipe out the *otradnoe* origin with a new beginning until, in despair, she gives herself to Rogozhin's knife—a Garden-of-Eden knife that separates the open and closed pages of a history book. Like all the other characters, major and minor, in the novel, Nastasya Filipovna is cut off from the past, and as de Tocqueville, student of that other country which, like Russia, had an ambiguous history, wrote: "Since the past has ceased to throw its light upon the future, the mind of man wanders in obscurity."[20]

The darkness of the past is dramatized in *The Idiot* as the absence of true parents. This is why the parallel between individual biographies and Russian national history is so close in Dostoevsky: *in each case the problem is to create a continuity without the benefit of antecedents.* The problem of forging a continuous identity, connecting past and present in any given individual life, is exacerbated by the cutoff between past and present in the sequence of generations. The three major figures of the novel—Myshkin, Rogozhin, and Nastasya Filipovna—are all fatherless. The other characters must all in their own way confront the failure of the fathers. Burdovsky discovers he is not Pavlishchev's son, but he is able to be his mother's son, a consolation denied to Ippolit, who dreams of disowning (*otkazat'sia*) his mother (his father is dead) and going off to live with Kolya Ivolgin, who will also give up *his* family (I, xxi).[21] Aglaya, the center of the family for all the Epanchins, disowns her parents in the end by running off with a phoney Polish nobleman and converting to Roman Catholicism—in Dostoevsky's world, a fate worse than death.

[20]Quoted in: Hannah Arendt, *Between Past and Future* (New York, Viking Press, 1961), p. 7.
[21]The old general is the most sustained example of the failure of the fathers. His constant insistence that he is related to those with whom he shares no blood, or that he knew other characters when they were still babies (hoping to signify, as with Myshkin, a connection between the generations), points to the debasement of such connections. Ivolgin is also important in the degree to which he points up the parallel between the two levels of past/present cutoff Dostoevsky is here working with, the generational (personal) and historical (national): he seeks to create the same specious connections between himself and Napoleon as he does with Myshkin.

The collapse of bridges between generations is marked in *The Idiot* by the failure of material inheritance. It will be remembered that money, which plays so enormous a role in the novel, always comes from the wills of a dead generation. Nastasya Filipovna's father dies in poverty, but leaves her to the guardianship of Totsky (who, as surrogate parent, leaves a sinister legacy indeed to his adopted child). Burdovsky seeks to establish the identity of his father in order to gain a part of his inheritance (II, 4); his problem is that of all the other characters: to discover the identity of his true parents. He differs from the others only in that he succeeds where they fail. Myshkin discovers his inheritance (135,000 rubles as we learn in IV, 5) amounts to much *less* than had been anticipated (II, 9). Radomsky, instead of receiving his uncle's enormous fortune, is saddled with only his shame; the old man shoots himself after squandering thousands of rubles in public funds (III, 2). It is, of course, at a crucial point in Radomsky's career (he has just resigned his commission) that the awful truth is revealed—by that profound student of the consequences that flow from ambiguous legacies, Nastasya Filipovna.

Rogozhin's relationship to his dead father is especially complex. The father "had a great respect for the *Skoptsy*," a sect of fanatical Orthodox Christians who castrate themselves (II, 3). Nastasya Filipovna (in the same chapter) says of the son that, "you'd have settled in this house, like your father, with those *Skoptsy* . . . you'd have been converted to their faith in the end . . . ," a parallel that brings out the sterility of both generations. The father's sexless passion is the accumulation of wealth for its own sake. And when at first glance it would appear that the son's passion for Nastasya Filipovna is sexual, it soon becomes clear that it is actually another genus of greed. He is a miser who takes very seriously the grim joke of Nastasya Filipovna's sale of herself to the highest bidder in the auction that concludes the first book of the novel. Having bought her, he seeks to hoard her—because she possesses him. Unlike others in the novel, Rogozhin comes into his father's money, and the sum is as great as had been anticipated; but its effects are as calamitous as the failure of the others to collect their inheritance.

All the attempts to smuggle something across the border of generations fail, another of the novel's symbols for the condition of discontinuity. As Hannah Arendt has written in the title essay of *Between Past and Future,* "The testament telling the heir what will be rightfully his, wills past possession for a future. Without testament or, to resolve the metaphor, without tradition—which selects and names, which hands down and preserves, which indicates where the treasurers are and what their worth is—there seems to be no willed continuity in time...."[22] The absence of such a pattern is central to the whole fabric of the novel, dramatized in a wide range of discontinuities, each of which has its symbolic condition: execution, epilepsy, seduction. To this list of fractures in identity we must now add that of the failed inheritance.

Money plays so important a role in the novel because of its status as a metaphor for exchange, a potential means of communication, as something that passes between people—or in wills—between generations. Money is significant as a system of conventional markers for value. What is more, unless there is *agreement* as to its value, it is worthless. There is a sense in which money is nothing more than a symbol of values that can be exchanged between people who may differ on all other matters. There can be no solipsism in economics; like words, money brooks no Carollian Humpty Dumptys who would insist that a coin is worth what they say it is. This is one of the reasons why money constantly crops up in semiotics and linguistics. Saussure, for instance, uses it as a metaphor for a fundamental operation of language itself:

> "To determine what a five-franc piece is worth one must...
> know: (1) that it can be exchanged for a fixed quantity of a
> different thing, e.g., bread; and (2) that it can be compared with
> a similar value of the same system, e.g., a one-franc piece, or
> with coins of a different system (a dollar, etc). In the same way a
> word can be exchanged for something dissimilar, an idea; be-
> sides it can be compared with something of the same nature,
> another word."[23]

But in *The Idiot* the generation of the fathers has not passed on to the sons those principles by which the worth of things may be determined. There is no common ground for value; thus money has the

[22]Hannah Arendt, *op.cit.*, p. 5.
[23]Ferdinand de Saussure, *Course in General Linguistics*, tr. Wade Baskin (New York, McGraw-Hill, 1966), p. 115.

opposite effect from that of exchange. It serves instead as a symbol for the *rupture* between generations. It marks that bottomless canyon that "inheritance" has failed to bridge. The inability of generations to transmit value from past to future is an extension of a pattern we have seen in the lives of the individual characters. They, too, cannot connect their own pasts and futures. In the lives of most of them there is a failure to sustain any of those moments which seem to define identity: Myshkin cannot will his moment of heightened awareness to his own future; thus he falls from ecstasy into epilepsy. Nastasya Filipovna falls from Eden into the world; Ippolit from a suicidal moment that would give his life significance to a "bad death" from a wasting disease. In these and other cases the future robs of its significance a past that was felt somehow to be privileged.

The major symbol clusters of the novel—execution, the Holbein Christ, epilepsy, Don Quixote, money—swirl around a core that is common to them all: the failure of *kairos* to effect *chronos*. There is no wholeness that will remain unsplintered throughout its unfolding in time: the man who promises to change his life if not executed in the next second, continues—when spared—to lead the same existence as before, the meaninglessness of which was clear from the vantage point of that exalted moment before the firing squad (I, 2). The promise of Christ's life is denied in the painting of his death: the cycle of biological time is unbroken: the Prince's moment of lucid self-awareness is wiped out in the epileptic fit that follows it. All the money, all the inheritances lead to a cutoff between past and present. No essence can withstand the battering of the moments as they pass by. The structure of a single moment's promise broken under the onslaught of a series of other such moments following upon it, constitutes the novel's central pattern. Its most paradigmatic expression is in the failure of *Heilsgeschichte*: Christ did not change the course of history; his promise of peace has been eroded by all the wars ever since. It is the collapse of this messianic legacy in the past that underlies all the other failed testaments from father to son in the book. Without the Christian inheritance, at a time when the *imitatio Christi* breaks down, each man must find his own way, seek his own identity without the aid of preexisting models. He must, in other words, become an idiot in the root sense of that word—someone on his own.

The Narrator in *The Devils*

by V. A. Tunimanov

In the novel it gradually becomes clear that Anton Lavrentievich G——v is the chronicler–witness of the recent events which took place in his town, and he also recounts this recent past. About himself G——v imparts very scant information: he "accidentally" admits into the chronicle certain remarks by other people, which somewhat reveal his "social" position. We know that he works somewhere, but it is not precisely indicated where. Liputin caustically introduces him to the tipsy Captain Lebyadkin: " 'It's Mr. G——v, a young gentleman of classical education and in close touch with the highest society' " (I, 3, ix).[1] G——v is a chronicler, and his personality is in the background and beyond the boundaries of the chronicle, a fact which also creates the necessary conditions for a sort of detached narration that almost completely rules out the "confession" of the narrator himself.

The only part of G——v's personal life that penetrates the chronicle is his short-lived and unrequited love for Liza Tushin. The chronicler describes his past feeling for Liza retrospectively and calmly: the story of the origin and dying of the feeling is given in "fragments" in the chronicle. At one time the chronicler runs errands for Liza, carries out her requests, performs services for her. It is true that the emerging function of the chronicler as the faithful servant and knight of the foremost town Amazon somehow dies of its own accord and

"The Narrator in Dostoevsky's *The Devils*" by Vladimir A. Tunimanov. Excerpted from a short monograph under the same title in *Issledovaniia po poetike i stilistike*, ed. V. V. Vinogradov et al. (Leningrad: Nauka, 1972), pp. 118–41. Copyright 1972 by Nauka, Leningrad, U.S.S.R. Reprinted by permission of the author and VAAP (All-Union Association of Author's Rights) in the U.S.S.R. Translated from the Russian by Susanne Fusso.

[1] Quotations from *The Devils* are from Fyodor Dostoevsky, *The Devils (The Possessed)*, translated with an introduction by David Magarshack (Penguin Books: London, 1953).

without any motivation. But in turn, the chronicler's fixed attention, his precise and detailed statement of the heroine's movements, of the slightest changes in her aspect, are motivated: "Liza, I observed, suddenly jumped up from her chair and for some reason as they were going out of the room followed them with a motionless stare to the very door. Then she sat down again in silence, but her face seemed to twitch spasmodically, as though she had touched some horrible snake" (I, 5, v).

In the chronicler's "ideological" biography the main thing he discloses is his sojourn in Stepan Trofimovich Verkhovensky's circle; this is recounted as an idle pastime, from the position of a man who has "matured" and renounced his former "delusions." The chronicler caustically recalls his own personal sojourn in the circle as well. The chronicler's irony is multi-directed, and this is one of the main conditions both of the narrative style and of the general atmosphere and structure of the novel. The irony partly affects the frightened citizens as well, and ridicules their absurd notions:

> At one time they used to say in the town about our circle that it was a hotbed of free-thinking, vice, and atheism; this rumor, by the way, always persisted. And yet all we did in our circle was to indulge in the most innocent, amiable, jolly typically Russian liberal chatter (I, 1, ix).

Also ridiculed are the groundlessness and abstract character of "political" conversations, the absurdity and irrelevance of the members of the circle:

> We also discussed problems of general concern to mankind, talked severely of the future fate of Europe and the human race, foretold in a doctrinaire fashion that after the fall of the monarchy in France that country would at once be reduced to the position of a secondary power, and we were firmly convinced that that would happen very easily and quite soon. We had long ago prophesied that the Pope would assume the role of a simple archbishop in a united Italy, and had no doubts whatever that this thousand-year-old problem was a trifling matter in our age of humanitarian ideas, industry, and railways. (I, 1, ix)

The chronicler himself is in the past no more than an extra, a claquer in the suite of Stepan, now with regret ("alas") recalling the past impersonal ("we") existence and, from a new position, asking: "But, gentlemen, don't we still hear today, and very often, too, sometimes, the same sort of 'charming,' 'clever,' 'liberal' old Russian nonsense?" (I, 1, ix). To be sure, the derision of the members of the circle and the townspeople also includes self-derision; denial borders on denial of one's own past, censure borders on self-censure.

Participation in Stepan's circle places the chronicler in a special relationship with the head of the town "liberals." G——v is Stepan's confidant. This is a comic feature, and Liza Tushin directly indicates its comic nature to the chronicler: " 'I have already formed an amusing idea about you: you're Mr. Verkhovensky's confidant, aren't you?' " (I, 3, viii). In fact, this is actually the chronicler's main occupation, which he carries out with a certain "anguish" and out of "boredom," simultaneously oppressed and amused by the lot that has fallen to him: "Let me observe in passing that I had to put up with a great deal during that unhappy week—never leaving the side of my poor affianced friend, in the capacity of his closest confidant" (I, 3, i).

The duties of a "closest" confidant remove the question of the chronicler's knowledge of, if not all, then of almost all the circumstances of Stepan's external and inner life, including the most intimate:

> It may be asked how I could possibly come to know so delicate a detail. Well, what if I witnessed it myself? What if Mr. Verkhovesky himself has on more than one occasion sobbed on my shoulder, while describing to me in lurid colours the smallest detail of his talk with Mrs. Stavrogin? (The things he told me on such occasions!) (I, 1, ii).

Such a "short" distance separating the chronicler from Stepan permits G——v to prophesy and guess subtle and forbidden stirrings of the "teacher's" soul, inaccessible to the common view: "It goes without saying that I had long since guessed that great secret of his and seen through it" (I, 3, i); "I had only been waiting for that word. Finally this secret word, hidden from me, had been uttered after a whole week of equivocations and grimaces;" "I guessed from the way he looked that he wanted at last to tell me something of the utmost importance, which he must have kept back till that moment" (III,9).[2]

The confidant "out of boredom" sometimes directly accuses and ridicules Stepan, pursuing, as a rule, high moral aims: " 'And such a sordid, such a . . . base thought could occur to you, Stepan Verkhovesky, in your lucid mind, in your good heart and . . . even before Liputin . . .' "; "Being still young, I could not help being indignant at the coarseness of his feelings and the ugly nature of some of his suspicions" (I, 3, i). The chronicler's penitential little words ("Oh, I was rude and discourteous, and I recall it now with regret") are far from always sincere, and often carry more venom than his direct accusations. The accusations are somewhat "neutralized" and softened not by the belated and frequently insincere repentances, but by the universality of the atmosphere of derision, into which the accuser himself also falls. Here the chronicler speaks extremely sharply about Stepan's estrangement from the world: "Such complete, utter ignorance of everyday reality was both touching and somehow repulsive" (III, 9). The chronicler himself, however, while ridiculing his friend's alienation from fundamentals [lit. "from the soil (ot pochvy)" —ed.] (the refrain "my poor friend" carries through the novel), has not so very far outstripped him in knowledge of the world, and is capable of the most improbable and stupid suppositions: "A wild and preposterous idea flashed through my mind" (III, 9). Caustically depicting Stepan's latest habits, the chronicler emphasizes that, besides other things, the former still loves "to dip into the champagne." It cannot be denied that this is a debasing trait, and one that produces an undeniably devastating effect in an unexpected context. But here again it does not befit the chronicler to stand in a pose of "high moral standards"; his "poor friend" is terribly communicative and prefers "to dip into the champagne" in company, where the libation may be enlivened by literary and frivolous conversation, or, in its absence, by the unvarying confidant-drinking partner: "As a rule, when we had met before and he had begun complaining to me, a bottle of vodka would

---

[2]To be someone's confidant almost always presupposes mutuality; such a "two-sided connection" is indeed formed between Stepan and the chronicler: "He, too, saw through me; I mean, he realized that I saw through him and that I was, indeed, angry with him, and he was angry with me for being angry with him and seeing through him."

almost invariably make its appearance after a little time and everything would become more cheerful" (I, 2, v); "Out of sorrow we also drank a little. However, he soon fell into a sweet sleep." Stepan's chatter and verbal nonsense are characterized by one of his most attentive listeners and "pupils." Stepan Trofimovich's speech at the celebration is commented on by the master of ceremonies who absurdly fusses with his rosette, and both these figures are undeniably comical. The sufferings of his panic-stricken friend are described by the frightened chronicler–citizen, stunned by what he has seen: "Mr. Verkhovensky and I, at any rate, at first shut ourselves up and looked on with apprehension from a distance"; "Mr. Verkhovensky and I, not without apprehension about the boldness of our theory, but encouraging each other, at last came to the conclusion . . . " (II, 2, i).

The chronicler's "eulogy" for Stepan took shape very early and clearly in the notebooks for the novel (with the exception of only a few nuances, which we omit); the main peculiarity of G——v's tone was also determined: "The chronicler pretends that he feels Christian pity for the darkening of a great character. He excuses Gr[anovs]ky, saying that it is all natural. . . ."[3]

This ironic, "pretending" tone begins at the very outset of the novel; after the excessively respectful epithets ("talented" and "much-revered") follows a slow but steady increase in irony. After the allusion to Stepan's constant histrionics, the phrase borrowed from Gogol, "he was a most excellent man," already sounds like a half-concealed sneer.

The simplest device for debasing Stepan's image is the direct contrasting of truth with fabrication, of real and precise facts with the "teacher's" fiction and chatter. The mysterious "whirlwind of concurrent events" is completely dispelled by the chronicler:

> It turned out afterwards that there had been no "whirlwind" and even no "events," at any rate at that particular instant. It was only the other day that I discovered, to my great astonishment, from a highly reliable source, that Mr. Verkhovensky had never lived in our province amongst us as an exile, as we were all led to

[3]N. E. Ignateva and E. N. Konshina, eds., *Zapisnye tetradi F. M. Dostoevskogo* [The Notebooks of F. M. Dostoevsky] (Moscow–Leningrad, 1935), p. 164. Stepan is conditionally called Granovsky in the preparatory materials for *The Devils*.

suppose, and that he had never even been placed under police supervision (I, 2, i).[4]

Once again returning to the notorious "whirlwind" that destroyed the career of the freethinker of the forties, the chronicler mercilessly contrasts the fruits of his "sorrowful friend" 's imagination to the truth: "And if the whole truth is to be told, the real cause of the change in his career was the . . . proposal that had been made before and renewed again by Varvara Petrovna . . . to undertake the education and the whole intellectual development of her only son" (I, 1, ii).

The "civic grief" stamped on Stepan's face during the card game prompts the chronicler again to appeal to "truth": "And to tell the truth he was very fond of a game of cards, which, especially in later years, led to frequent and unpleasant squabbles with Mrs. Stavrogin, particularly as he was always losing" (I, 1, ii).

The second device for debasement is also simple: a high-flown and respectful preamble, then a whole system of qualifications, a certain hesitation after them and finally a full negation of what was said at the beginning:

> And yet he was undoubtedly a highly intelligent and talented man, a man who was, as it were, even a scholar, though so far as his scholarship was concerned . . . well, he did not really make any important contribution to scholarship, indeed none at all, I believe (I, 1, i).

Here the debasement is consistently carried to its furthest limit, to zero. Precisely here (and this is characteristic of the "eulogy") there follows a partial "rehabilitation" of Stepan: "But, then, that happens again and again in Russia with men of learning" (I, 1, i).

Still another (and frequent) device for the comic debasement of the "teacher" is the synonymic comparison of extremely heterogeneous and unequal concepts and names. According to the chronicler's description, Stepan ". . . looked almost like a patriarch or, to be more

---

[4]Let us note that a second "whirlwind of concurrent events" was destined to bewilder Virginisky (in general, various sorts of psychological and ideological parallels appear frequently in *The Devils*)—an ironic subtext is retained here as well, although it is impossible to deny the existence of the "whirlwind." And, incidentally, the "whirlwind of concurrent events" is one of the main principles of the chronicle's system.

exact, like the portrait of the playwright Kukolnik" (I, 1, v).[5] Yet another time, Kukolnik falls into a strange synonymic relationship, that destroys the pathetically emotional tone of the chronicler's exclamations:

> This man whom we had looked upon as a prophet for twenty years, our preacher, teacher, patriarch, the Kukolnik who had borne himself so grandly and majestically before us all, whom we regarded with such admiration, thinking it an honor to do so— suddenly this man was sobbing . . . (II, 9).

The irony here, however, is ambivalent—the worship of "our Kukolnik" is strange and absurd.

The "pretending" G——v often justifies himself by saying that he didn't quite want to say what he just said, since he was recounting it not in the usual sense but in a quite special one. The majority of such stipulations are insincere and produce the reverse impression:

> I used the expression "flung himself into the arms," but don't let anyone jump to any rash and improper conclusions; those arms have to be understood only in the highest possible moral sense. These two remarkable beings were joined forever in a union that was most refined and delicate (I, 1, i).

The solemn intonations and grandiloquent words, more than anything else here, promote the appearance of "rash" and "improper" considerations. And the "most refined and delicate union," after the series of anecdotes and details, appears in an utterly ironic light. We can also detect an analogous phenomenon in the chronicler's other justifications and stipulations: "I don't claim for a moment that he had never suffered for his convictions, but I am fully convinced now that he could have gone on lecturing on his Arabs as much as he liked if he had only given the necessary explanations" (I, 1, ii);[6] "I

---

[5]The "real" reason for such a strange and comic resemblance is specially explained in parentheses. It appears that, in memory of her childhood love for the lithograph of the poet, Varvara Petrovna "kept that picture among her most intimate treasures, so that it is quite likely that she designed Mr. Verkhovensky's clothes in such a style that they somewhat resembled the clothes worn by the playwright in the picture" (I, 1, 5).

[6]"Necessary explanations" in reference to Arabs is a further example of how complicated the chronicler's irony is.

wish merely to point out that he was a man of a tender conscience (sometimes, that is), and that was why he was so often depressed" (I, 1, ii); "Mr. Verkhovensky sometimes talked of art, and very well, though a little abstractly. Occasionally he would recall the friends of his youth—all names who had made their mark on the history of Russian progress—he recalled them with emotion and reverence, though not without envy either" (I, 1, ix).

Even such an indisputably major and sincere feature of Stepan as his love for art and refinement cannot avoid the all-penetrating scoffing of his "pupil"-confidant: "So far as books are concerned, I should point out that in later years he seemed to avoid reading. . . . It also frequently happened that he would take De Tocqueville with him into the garden, while he secretly carried a Paul de Kock in his pocket" (I, 1, v).

The chronicler's statements ("But anyway, these are trifles"; "But that too, of course, is a petty detail") are sly; it is precisely on petty details and trifles that he concentrates his attention, revealing, so to speak, the cherished domestic secrets of "our preacher," showing him in a mire of base details:

> Our friend had certainly acquired not a few bad habits, especially during recent months. He let himself run to seed visibly and rapidly, and it is quite true that he had become slovenly. He drank more, he was more easily moved to tears, and his nerves grew weaker. He had become far too sensitive to everything of artistic value. His face had acquired a strange faculty for changing extraordinarily rapidly, from the most solemn expression, for instance, to the most ridiculous and even stupid (I, 2, v).

An accent on petty details is the essential peculiarity of the chronicler's narration in general, and especially when he is speaking of Stepan. The orientation towards "chattering" about trifles, the concentration on petty details, are proclaimed by Dostoevsky in the notebooks for *The Devils*: "No matter how superfluous, and idle, and verbose it seems, in essence it is in close connection with the very core of events. It is always this way in reality. An unsuspected thing, a trifling thing, suddenly becomes the main thing, and everything else only revolves around it as something secondary and accessory."[7]

[7]*Ignateva and Konshina*, p. 240.

N. M. Chirkov is correct when he writes: "The narrator tirelessly notes various petty details, various weaknesses of old man Verkhovensky: his posing, his affected estheticism, his predilection for wine, for playing 'a little cards,' even his attacks of choler. We have here not only the debasement of the hero, the desire to exhibit him in the most comic aspect, but even a sort of rapture in the exposure of his, in the final analysis, insignificant existence as a mere hanger-on."[8] Another of Chirkov's theses is partially correct: "Dostoevsky constantly leaves an unexplained residue in the explanations of his characters' actions. From this arises one of the writer's devices—reticence in the depiction of one or another of the characters' mental movements. For such an end the form of first-person narration is also very convenient. The narrator, unlike the omniscient author, naturally cannot know everything."[9] But Chirkov selects an unsuccessful illustration for his thesis about inexplicability and reticence. Here is what he writes about Stepan's fatal rendezvous with Varvara Petrovna: "The narrator does not inform the reader what in fact took place between them. Why, after a friendly parting, did Varvara Petrovna suddenly whisper these words? The narrator offers no commentary at all. He leaves it to the reader to guess about everything. The entire psychological aspect of this scene is built on an obviously intentional reticence."[10]

Let us quote the scene:

> Then one day, at night-fall, they parted very amicably after a highly animated and poetical conversation, pressing each other's hands warmly at the steps of the cottage which Mr. Verkhovensky occupied. Every summer he moved from the huge Skvoreshniki mansion into the little cottage which stood almost in the garden. He had only just gone in and, sunk into unhappy meditation, taken a cigar and without lighting it stopped, weary and motionless, before the open window, gazing at the little white clouds, light as fluff, gliding round the bright moon, when suddenly a faint rustle made him start and turn round. Mrs. Stavrogin, whom he had left only four minutes earlier, was again standing before him. Her yellow face was almost blue, her lips

[8]N. M. Chirkov, *O stile Dostoevskogo* (Moscow, 1963), p. 55.
[9]*Ibid.*, pp. 65–66.
[10]*Ibid.*, p. 66.

were pressed tightly together and twitching at the corners. For ten full seconds she looked into his eyes in silence with a firm, implacable gaze, and then she whispered rapidly: "I shall never forgive you for this!" (I, 1, iv).

If one considers that Varvara Petrova "was sensitive and observant" and "soon guessed the meaning of the strange expression on her friend's face," and that "he was a little too innocent at times," then it is quite easy to find the key to this "tragic" (for Stepan) scene. What sort of explanatory commentaries are necessary, when the main point is splendidly revealed, better than by any explanations, by the cigar in the hands of the "weary" Stepan. In any case the cigar and the "innocently open" expression on Stepan's face tell Varvara Petrovna not only much, but everything, and this "everything" also becomes evident at the same moment to the "hanger-on" himself, filling his further existence with horror and the expectation of catastrophe. By the way, we may also find direct confirmation in the novel of the fact that it was precisely the cigar that played such a fatal role. The dying Stepan is spiritedly and maliciously reminded of the past by his old friend:

"Remember the cigar?"

"My friend," he mumbled, horrified.

"Your cigar—in the evening—by the window—the moon was shining—after the little conversation—in Skvoreshniki? Do you remember it? Do you remember it?" she cried, jumping up from her chair, seizing his pillow by the two corners and shaking it together with his head. "Do you remember, you futile man, you futile, disgraceful, cowardly, always, always futile man?" she hissed in her ferocious whisper, barely restraining herself from screaming. (III, 7, iii)

The cigar is, of course, a petty detail, but the sort that is shifted out of the order of secondary signs into the center, out of the "accessory" into the major, and all the emotions and the "secret" psychological process are concentrated around this supposedly "trifling" detail. It is the same in other cases. Thus in Dostoevsky the principle of "reticence," "insufficiency," "the incompletely spoken," is combined with a "redundancy" of information. Reticence and holding back follow from Dostoevsky's general anthropological and philosophical views, according to which the essence of things and phenomena is hidden so deeply that not even the subtlest scientific analysis is capable of discovering it with mathematical precision: there always remains an "irrational" and inaccessible residue, in which, perhaps, the solution is also contained. Between Kirillov and the chronicler a curious exchange takes place:

> ". . . Liputin was weak, or impatient, or unreliable, or—envious."
> The last word surprised me.
> "I'm afraid you've used so many adjectives that it would be strange if one of them did not apply to him."
> "Or all of them together."
> "Yes, that's true too." (I, 3, viii).

The whole point is that it is impossible to place Liputin (or anyone else) in some sort of category that exhausts his essence. He fits into many categories, and one can expand the number of them almost to infinity. This does not at all contradict the presence of a multitude of facts and "factlets," everyday details that create an impression of "redundancy" and "needlessness." On the contrary, the petty details are good in that by their insignificance they countervail the power of categories and make that power illusory.

The narrator–chronicler is not an omniscient author but, all the same, his knowledge does not so strongly differ from the omniscience of the author–demiurge; he knows much, even that which, in the opinion of Ya. O. Zundelovich, he should not and cannot know. Zundelovich is quite bothered, in particular, by the fact that the chronicler, having admitted his own poor state of information, suddenly forgetting about it, begins to prophesy in the manner of an omniscient, all-seeing author. Zundelovich takes the chronicler's reservations and admissions quite seriously, not noticing his irony and "reverse" intonation, and, convicting him and Dostoevsky of inconsistency, concludes that there are artistic errors and failures of the "authorial voice" in the novel. Let us cite some passages from Dostoevsky in the framework of Zundelovich's commentary and conclusions:

> . . . I want to emphasize that in other cases the chronicler insists especially sharply on his lack of information: "Of course, no one has a right to expect from me, as the narrator, too exact an account concerning one point: for we are dealing with a mystery here, we are dealing with a woman."

This affirmation of his reportorial limitation seems simply paradoxical when, on the other hand, the chronicler very often knows things which in his capacity it is not prescribed for him to know, as for example in the narrative of the nocturnal conversation between the spouses von Lembke, when the chronicler—suddenly reminding us of his existence—declares: "I think he [Lembke] fell asleep at about seven in the morning."

This kind of unexpected failure of the authorial voice attests again and again that Dostoevsky did not find a balanced correlation among his given manners of narration.[11]

It is imprecise to call the chronicler's supposition "knowledge" (it is his hypothesis—"I think"). Otherwise, though, it would seem hard to object to anything Zundelovich says. All the same he is in essence mistaken; the passage from the novel, in which the chronicler supposedly "insists especially sharply" on his lack of information, is broken off in the middle of a sentence, and the thought is distorted thereby. Let us restore the sentence:

Of course, no one has a right to expect from me, as the narrator, too exact an account concerning one point: for we are dealing with a mystery here, we are dealing with a woman; but one thing I do know: on the previous evening she had gone into Mr. Lembke's study and stayed with him there till long after midnight (III, 1, ii).

And further:

Mr. Lembke was forgiven and comforted. Husband and wife came to a complete understanding, everything was forgotten, and when towards the end of the interview von Lembke, in spite of everything, went down on his knees, recalling with horror the main and final incident of the previous night, his wife's exquisite little hand, and afterwards her lips, checked the passionate outpourings of penitent speeches of the chivalrously delicate gentleman, rendered powerless with emotion (III, I, ii).

Where is there any sharp insistence on lack of information here? One could rather speak of a fantastically detailed ("redundant") knowledge. Here the chronicler does not at all yield to the omniscient author: he knows everything and, a worthy representative of the

[11]Ia. O. Zundelovich, *Romany Dostoevskogo: stat'i* (Tashkent, 1963), p. 115.

town, cannot keep from recounting these postmidnight conjugal relations in a "high" and "idyllic" style; he gossips with relish, tearing the veil from family mysteries. Zundelovich takes the chronicler's "rhetorical" derogation at face value and, having freed G——v's speech of irony, sets up a formula to which he is so rigidly attached that he is led to distort the text and draw rigid conclusions.

Zundelovich adopts a prejudiced and unjust attitude not only to the chronicler, but also to the "most venerable" Stepan Trofimovich Verkhovensky. In particular, Zundelovich adheres to the idea that the Gogolian theme of the road is parodied in *The Devils* (in the chapter "Stepan Verkhovensky's Last Pilgrimage"). In this debasement and parodying, a special role, in the scholar's opinion, is played by the idea of the post-horses, and by the "gallicisms" used by Stepan (" '*Vive la grande route*, and what happens then is in the lap of the gods' "):

> By this gallicism (of which Stepan is so fond and which almost completely serves as the means for his speech characterization) the theme of the road is vulgarized once and for all, and the grandiloquent inhabitant of 'our town' is once again thrown down from the 'poetic heights' by the author.[12]

Another student of Dostoevsky, Chirkov, treats Stepan's last journey and the theme of the road in an absolutely opposite manner:

> But the final fate of this hero introduces a note of high pathos, which sharply contends with the narrator's systematically debasing and debunking tone. Against all expectations and suppositions, in defiance of the narrator's elucidation, which suggests to the reader that it is impossible to expect anything serious of Stepan, the hero breaks with his past and goes out, according to Dostoevsky's thought, onto the highway. . . . Stepan is ludicrous with his childish ignorance of life, his French language in a Russian village, but behind this step of his the writer forces one to feel the breathing of death, a sort of higher human necessity."[13]

Later Chirkov passes to broad generalizations and surprising parallels: he recalls Don Quixote, the attractive elders of Dostoevsky's late novels (Makar Dolgoruki and Zosima) and even Leo Tolstoy ("Ste-

[12]*Ibid.*, p. 132.
[13]N. M. Chirkov, *O stile Dostoevskogo*, pp. 55–56.

pan's departure from the house and his going out onto the highway involuntarily turned out to be a great prototype. In this Dostoevsky, unbeknownst to himself, anticipated the finale to the life of his contemporary—'the great writer of the Russian land' ").[14]

Chirkov gets carried away with parallels, but on the whole his remarks are more just than Zundelovich's verdicts. Stepan's "enlightenment," the poetic outing of a liberal of the 1840s, enters into the sphere of the novel's central problems. In general, the "comic" and the "lyric" in Stepan's image presented themselves to the author in an indissoluble unity. In his notebook Dostoevsky observes: "—And yet Gr. sometimes had occasion to truly rise to the lofty (when he was in sorrow and was frank) with Prince Sh. But these were only occasions;" "Gr.—must without fail be made brilliant and likable and nice, without at all hiding his deficiencies."[15]

Although the caustic voice of the chronicler dominates in the novel, one cannot speak of the hero's sudden rebirth before death, in defiance of his past. Even earlier the touchingly naïve and pathetic peeps through in the "poor friend" 's aspect. In Stepan's speech at the celebration, the parodic and comic does not annul the lyric transport, nor the sincerity, nor the "loftiness" of the "teacher" 's thoughts, which in many respects were also shared by Dostoevsky himself. The ironically parodic and debasing are also present in the chapter "Stepan Verkhovensky's Last Pilgrimage." No abrupt violations, or even deformations, occur in the hero's image as it has taken shape, nor any hosannas or glorification; only the poetic motifs are intensified, splendidly set off by the chronicler's irony and by comic details. In the novel, the chronicler and Stepan each has an individual tone and vocabulary; to violate what has already taken shape would mean destroying the whole. Let us recall Dostoevsky's words in a letter to N. A. Lyubimov of August 7, 1879:

> It goes without saying that many of the teachings of my elder Zosima (or rather, the manner of their expression) belong to his character, that is to his artistic representation. Although I hold entirely the same views that he expresses, if I were to express them personally *as myself*, I would express them in a different

[14]*Ibid.*, p. 56.
[15]*Ignateva and Konshina*, p. 164.

form and in different language. But he *could not* express himself in a different language or *in a different spirit* than that which I imparted to him. Otherwise an artistic character would not have been created.

It is the same in the case of Stepan: his thoughts about the road, his interpretation of the Gospel, and his dying words are entirely shared by the author, but the manner of expression is personal, individual, peculiar to Stepan. Dostoevsky's hero is pitiful, touching and ludicrous at the time of his last wanderings: in the half-diffuse senile stream of thoughts, Fedka and the purse, cow and cart, and peasant woman, Russian and French words are strangely combined:

> It was Peter Ilyich, though, who talked at the club about horse-breeding and I mulcted him, *et puis*, but there is something behind that cart and—yes—I believe there's a peasant woman in it. A peasant woman and a peasant—*cela commence à être rassurant*. The woman behind and the peasant in front—*c'est très rassurant*. There's a cow tied by the horns to the back of the cart, *c'est rassurant au plus haut degré* (III, 7, i).

Stepan's conversation with the folk, for whom he is lord and foreigner, is absurd: his profound opinions, giving him away as an aesthete and lover of the elegant, are absurd; his gestures are inappropriate: "He filled his glass, got up and with a certain solemnity, crossed the room to the other corner where his companion on the sack . . . had seated herself" (III, 7, i); "With the gesture of a man saving himself, he turned to her and offered tea." He is strangely absent-minded and continually lapses into oblivion, the course of his thought is broken and capriciously associative; a thought latches onto objects that casually fall into his field of vision, and slips on by; his speech is breathless and inconsistent:

> I feel that I'm speaking well. I shall speak to them very well, but—what was it I was going to say? It was something important. I keep losing the thread and I cannot remember . . . I'm awfully, awfully confused. I can't remember what I was going to say . . . I think I'm going to fall asleep. My head's swimming. It's going round and round and round. (III, 7, ii)

His story, transmitted in a double refraction (that of the gospel woman and of the chronicler), is a last pitiful confession—the tragicomic "fantasia" of a hanger-on and unsuccessful man, the apotheosis of the "sincere" lie, after which Stepan, as is prescribed for a man who feels his dying hour approaching, confesses his sinful and mendacious life:

> My friend, all my life I've been lying. Even when I spoke the truth. I never spoke for the sake of the truth, but for my own sake. I knew it before, but it is only now that I see it . . . The trouble is that I believe myself when I am lying. The hardest thing in life is to live and not to lie, and—and not believe your own lie, yes, yes, that's it exactly! (III, 7, ii).

Having cleansed himself of lying, Stepan ends up fully prepared for the expression of the main pamphleteering idea of the novel, without, however, changing his favorite manner of interspersing Russian words with French ones—it would be strange to suppose that the gallicisms are called upon here to compromise his thought.

> "My friend," said Mr. Verkhovensky in great excitement, "*savez vous*, this wonderful and extraordinary passage [Luke 8:32–36—ed.] has been a stumbling-block to me all my life—*dans ce livre*—so that I remembered that passage from childhood. But now an idea has occurred to me; *une comparaison*. An awful lot of ideas keep occuring to me now. You see, that's just like our Russia. These devils who go out of the sick man and enter the swine—those are all the sores, all the poisonous exhalations, all the impurities, all the big and little devils, that have accumulated in our great and beloved invalid, in our Russia, for centuries, for centuries! *Oui, cette Russie, que j'aimais toujours.* But a great idea and a great will shield her from on high, as with that madman possessed of the devils, and all those devils, and all those impurities, all those abominations that were festering on the surface—all of them will themselves ask to enter into the swine. And, indeed, they may have entered into them already! They are we, we and them, and Peter—*et les autres avec lui*, and perhaps I at the head of them all, and we shall cast ourselves down, the raving and the possessed, from the cliff into the sea and shall all be drowned, and serves us right, for that is all we are good for. But the sick man will be healed, and 'will sit at the feet of Jesus', and all will look at him and be amazed. My dear, *vous comprendrez après. Nous comprendrons ensemble.* (III 7, ii)

Having made his contribution to the pamphleteering element in the novel, Stepan before death utters a fiery, poetic speech glorifying a great thought and the eternal human laws (here he actually does not use gallicisms):

> The mere presence of the everlasting idea of the existence of something infinitely more just and happy than I, already fills me with abiding tenderness and—glory—oh, whoever I may be and whatever I may have done! To know every moment, and to believe that somewhere there exists perfect peace and happiness for everyone and for everything, is much more important to a man than his own happiness. The whole law of human existence consists merely of making it possible for every man to bow down before what is infinitely great. If man were to be deprived of the infinitely great, he would refuse to go on living, and die of despair. The infinite and the immeasurable is as necessary to man as the little planet which he inhabits. My friends—all, all my friends: long live the Great Idea! The eternal, immeasurable Idea! Every man, whosoever he may be, must bow down before what is the Great Idea. Even the most stupid man must have something great. Peter, my boy—oh, how I wish I could see them all again! They do not know—they do not know that the same eternal Great Idea dwells in them too! (III, 7, iii).

This is a different, higher philosophic-ideological level of the novel, poorly correlated with the pamphlet. It is natural that Stepan, proclaiming the laws common to all mankind, is "removed" from the common course of the chronicle, cut off from the basic tragedies and catastrophes, and knows nothing of his son's latest deeds in town and of the fate of Shatov. His "great thought" is outside these nightmares and shocks.

Stepan runs away from the town tragedies. He also runs away from his confidant-chronicler, thereby arousing in him a whole whirlwind of contradictory considerations. Throughout practically the whole novel Stepan is shown in the ironically refracted light of the chronicler's "eulogy," which brings him down from the liberal heights into base reality, and ridicules his personal life, creative work, and conversational manner; he is, it seems, examined from all sides by his "pupil," mastered, and hidden once and for all under the rubric "man of the forties." The chronicler's information about the life and habits of his "sorrowful friend" is unusual but, it turns out, even such a seemingly "redundant" knowledge is not complete.[16] The chronicler, in recounting Stepan's last pilgrimage, unexpectedly turns out to be far away from him, and reconstructs the circumstances which escaped his view according to the testimony of others. Under the pressure of new facts, he is compelled to amend the image that he has drawn of the "teacher." The chronicler begins the story with a firm, often repeated "I am convinced":

> I am convinced that Stepan Verkhovensky was very much afraid when he realized that the time he had fixed for his mad enterprise was approaching. I am convinced that he suffered greatly from fear, especially on the night before he had set off—that terrible night . . . but I am convinced that he could never before have imagined himself alone on the highway without horror, and in such a condition, too. (III, 7, i)

With this the chronicler's "conviction," based on many years' experience and knowledge of his friend, is exhausted; and although subsequently G——v goes over the possible versions that could have diverted Stepan from his "mad enterprise," he himself already doubts the justness of his own suppositions. He cannot fail to admit that in Stepan's final transport there is something that does not yield to the traditional explanations, something of the sort that would have happened "in spite of everything":

> But that made no difference: however clearly he realized the horrors awaiting him, he would have gone out and taken to the road! There was a feeling of pride in what he had undertaken that fascinated him in spite of everything. Oh, he could have accepted Mrs. Stavrogin's magnificent conditions and have remained dependent on her charity "*comme un* ordinary hanger-on!" But he had not accepted her charity and had not remained. (III, 7, i)

[16]The chronicler sincerely admits his shortsightedness and mistakes; he missed the birth of something new behind the usual words and gestures: "But it was this fastidiousness and sarcasm, which still clung to him in spite of all shocks, that put my mind at rest at the time: a man who had apparently changed so little compared with what he had been, was most certainly not disposed at that moment to do anything tragic or untoward. That was how I reasoned at the time, and goodness me, how wrong I was! I did not take enough into consideration . . ." (III, 2:i)

Later, the voice of the chronicler, while not devoid of the sincerity of lyricism, is constantly broken in upon by the traditional ironic notes, which at times attain the causticity of the first pages of the novel. The chronicler, forced several times to admit the fact that Stepan's flight and actions had affected him, chooses, where possible, the traditional "everyday" explanations for the incomprehensible: "And indeed I was very surprised to learn from Mrs. Stavrogin afterwards, that he was not afraid of death at all. Perhaps he simply did not believe her, and still regarded his illness as a trifling one" (III, 7, iii). The chronicler is inclined to explain Stepan's enlightenment and unexpectedly awakening interest in religion through the familiar characteristics of the head of the town liberals:

> Whether he was indeed converted, or because the majestic ceremony of the administration of the sacrament moved him deeply and awoke the artistic sensibilities of his nature, but, I am told, he uttered with great feeling some words which were in direct contradiction to his former convictions. (III, 7, iii)

Stepan, who has escaped from control, performed unexpected acts and "suddenly" said so much that is unusual, is by all possible means "driven" back into his previous limits by the chronicler, who thereby saves the artistic nature of the image. Stepan's flight is a breakdown of tradition, stagnation; it is an elemental movement. The "fall from a height," as applied to many characters (Stepan, Lembke, Liza, the petty bourgeois) is one of the novel's central motifs; various sorts of liberation of the elemental, often destructive, energy hidden in man are compared. This energy casts Stepan into the wide world, onto the highway; his last pilgrimage purifies the soul and enlightens the mind of the liberal of the forties. Stepan (like, by the way, Varvara Petrovna) is almost entirely within the chronicler's field of vision (of visibility).

As a member of the liberal circle,[17] the chronicler is personally

---

[17]The members of the liberal circle automatically pass, so to speak, from the father to the son, into the "organization" of Pyotr. Thus is the connection of the "revolutionary" generations schematically realized in the novel. The chronicler does not take part in the "organization" of Pyotr, remains by the side of the "father" as his loyal confidant and friend, and together with his "teacher" takes up a negative position towards the "nihilism" of the latest pattern.

acquainted with the participants in the evenings at Stepan's, but, although his relationship with them has a rather "general" and "perfunctory" *(uslovnyi)* character, he is usually quite opinionated and emotional in his view of them. Thus, outlining the figure of the senior member of the circle, Liputin, the chronicler does not restrain himself or mask his personal feelings: ". . . the insignificant and almost abject figure of the little provincial official, a jealous husband and coarse family tyrant, a miser and a moneylender . . ." (I, 2, iii). This is no longer debasement, but an unambiguous, unconditional conviction and sentence. The chronicler is connected with Liputin by complex relations of contempt-curiosity, repulsion-attraction (and also, like Stepan, the chronicler openly fears Liputin):

> He talked for a quarter of an hour, and so amusingly that I could not tear myself away. Though I could not stand him, I must admit that he had the gift of making people listen to him, especially when he was very angry about something. (I, 3, i)[18]

The chronicler's relationship to Virginsky is more complex: sympathy and pity are combined here with outright caricature. In the depiction of Virginsky, Dostoevsky's sad irony regarding his own Fourierist enthusiasms (memories of his former brightly burning "spiritual fire") is perceptible:

> Virginsky himself was a man of quite remarkable purity of heart, and, indeed, I rarely met with a more honest spiritual fire. "Never, never will I abandon these bright hopes," he used to say to me, with shining eyes. Of those "bright hopes" he always spoke quietly, with sweetness, in half a whisper, as though in secret. (I, 1, viii)

The chronicler perceives Shatov almost entirely externally: his manners and isolated oddities (comic details) are outside pamphleteering accusation, which is completely understandable—Shatov is just as much the spokesman for the author's position in the novel as the chronicler is. The latter even lacks Shatov's "directness":

> Whenever I had gone to see him before (which was not often) he

---

[18]This same "sorcery" conditions Liputin's success in the circle: "But we liked his keen intelligence, his inquiring mind, and his peculiar malicious cheerfulness" (I, 1, viii).

would invariably sit scowling in a corner, answer sullenly, and it
was only after a long time that he grew animated and began
talking with pleasure. Even then he always scowled when saying
good-bye, and opened the door for you as though he were getting rid of a personal enemy (I, 4, iv).[19]

The chronicler also notes, "In our company he was always sullen and
uncommunicative . . ." (I, 1, viii). The taciturn and silent Shatov is
nearly the first orator in the novel who spiritedly and loquaciously sets
forth "Slavophile" ideas. Shatov exists independently of the chronicler. Ideological aims demanded precisely this presentation of the
figure of Shatov, and such a "free" connection between him and the
chronicler. Shatov's "freedom" is also expressed in his ironic certifica-
tions of the chronicler: " 'You're of course a "moderate liberal," ' "
Shatov said, smiling, too" (I, 4, iv). Shatov's views are not directly
affirmed in the novel. If one looks retrospectively at Dostoevsky's
creative work in the 1870s, one may easily note that the writer attempted to contrast the new, "demonic" ideas with the idea of the
exceptional charactor of the Russian nation in its "populist" variant.
In *The Devils* this tendency is also perceptible. In the overall structure
of the work, however, Shatov—the hero-victim of the nihilist circles
and advocate of the theory of the "God-bearing people"—is not put on
a pedestal: he is also a participant in the round-dance of the "possessed." It is true, though, that in accordance with Dostoevsky's pamphleteering conception, more space is alloted to Shatov for the prop-
agation of ideas than to the spokesmen of opposing ideas.

The chronicler's cursory direct knowledge far from rules out the
accuracy and precision of his deductions and conclusions. The image
of Karmazinov and his work is almost entirely refracted through the
chronicler's "I" narration. The brevity of the description of Shigalyov
is marked by aphoristic concentration and the precisely captured essence of the "theoretician":

Never in my life have I seen such dejection, gloom, and despon-
dency on the face of a man. He looked as though he were expect-

[19]Now and then the chronicler reveals an understanding of Shatov's "inner" world: "Knowing Shatov, I can say with certainty that he could never
have allowed himself to dream that a woman might say to him: 'I love you' "
(III, 5, i).

ing the end of the world not at some indefinite time, according to prophecies which might never come true, but with absolute definiteness—say, the day after tomorrow, at exactly twenty-five minutes past ten. We hardly said a word to one another on that occasion, but merely shook hands like two conspirators. I was particularly struck by his ears, which were of unnatural size, long, broad, and thick, sticking out in a most peculiar way. His movements were awkward and slow. If Liputin did sometimes dream of the phalanstery being established in our province, Shigalyov most certainly knew the day and the hour when it would come to pass. He made an ominous impression on me . . . (I, 4, iv).

The chronicler's description of Shigalyov is a very rare case of an exhaustive and categorical characterization of a character at "first glance." The ideologue-theoretician of the human anthill is the most "integral" character in the novel. In his theoretical constructions everything is straightforward, methodical and clear, and written all over the physiognomy of the "pure" socialist, and for this reason the chronicler's first glance is so precise and true. One's impression upon meeting Shigalyov can only be formulated in the most general way (you liked him or you didn't); there is no place here for indignation or pity. Pity presupposes the presence of some sort of human feelings and ideas, but for Shigalyov all feelings are killed by the "program."

The chronicler's relationship to the mediocre Erkel is more complex. The chronicler sincerely pities the young murderer (as do many others in the town): "I speak so much about him because I am very sorry for him" (III, 4, i). But at the same time, Erkel's cold energy, his unquestioning readiness to carry out any order, inspire horror in the narrator. The strange and silent "boy"—the most loyal and devoted minion of Pyotr Stepanovich Verkhovensky—is simply destined for "punitive" measures: "To carry out orders was an absolute necessity for his petty, unreasoning nature, which always yearned to submit itself to someone else's will—oh, of course, only for the sake of the 'common' or 'great' cause."

For all his simplicity and ordinariness, Erkel is illuminated by the chronicler in a more complex manner than is Shigalyov. The ordinary Erkel is subjected to a detailed, scrupulous and concentrated analysis, which consists of a chain of clear-cut definitions, resembling aphorisms in form and type (in general the secondary characters of the chronicle are primarily described on a generalized level): "Erkel belonged to that type of 'little fools' who lack only the higher forms of reasoning powers; but he had plenty of the other, the lesser, reasoning powers, even to the point of cunning" (III, 5, ii). The description is precise and condensed; the thought is firmly formulated and rejects in advance the possibility of any other interpretations.

But precision of description and truth of deductions do not always mark the chronicler's "vision." Let us take one of the complex cases: the chronicler's perception of Kirillov. Most of the characters in the chronicle are known to Anton Laventievich G——v before the starting (zero) point of the narration. Kirillov is an exception; his closed way of life is hardly conducive to personal contact, his unsociability and possession by ideas hinder a true understanding of him. The chronicler sees and hears Kirillov, converses with him—and doesn't understand him; he seizes upon the external, that which is intelligible to the eye and ear, but is not capable of penetrating inside. The chronicler meets Kirillov's ideas with unconcealed mockery, which does not escape even the man possessed by the theory of the saving power of suicide: " 'I'm sorry you seem to be laughing,' he added half a minute later." G——v's reaction to his strange conversation with Kirillov is terse: " 'He's mad as a hatter, of course,' I decided" (I, 3, viii); "I mentioned, by the way, my conversation with Kirillov, adding that Kirillov was probably mad" (I, 3, x).

Shatov's judgments about Kirillov (and not only about him) are partial and consequently unjust; the chronicler's opinion after a first acquaintance is superficial but neutral. Shatov rejects the chronicler's superficial idea that Kirillov is insane; in turn the chronicler disagrees with the unjust inclusion of Kirillov among the punsters:

> "Russian atheism has never gone farther than a pun," Shatov muttered, putting in a new candle in place of the burnt-out end.
> "No, that man did not give me the impression of a punster. I don't think he knows how to talk, let alone make puns." (I, 4, iv)

The true Kirillov reveals himself in his conversations with Stavrogin, Pyotr Verkhovensky, and Shatov. The chronicler is absent from all these conversation scenes.

As a character the chronicler is a passive and puppetlike figure, and although he often bustles about, in essence he takes almost no part in the action; what he hears and sees is important, and significantly less important is what he says and does during the events. Part of his function is the collection and systematization of material, and this is the most extensive field of his activity. Finally, part of the chronicler's function is the interpretation of what he has seen, and here he may display exceptional subtlety and depth, or not display it, or simply forego a definite decision. The chronicler's information may also fluctuate from complete knowledge (and here he resembles the omniscient author) to half-knowledge and even incorrect knowledge (and here he is a fallible and mortal man, whose judgments and interpretations are often mistaken). The chronicler may also displace the temporal point of the story: a later, total knowledge is superimposed on his former knowledge; but often G——v "confiscates" this his later understanding of things, transferring the narration entirely into the past. The total point of view (after the catastrophe) is present in the novel in the form of a ramified system of allusions; this projection of results is carried out vaguely (basically regarding details) and unevenly—the story of the chronicler's gradual learning and "enlightenment" form an essential aspect of the dynamism and interest of the novel's development. This story of learning is not emphasized, and in general the chronicler often foregoes explanations; as a result, the characters acquire "independence" and depart from the importunate accompaniment of the chronicler's voice. Narration "from the chronicler" recedes, and scenes without the chronicler's participation at all, or with his minimal participation, come to the fore. The conditionality and, to a certain extent, "outsider's position" of the figure of the chronicler permit the changing of the "scenery" in the narration to take place almost unnoticeably and painlessly for the unity of the chronicle's system; G——v disappears just as easily and unconstrainedly as he appears again. Dostoevsky apparently considered any special notifications to the reader about the change of "scenery" to be superfluous, although, judging by his notebooks, they were planned: "I sat with Gr—— for the third time and listened to his heated conversation with Sh. In general, even if I describe conversations *tête à tête* [*sam drug*]—don't pay any attention: either I have firm data, or, perhaps, I *make it up* myself—but be assured that everything is true. For I have adopted the system of *a chronicle*."[20]

Is it possible to contrast the scenes *"tête-à-tête"* with the scenes that have the chronicler's presence and his "I" narration? Yes and no. The scenes without the chronicler (either based on data received by G——v from others, or made up by him, or, perhaps most frequent of all, representing a combination of fantasy, personal experience and the interpretation of others' opinions) seldom contradict the direct narration of the chronicler, and if they do contradict it, it is in accord with the artistic task. The chamber conversation scenes are an indispensible admission into the chronicle: the chronicler's direct presence in them would, naturally, be very hard to motivate; in some cases it would be "immodest," in others simply impossible. The chronicler must inevitably turn into a storyteller and conjecture substantial *"lacunae"* in the chronicle through his imagination. The crowd scenes, in which the chronicler for a number of reasons does not participate either, are a cross between various sources of information and his imagination. (See in the drafts: "In the discussion of the meetings, make a remark as the chronicler: Perhaps, they had still other meetings—and surely they did—I don't know, but the matter, probably, happened this way. . . .")[21]

In *The Devils* there are three basic forms of narrative: (a) narration "from the chronicler," in which the narrator's voice dominates; (b) scenes with the chronicler's participation, in any of which his role may be most different; (c) scenes without the chronicler—intimate, chamber scenes, with the complete or almost complete disappearance of G——v. There is also the combined form of narrative—the crowd scenes.

The establishment of the true proportions among the various forms of narrative, and the methods of linking them, formed Dostoevsky's main "artistic" concern. The vacillations in the process of work on *The Devils* were most various, but on the whole one may speak of a gradual intensification of a tendency toward limiting the "explan-

[20]*Ignateva and Konshina,* p. 137.
[21]*Ibid.,* pp. 136–137.

atory" and "ideological" function of the chronicler. The broadly out-
lined connection between Stavrogin and the chronicler was especially
weakened. In the original outlines, Stavrogin's actions and words
were to be more often accompanied by rejoinders and explanations
"from the chronicler":

> In the chronicler's voice at the middle or end of his novel: In
> general Stavrogin had such-and-such an aim; however, that is
> according to Ush——v's[22] testimony. I don't know what their
> business there in Switzerland was, but I have correctly defined
> the essence of their movement, their philosophy, the sense of
> their actions: I'll vouch for that.[23]

It was also assumed that after Stavrogin's death the chronicler would
sum up, give an analysis of the prince's character, in a special ("indispensable") chapter, "Analysis":

> The chronicler, after the prince's death, is to make an analysis of
> his character (indispensably, a chapter called *Analysis*). Saying
> that this was a strong, predatory man, who became entangled in
> convictions and who out of endless pride desired and could
> only be convinced of that which was completely *clear* . . . etc.[24]

The "Analysis" chapter was never realized, and the story of the
chronicler's gradual knowledge of Stavrogin, begun in such promis-
ing detail in the first part of the novel, subsequently came to naught;
the character passed into other spheres of the narrative, having fallen
out of the plane of narration "from the chronicler." G——v avoids
personal explanation of Stavrogin's character, leaving that for the
prince himself to do in a letter, and for the other characters in the
chronicle (Kirillov, Shatov, Khromonozhka [Marya Lebyadkin], Pyotr
Verkhovensky, Liza Tushin). Moreover, not only the line from the
chronicler to Stavrogin, but also from Shatov to Stavrogin, was cur-
tailed; thus, in the notebooks a whole series of conversations between
Stavrogin and Shatov was planned, but in the final text only a single
conversation remains, which ends with the prince's assurances that he
will not visit Shatov again.

[22]This was Dostoevsky's conditional name for Shigalyov in the notebooks.
[23]*Ignateva and Konshina*, p. 138.
[24]*Ibid.*, p. 317.

In the first part of the novel, Stavrogin is the object of G——v's
intense and unremitting attention; the latter is interested and bewil-
dered by the prince's strange and romantic life, and, like a conscientious chronicler, renders Stavrogin's history, relying on the rumors,
opinions, and legends of others, for want of his own information. One
of G——v's functions is to interpret and classify opinions. Another, no
less important role of the chronicler also comes to the fore here: the
keen personal attention of G——v as an observer, who tries to find
out the truth, the "essence" of Stavrogin by means of the comparison
of a personal, subjective view to the general view. Marya Lebyadkin,
Pyotr Verkhovensky, Liza, Shatov, and Kirillov penetrate to the "essence" of Stavrogin, each in his own way and with varying degrees of
precision. The chronicler participates especially intensively in the
general movement at the beginning. The chronicler's first personal
impression is surprise: the legendary Stavrogin of the others' stories
turns out to be quite different from the real Stavrogin. For the time
being the chronicler's surprise bears only a relatively personal character (he is one of many who are surprised); but neither is it temporary
and casual, and it has actual, real roots. It is completely understandable and explicable and does not entirely refute Stavrogin's legendary
biography, all the more since that biography is not completely legendary (a statement that has the force of proof, since here also the
chronicler superimposes later knowledge on the temporal point of
view):

> I was not the only one to be surprised: our whole town was
> surprised, and our town, of course, knew Mr. Stavrogin's biog-
> raphy, and in such detail that one could hardly imagine where
> they could have got it from and, what was even more surprising,
> half of the stories about him were quite true. (I, 2, i)

The chronicler, joining in the general chorus, is not distinguished
from it only at first. He refuses to explain Stavrogin's provocative and
strange actions, and this in itself is a marked personal position:
G——v has a large choice of interpretations, but he places them all
under suspicion, and, what is particularly remarkable, he holds to his
previous opinion even "now," that is, after everything that has happened: "For my part, I don't know to this day how to explain it, in
spite of the incident which occurred soon afterwards and which ap-

parently explained everything and, it would seem, set everybody's mind at rest" (I, 2, ii). "Everybody"—but not the chronicler.[25]

The scene at Varvara Petrovna's with Stavrogin and the others is the culmination of the first part and the culmination of the narration about Stavrogin "from the chronicler." The chronicler is the "leader" in this scene, the observer and commentator. Stavrogin appears and the chronicler's gaze is immediately riveted to him: alterations, which give rise to questions, are noted:

> But now—now, I don't know why, he looked to me at the first glance as quite incontestably handsome, so much so that it was impossible to say that his face was like a mask. Was it because he was just a little paler than before and had apparently gone thinner? Or was it perhaps because some new idea was now reflected in his eyes? (I, 5, v)

The chronicler draws attention to Stavrogin's smile, gestures, walk, facial expression (and how it changes), and vocal intonation. He describes them with the precision of a stenographer whose attention the subtlest momentary movements do not escape: "here he exchanged a momentary glance with him," "he spoke with a certain peculiar twist to his face." It is as though the chronicler stops time or stretches an instant into infinity: "So passed five seconds"; ". . . the whole scene did not last more than ten seconds. Still, a great deal happened in those ten seconds" (I, 5, viii). Around a few seconds, which hold so much, the past and present are concentrated. The chronicler's total point of view, achieved as a result of long searching and collecting of facts, is summarized; a long tirade about the heroes of the past (Lunin and Lermontov), similar to Stavrogin in some ways but also different in many others, is introduced; early and late judgments are persistently combined into a single focus:

> I repeat again: I thought him at the time and I still think him

---

[25]Almost nothing is said in the novel about the personal relationship between G——v and Stavrogin, except for a single casual and obscure hint. Perhaps Dostoevsky contemplated a closer connection, even conversations, but nothing remained of these plans but a single stroke: "Let me also add that four years later, in answer to a discreet question from me about that incident at the club, Stavrogin said, frowning, 'Yes, I was not quite myself at the time' " (I, 2, ii).

(now that everything is over) the sort of man who, if he received a blow in the face or a similar insult, would have killed his adversary on the spot and without challenging him to a duel (I, 5, viii).

The chronicler's hearing and vision are strained and sharpened to the utmost, his gaze strives to break through the outer shell and penetrate to the inside. Of course the chronicler sees the whole scene "from the outside," but he sees so keenly and penetrates so deeply that his vision achieves supernatural dimensions, approaching in intensity and precision the vision of the infallible and "omniscient" author. The chronicler of course does not simply describe what he saw then: he projects his whole experience, a huge sum of facts, and his final (by the time of the chronicle's creation) knowledge. The chronicler's reticence is, obviously, a proper means for promoting the carrying out of an aim that was essential for Dostoevsky—the interest of the narrative. But this is not all; interest is already achieved by the fact that the chronicler limits himself to an allusion to other facts known to him, which will be communicated subsequently in their own place and their own time. Something else is more important. The reader is informed that the chronicler knows quite a lot about Stavrogin and, despite such an extreme and comprehensive state of information (close to "omniscience"), he cannot explain Stavrogin's conduct with complete assurance. In other words, it is explained at the outset that there will be no final summation, the reader will not receive complete solutions and much will remain obscure at the very end of the novel; by this itself the reader is invited by the author to take whatever personal participation is within his powers in the disentanglement of knots and the guessing of "psychological" rebuses.

Beginning with the second part of *The Devils*, perceptible changes in the narration take place; the connection between the chronicler and Stavrogin also undergoes deformation. Even later the chronicler observes Stavrogin, but his vision loses its keenness; he sees little and poorly: "I saw them meeting in the doorway: it seemed to me that both of them stood still for a moment and looked rather strangely at one another. But I may not have seen them properly for the crowd" (II, 5, ii). Even when G——v is presented with an opportunity of demonstrating his talent for penetrating "within," he does not make use of that opportunity. The chronicler also foregoes personal judgments about the hero, with one small exception—the introduction to

Stavrogin's letter (in a narrow sense—a stylistic remark; in a broad sense—an accusation): "Here is the letter, word for word, without the correction of a single mistake, in the style of a Russian landed gentleman who has never mastered Russian grammar in spite of his European education" (III, 8).

Stavrogin's letter is a fragment of a hero's never-quite-formulated confession—a confession summing up the failure of a life. The letter contains no discoveries, nothing specifically new; it confirms the opinion of others about Stavrogin, freeing these evaluations of superfluous emotionalism and transience. In the combination of narrative forms chosen for the account of Stavrogin's history, the leading one is objective narration (chamber scenes, conversations *tête-à-tête*, without the presence of the chronicler). The others (narrative by the chronicler and confession) occupy a subordinate, secondary place on the whole, although the proportions are different in the first part of the novel—partly, perhaps, explainable by the vacillations,[26] which concluded in the victory of objective narration by an all-seeing author standing outside the action.

The images of Stavrogin and Pyotr Verkhovensky demanded a different style of narration, different forms, than Stepan:

> "Nechaev and the prince without explanations, but in action, and for St. Tr——ch *always with explanation*"; "The tone consists in not elucidating Nechaev and the prince. Nechaev begins from gossip and commonplaces, and the prince is revealed gradually [by narration] in action and without any explanations"; "The *main thing* is that throughout the novel it never be fully explained why Nechaev came"; "The whole situation and progress of Nechaev must be that the reader sees absolutely nothing but a few buffoonish and strange characteristic features. I must not do like other novelists, that is, trumpet from the very beginning that here is an unusual man. On the contrary, I must hide him and only gradually uncover him through artistic features (for example, the difference between his intellect and cunning and his utter ignorance of reality)."[27]

Thus, the image of Stepan is revealed by means of narration "from

---

[26]The materials in the notebooks convincingly show how strong these vacillations were.

[27]*Ignateva and Konshina*, pp. 271, 273, 288.

the chronicler," the images of the prince and Pyotr Verkhovensky, in dialogue and in action; these are two basic and opposing narrative principles. By the combination of heterogeneous narrative forms, the dynamic flow of the story is achieved, the problem of interest is solved, the functions and boundaries of the chronicler's activity and the variety of distances between chronicler and characters are defined.

Stepan Verkhovensky and the Shaping Dialectic of Dostoevsky's *Devils*

by Gordon Livermore

Writing to Apollon Maikov on March 2, 1871, after completing Part I of *Devils*,[1] Dostoevsky explains that Stepan Trofimovich Verkhovensky, to whose biography the novel's introductory chapter is devoted, is a "secondary character," but one "whose story is closely bound up with other (principal) events of the novel." Therefore, Dostoevsky writes, "I took him as the cornerstone, as it were, of the whole." Dostoevsky's remark appropriately suggests Stepan's "secondary" yet, paradoxically, central role in *Devils*. Not only is Stepan's story bound up with the principal events of the plot, but in his position as the novel's "cornerstone" he also introduces its central thematic conflict. Focused in the antagonism between Stepan and his son Pyotr, this conflict is repeated in numerous variations throughout the novel and ultimately mirrored in its structure. Its roots lie in Stepan's idealist sensibility and persistent impulse to leap, in Vyacheslav Ivanov's terms, *a realibus ad realiora*,[2] from "lower" to "higher" reality, from particular to general, from fact to idea.

"Stepan Verkhovensky and the Shaping Dialectic of Dostoevsky's *Devils*" written for this collection by Gordon Livermore. Copyright © 1983 by Prentice-Hall, Inc.

[1] I have chosen to translate Dostoevsky's *Besy* as *Devils*, rather than *The Devils*, in the belief that the initial definite article inappropriately invites a narrowly specific interpretation of the author's suggestive metaphorical title.

[2] Ivanov uses the phrase *a realibus ad realiora* to identify the general direction in which he says Dostoevsky's "realistic symbolism" leads the reader: "from reality on a lower plane, a reality of lesser ontological value, to a more real reality." Vyacheslav Ivanov, *Freedom and the Tragic Life: A Study in Dostoevsky*, trans. from an expanded version of Ivanov's "Dostoevskii i roman-tragediia" (1911) by Norman Cameron and ed. by S. Konovalov, 3rd ed. (New York: Noonday Press, 1960), p. 49.

As critics have generally recognized, Stepan, modeled quite loosely on the liberal Hegelian historian Timofei Granovsky, represents a synthetic portrait of the progressive, Western-oriented Russian intellectuals who shaped the ethos of the nascent Russian intelligentsia in the "remarkable decade" of 1839–1848. Dostoevsky later referred to Stepan, in the July–August issue of his *Diary of a Writer* for 1876, as a "type of the idealist of the Forties." Before his confrontation with the nihilists at the literary matinee, Stepan remarks that he is making a stand "for the sake of a great idea" (II, 10, iii).[3] Earlier the narrator has mentioned Stepan's need to believe that he was fulfilling the "higher duty of the propaganda of ideas" (I, 1, ix). The specific idea that Stepan defends at the matinee is the necessity of art. But the sense of urgency he feels about *ideas* in general is essential to both his identity and his implicit aesthetic. Stepan not only "represents an idea" *(predstavliaet ideiu)*, as he is identified when he visits Petersburg in 1859–60 (I, 1, vi), he represents an essentially idealist belief in the importance, efficacy, and "higher" reality of the Idea.

Previous critics have noted that Stepan's surname, Verkhovensky, suggests the role of leadership or supremacy—*verkhovenstvo*—for which Stepan contends with his son Pyotr in the novel. But in addition to this connotation, the root *verkh* ("height," "summit") can also be taken to allude to Stepan's elevated, idealistic view of human nature and his personal gravitation toward "higher" reality. Used figuratively, the adjective *vysokii* ("high," "lofty") and its comparative-superlative degree, *vyshii*, are repeatedly either associated with Stepan or on his lips. The words suggest the pull of his vision away from mundane and material reality toward the "higher" world of the idea and the ideal. Thus the narrator remarks, for example, that Stepan was "noble, with higher aspirations" (I, 2, viii); that Stepan's article on medieval knights adduced "some higher and exceptionally noble idea" (I, 1, i); and that his epic poem was marked by a "note of higher humor" (I, 1, i).

Throughout the novel, of course, the association of the "lofty" or the "higher" with Stepan has ironic overtones. It is repeatedly connected with his evasion of *realia*, of both the practical demands of life and the practical consequences, or inconsequence, of his words and

---

[3]Quotations from the novel are my translations from the text of *Besy* as it appears in F. M. Dostoevskii, *Polnoe subranie sochinenii*, ed. V. G. Bazanov et al., X (Leningrad: Nauka, 1975).

actions. Thus, with reference to Stepan and his circle, the narrator speaks ironically of "higher liberalism" and the "higher liberal, that is," he says, "the liberal without any purpose whatsoever" (I, 1, ix). Stepan's belief that he was fulfilling the "higher duty of the propaganda of ideas" has provided him with an excuse for doing *nothing* for twenty years. Instead of liberating Stepan from attachment to the mundane and the material, the upward cast of his vision toward the "higher" has served mainly to divert his attention from his chronic irresponsibility and indulgence in the pleasures of card and drink at the expense of his patroness Varvara Petrovna Stavrogin. When Varvara confronts him with the record of his offenses in the course of their long relationship, Stepan concedes: "Yes, I sponged off you." But he defends himself characteristically: "Sponging was never the highest principle of my actions. That just happened of itself, I don't know how . . . I always thought that there remained something between us higher than food . . ." (II, 5, iii).

Altogether, Stepan's life in the novel—as presented through the somewhat disillusioned eyes of his former confidant, the narrator—constitutes an extended, ironic commentary on his gravitation toward the "higher" realm of ideas. The vague, abstract and allegorical quality of his own narrative poem, which the narrator identifies as "an allegory in lyrical-dramatic form that recalled the second part of *Faust*" (I, 1, i), is symptomatic of his essential mode of perception, his compulsion to abstract and intellectualize, and his inclination to see reality as idea and symbol. If the true forms of things are obscured for Plato's cave dwellers by an illusory veil of sensory appearances, one could say that the concrete and particular dimension of existence is often obscured for Stepan by an insubstantial yet surprisingly opaque veil of forms and ideas.

Telling of "Stepan Trofimovich's Last Wandering," the narrator mimics his friend's characteristic sensibility as he attempts to present the symbolic dimensions of setting out on the highway, as Stepan might have conceived it: "The highway—that is something long, long, to which no end can be seen; the highway is like human life, like the human dream. In the highway there is an idea . . ." (III, 7, i). The narrator suggests, moreover, that Stepan's attention to the symbolic significance—the idea—of his journey would have precluded any concern with the particular, practical details of travel: "In the highway there is an idea; but what sort of idea is there in an order for post horses? In an order for post horses the idea comes to an end. *Vive la grande route*, and beyond, whatever God provides."

Stepan's habit of according precedence to the abstract over the concrete, to the idea over actuality, fosters a tendency to confuse his intentions with actions. As he suggests in defending himself to Varvara, the "higher principle" or idea of his actions is more compellingly real to him than the substance. When, for example, the narrator asks him, following his "inventory," whether he belongs to some sort of secret society, Stepan confesses that he cannot say for sure: "When you belong with all your heart to Progress and . . . who can be secure: You think you don't belong, and suddenly you take a look, and it turns out that you do belong to something or other . . ." (II, 9).

This same sensibility is manifested in Stepan's habitual inclination to substitute symbolic gesture for responsible action, action taken in full consideration of the attendant circumstances and probable consequences. Characteristic of this inclination is the "beautiful idea" that Stepan conceives of presenting his son Pyotr with the "absolute, highest, *maximum* price" of 15,000 rubles for the latter's estate, the value of which Stepan has squandered to cover gambling debts. The narrator tells how Stepan unfolds to Varvara a dramatic "little scene" in which he would suddenly place the money before Pyotr and then, with tears in his eyes, press *"ce cher fils"* to his breast (I, 2, viii). Thus Stepan implicitly hopes to redeem, with a single, dramatic gesture, a lifetime of neglecting his son. He suggests, moreover, that the gesture would have further, symbolic significance and would vindicate the ideology of his generation: "He hinted that this would even impart a certain, particularly noble luster to their amicable bond . . . to their 'idea.' It would exhibit in such a disinterested and magnanimous light the fathers and, in general, the people of the previous generation in comparison to the new, frivolous and 'social' youth." Though Stepan supplies the "idea" for this symbolic scene, he depends on Varvara to provide the money. Of course, what is wanting for the enactment of his imagined scene is not only the substantial matter of 15,000 rubles, but also the existence of a son who has been reared in the role of *"ce cher fils."*

It is appropriate that Pyotr, who has been virtually abandoned by Stepan as a child and is thus a glaring instance of his father's neglect of *realia*, should emerge in the novel as a bitter antagonist of Stepan's idealism and intellectualism and a strident spokesman for the "realism" that was being advocated during the 1860s by Chernyshevsky and the revolutionary democrats. Against Stepan's gravitation toward the idea, Pyotr echoes the revolutionary democrats' frequent appeal to facts as the touchstone of truth when he tauntingly advises his father concerning the lecture Stepan is preparing: "And try, if you can, to make it without nonsense: facts, facts, and facts. . . ." (II, 4, ii). Against Stepan's proclivity for thought, Pyotr embodies in an anti-intellectual extreme the urge toward revolutionary action.

Pyotr elicits the commitment to such action at the meeting recounted in the chapter "At Our People's," following an abbreviated debate that offers a variation in a minor key of the conflict between himself and his father. His opponent in the debate is a local teacher of literature and amateur poet—by virtue of his vocation, a distant double for Stepan—who opposes precipitous destructive action in favor of further "discussions and opinions about the future social order" and the achievement of gradual change through propaganda (II, 7, ii). But according to Pyotr, the only alternative to immediate revolutionary action is purely imaginary progress, "the composition of social novels . . . the clerical predetermination of human destinies a thousand years in advance on paper . . . slow, paper dreaming." Pyotr finally contrives to secure a pledge to revolutionary action and to terminate debate at the meeting with a question that epitomizes the sense of urgent movement that he embodies in the novel: "I ask all the honorable company not to vote, but directly and simply to declare, what do you find jollier: a snail's pace in the swamp, or full steam ahead across the swamp?"

The violent revolutionary action that Pyotr proposes is figuratively expressed at the meeting—at first facetiously—in terms of "one hundred million heads." The notion of decapitation, which is also suggested in the axe that decorates the revolutionary proclamations in *Devils*, recalls a fear for the safety of his head that Stepan has expressed on several occasions in the novel. The narrator mentions in his introductory chapter that Stepan went about on the eve of the Emancipation anxiously muttering to himself a fragment of verse: "The peasants are coming and carrying their axes./ Something dreadful is going to happen" (I, 1, ix). In response to Liputin's taunting observation that the heads of former serf owners might indeed be in danger, Stepan has replied: "*Cher ami*, believe me, *that* . . . will be of no use either to our landlords, or to all of us in general. Even without our heads we shall not be capable of organizing anything, despite the fact that our heads, more than anything, interfere with our understanding." Stepan betrays a similar anxiety in his later challenge to his son Pyotr: "Do you understand that if you have the guillotine in the foreground it is only because chopping off heads is the easiest thing of all, whereas having an idea is the most difficult thing of all" (II, 1, ii).

Both Stepan's anxiety for the security of his head and the decapitation that Pyotr threatens are symbolic as well as literal. Associated with his idealistic sensibility and self-defined vocation as "poet and thinker" (II, 9), the head is the symbolic center of Stepan's identity. Conversely, it is the symbolic target of the anti-idealistic and anti-intellectual contempt that Pyotr voices in the novel.

Accordingly, the disruption of the literary matinee by Pyotr's cohorts, with its mocking rout of the intellectual and literary celebrities, represents a kind of comic–symbolic decapitation. Significantly, Stepan's abortive defense of beauty, with its implicit appeal to the "higher" order envisaged by the artist's imagination, yields to the frenzied orator who proclaims the senselessness (*bestolkovshchina*) and disorder (*besporiadok*) of Russian reality (III, 1, iv). His declamation is met with wild applause and, amidst the uproar, an approving shout from the audience: "That's the business! That there's the business! [*Vot eto delo! Vot tak delo!*] Hurrah! Nossir, that's none of your aesthetics!" This shouted opposition of *delo* to *estetika* epitomizes the nihilists' rallying cry against Stepan and the idealists; it simultaneously suggests the nihilist's demand for unadorned, concrete reality instead of the idealized images of art and for action instead of speculative thinking and visionary dreaming. Ironically, the cry rings out at the matinee as a voice of approval for the mindless chaos that sweeps the hall.

Pyotr, however, is not simply the antithesis of his idealist father. These apparent opposites are ultimately bound in dialectical unity. Pyotr's realism, of course, is essentially a pose, as Stavrogin first suggests when he remarks ironically of Pyotr: "Note that as a realist he cannot lie, and that the truth is dearer to him than success, except for those special cases in which success is dearer than the truth" (I, 5, vii). Pyotr is first and foremost a liar. But his affinity with Stepan is not just the distant kinship between the artist and the liar, or between the self-deceived dreamer and the cynical master of deception. For example, in a conversation with Stavrogin, Pyotr echoes with a cynical twist his father's tendency to lose sight of the distinction between the symbolic and the literal: He complains that "the fools," his local recruits, "reproach me for having deceived them about the central committee and its 'innumerable branches' . . . But what sort of deception is there here: The central committee is you and I, and there will be as many branches as you like" (II, 6, vii). It is ironically appropriate that the final public judgment of Pyotr should attribute to the son shortcomings that might well describe the father, including "a complete ignorance of reality . . . and a terrible abstractness" (III, 8). Indeed, Fedka the convict has remarked on Pyotr's inclination to operate on the basis of prematurely concocted schemata of reality: "I tell you, sir, it's plenty easy for Pyotr Stepanovich to live in the world, because he himself imagines [*predstavit sebe*] a person and then lives with the one he imagines" (II, 2, i).

Early in the novel, Stepan evaluates his son and finds him wanting in terms of rather typical idealistic criteria. He remarks that he has found Pyotr to lack any "sense . . . of something higher, something fundamental, any embryo of a future idea" (I, 3, iv). Pyotr may, indeed, lack a sense of the "higher" in Stepan's definition, but he shares his father's inclination to spurn concrete and particular reality for less substantial and more abstract realms. On closer examination, Pyotr's summons for movement "full steam ahead"—the very appeal to revolutionary action that epitomizes his anti-intellectual and anti-idealist opposition to his father—amounts to a mere abstraction, a metaphorical *idea* of action that is no more specific than the "highway" on which, as the narrator conjectures, Stepan later embarks. Or, at the most, the action for which Pytor appeals is concrete only insofar as it amounts to a wholesale, destructive assault on *realia*. In his early remarks on Pyotr, Stepan has commented: "I took him for a nothing [*nichto*], *quelque chose dans ce genre*" (I, 3, iv). His words prove prophetic: Pyotr emerges in the novel as a *bes* of nothingness, a spirit of negation. In the chapter "Ivan Tsarevich," he exclaims to Stavrogin: "We shall proclaim destruction—why, oh why is that little idea so fascinating! (II, 8). In effect, Pyotr's "little idea" of destruction translates into action the purely intellectual negation of concrete and particular reality that is inherent in the very process of abstraction and is constantly implicit in Stepan's gravitation toward *realiora*. But whereas Stepan appeals to a "higher" order of ideas and idealized forms, Pyotr, under the banner of *realia*, embodies the total abstraction of pure negation. Hostile toward his father's idealism, he simultaneously echoes the hostility toward concrete *realia* that is apparent in such utterances of Stepan's as his exclamation that "Russians should be exterminated for the good of humanity" (II, 1, ii).

If Stepan's tendency to negate *realia* receives its full dialectical development in Pyotr, it is also echoed in numerous other characters in *Devils*. The novel offers repeated examples of characters who, following Stepan's model, evade or deny the concrete and particular dimension of reality in their eagerness to affirm the abstract and symbolic. This tendency manifests itself most distinctly, perhaps, in Ivan Shatov, whom the narrator portrays in the introductory chapter as "one of those ideal Russian beings who are suddenly struck by some powerful idea and are, as it were, crushed by it all at once and sometimes even forever" (I, 1, viii).[4] Shatov, of course, is one of several characters in the novel who insist on turning Stavrogin into a symbol and cannot come to terms with Stavrogin's specific, contradictory reality. It is symptomatic that, on the occasion of Stavrogin's visit to Shatov in the "Night" chapter that begins Part II of the novel, Shatov repeatedly attempts to evade or negate the concrete and personal level of Stavrogin's identity and of his own relationship with Stavrogin, insisting that they exist on some superior level of generality. Thus, in reference to their conversation some years earlier in which Stavrogin sowed the seeds of the ideas Shatov now preaches, Shatov insists: " 'Our' conversation never existed at all: There was a teacher, prophesying tremendous words, and there was a pupil who had risen from the dead. I am that pupil and you are that teacher" (II, 1, vii). Just moments earlier he has elevated them to an even higher level of abstraction: "I ask respect for myself, I demand it!" he shouts at Stavrogin. But then he adds: "not respect for my personality—to hell with it—but for something else . . . We are two creatures and we have come together in infinity, for the last time in the world" (II, 1, vi).

[4]The narrator's adjective for Shatov, "ideal'nyi," suggests "ideal" in the ironic sense of "existing solely as an idea or mental image."

Shatov's words here to Stavrogin are later parodied when Governor von Lembke visits his wife Yulia in her bedroom to air his complaints against her. Von Lembke insists: "We are not in the boudoir of an affected lady but are like two abstract creatures on a balloon who have met in order to speak the truth" (II, 10, i); the Russian, *vozdushnyi shar*—"aerial sphere"—gives a pretentiously etherial sound to what is, in fact, a balloon).

One could say that Shatov's desire to abstract his conversations with Stavrogin from the circumstances of their lives and locate them purely in the realm of ideas amounts to an attempt to place them wholly in the dimension of the novel that Edward Wasiolek has called the "metaphysical drama." Wasiolek contrasts this component of the novel to that which he calls the "political pamphlet,"[5] the dimension of *Devils* that bears the distinct imprint of Dostoevsky's original intentions when he set out, as he claimed in a March 24, 1870, letter to Nikolai Strakhov, to write a piece for which he anticipated success "in a tendentious rather than artistic sense," and which he was quite prepared to see "turn out to be nothing but a pamphlet." In contrasting "metaphysical drama" to "political pamphlet," Wasiolek joins a number of critics who have identified an unresolved conflict in *Devils* between the tendentious "pamphlet" that Dostoevsky first began to write and the philosophical dialogue that focuses in Stavrogin, Shatov, and Kirillov and seems to have migrated to *Devils* along with Stavrogin from Dostoevsky's inchoate *Life of a Great Sinner*, the projected magnum opus which the author reluctantly abandoned shortly after beginning *Devils*. Wasiolek expresses a widely held critical opinion when he observes that "there are two centers of gravity in the novel . . . the political pamphlet and the metaphysical drama, and they have only the weakest of structural ties."

But the plainly misguided nature of Shatov's impulse to locate his conversation with Stavrogin solely in a timeless and abstract realm of ideas (and his wrongheadedness is underscored by von Lembke's later parodic echoing of his words) might be taken as a kind of signal that the "higher" metaphysical dialogue in *Devils* is not meant to be regarded in abstraction from the overall context of the novel. This

[5]Edward Wasiolek, *Dostoevsky: The Major Fiction* (Cambridge, Mass: M.I.T. Press, 1964), pp. 110-111.

provides a clue that the tension between levels of plot or "centers of gravity" in *Devils* is not merely extraneous to the novel's design, not just some fortuitous birth defect that can be traced to the circumstances of its gestation. One need not claim unqualified aesthetic success for *Devils* in order to argue that the division between the novel's satirically treated social and political intrigue, on the one hand, and the philosophical drama that centers in Stavrogin and his satellites, on the other, can be viewed as a formal correlative to the novel's principal thematic conflict, to the pervasive tension between *realia* and aspired-to *realiora* that manifests itself first in the introductory story of Stepan Verkhovensky.

Far from being downplayed or muted in *Devils*, the tension between levels of reality appears to be repeatedly underscored. It is emphasized, for example, by implicit plays on the motifs of mystery and revelation. The novel's intrigues develop around secrets and enigmas, and repeated references to the unknown, the secret, the mysterious, the hidden and the enigmatic create a threat of related verbal motifs that is woven throughout the novel. For example, the word *taina* ("secret," "mystery") and related words derived from the same root are repeatedly applied to a variety of *realia*—persons, actions, and circumstances—belonging to the political and social intrigues. In response to the novel's secrets, the characters undertake a series of investigations and inquiries, and their aspirations to uncover the truth are marked by repeated uses of the verb *otkryt'* ("to discover/reveal") and the noun *otkrytie* ("discovery," "revelation"). Thus, the governor's wife Yulia von Lembke pursues the "discovery" *(otkrytie)* of the political conspiracy that she believes "is most certainly concealed" in the province (II, 6, i). Liza implicitly challenges Stavrogin to acknowledge his marriage to Maria Lebyadkin when she mentions Captain Lebyadkin's offer to "reveal [*otkryt'*] certain secrets [*tainy*] about you" (II, 10, iii).

In contrast, the protagonists of the metaphysical drama are more concerned with ultimate mysteries and revelation—not with mundane *otkrytiia* but with *otkrovenie*, a native Slavic calque on the borrowed Greek word *apokalipsis*. Appropriately, the idea of ultimate relevation is first introduced in connection with Stepan Verkhovensky, the real progenitor of the metaphysical drama, whose allegorical epic ends with man's completion of the Tower of Babel, deposition of the

"former lord," and commencement "of a new life with a new insight
into things" (I, 1, i). Kirillov actually reads the Biblical Apocalypse to
Fedka the convict (II, 6, vi), and the idea of apocalypse permeates
Kirillov's own thinking. Shatov dedicates himself to what he believes is
the ultimate relevation, the "new word, the final word, the sole word
of renewal and resurrection" (II, 1, vii). And the narrator associates a
kind of rigorously scientific apocalyptic vision with Shigalyov—a
minor figure in the metaphysical drama—when he first introduces
him as a man who "looked as though he were expecting the destruction of the world, and not just some time, according to the prophesies,
which might not be fulfilled, but quite definitely like the day-after-
tomorrow, at precisely 10:25 A.M." (I, 4, iv).

Throughout the novel, references to the "secrets" and pursued
"discoveries" of the mundane intrigues inevitably invite consideration
of the contrasting "mysteries" and pursued "revelations" of the
metaphysical drama. And the converse holds, as well. For example,
the House of Fillipov, which both Shatov and Kirillov inhabit, constitutes a central point of conjunction between the two levels of mystery
and inquiry in the novel, a kind of escalator *a realibus ad realiora*. After
discovering the "mysterious [*tainstvennoe*] murder" of Shatov (III, 6, ii)
and the suicide of Kirillov, the investigating authorities conclude that
this house has harbored the secrets of the political conspiracy, if not
the nucleus of the suspected secret society itself. Pyotr has earlier told
von Lembke that Kirillov "is hiding" *(taitsia)* there (II, 6, iii); and the
murderer Fedka has in fact been hiding there, entering and leaving
by way of a "secret passage" *(tainyi khod*; III, 4, ii). Ironically, however,
the house has figured most notably in the novel as the principal setting of the metaphysical drama with its focus on ultimate mysteries
and ultimate revelation. Yet the ultimate effect of this ironic contrast
is to underscore the collapse of *realiora* into *realia* that finally trans-
pires at the House of Fillipov. Thus, as he writes his suicide note,
Kirillov, whose nocturnal existence in the house reflects his extreme
withdrawal from *realia*, twice echoes in an apocalyptic frenzy Christ's
avowal that "there is nothing hidden [*tainoe*] that shall not be made
manifest" (III, 6, ii). But the suicide note's only demonstrable service
of revelation is to provide the first tentative clue in the police investigation of the murders and devastation in which the political and social
intrigues culminate.

On the level of *siuzhet*, the transitions between mundane intrigue and metaphysical drama in *Devils* are often conspicuously abrupt and tend to accentuate the incongruity between the two planes of focus in the novel. For example, the sequences in Part I in which the narrator visits Kirillov and Maria Lebyadkin, seeking clues regarding the social intrigue, unexpectedly shift the novel's focus *a realibus ad realiora*. Instead of satisfying the narrator's curiosity with facts about the Lebyadkins' role in the mounting social intrigue, Kirillov expounds his monomaniacal preoccupation with suicide and the existence of God, and Maria Lebyadkin introduces an unexpected aura of other-worldly mystery. As the Soviet critic Vladimir Tunimanov has suggested, one need not agree with Vyacheslav Ivanov's specific, symbolist exegesis of this scene to recognize the vague ambiance of allegory that surrounds the Lebyadkin woman here. Thus, Tunimanov observes: "Everyday life here gravitates toward 'otherworldliness,' and objects are displaced from their ordinary series to a symbolic one; the narration is shifted from the quotidian realistic level to a higher, symbolic one."[6]

Shortly following these scenes, their abrupt transitions *a realibus ad realiora* are satirized in the scene in which Varvara Stavrogin interrogates Captain Lebyadkin in her drawing room. Varvara has pressed Lebyadkin to explain "why" his sister might, as he has said, accept charity from her and from no one else. Lebyadkin contrives to evade her question by absurdly diverting the conversation to the plane of the metaphysical. "You expect an answer to 'why?' " he replies. "That little word 'why' has suffused the entire universe from the first day of creation, madam, and all of nature cries every minute to its creator, 'why?,' and for seven thousand years now has received no answer. Could it be that Captain Lebyadkin alone must answer, and would that be just, madam?" (I, 5, iv).

An equally comic transition, in the opposite direction, marks the final descent from *realiora* at the House of Fillipov: Kirillov, on the threshold of the suicide that is supposed to mark the advent of the man–god, suddenly wants to draw a cartoon face with outthrust

<hr/>

[6]V. A. Tunimanov, "Rasskazchik v *Besakh* Dostoevskogo," in *Issledovaniia po poetike i stilistike*, ed. V. V. Vinogradov, V. G. Bazanov, and G. M. Fridlender (Leningrad: Nauka, 1972), p. 148.

tongue on the note that Pyotr is dictating, but he finally settles for signing the note: *"Liberté, égalité, fraternité ou la mort!, de Kiriloff, gentilhomme-seminariste russe et citoyen du monde civilisé!"* (III, 6, ii). And thus, utterly obscuring the professed apocalyptic aim of his suicide, he plunges absurdly from the pinnacle of the metaphysical drama to the ridiculous depths of the political pamphlet.

Just as Pyotr Verkhovensky is the product of Stepan's neglect of *realia*, so the wave of destruction that Pyotr instigates and in which the "political pamphlet" climaxes is at least facilitated by the other intellectuals' preoccupation with the "higher" concerns of the "metaphysical drama." Pyotr takes advantage of Stavrogin's noncommittal attitude, rooted ultimately in the latter's deep philosophical irresolution, to induce Fedka to murder the Lebyadkins, ostensibly on Stavrogin's behalf; the murderer, in turn, evidently sets the fire in the river district in an attempt to conceal his victims' bodies. Shatov's desire to resign from the revolutionary society, which he joined because of one theoretical enthusiasm and now quits because of another, provides the occasion for Pyotr's attempt to ensure his local quintet's allegiance by implicating them in Shatov's murder. Shigalyov's indifference to all but the integrity of his theory causes him to decline to participate in the murder "solely because all this business [*delo*], from beginning to end, literally contradicts my program" (III, 6, i); but his exclusive preoccupation with theory also makes him decline to avert the murder by warning Shatov. Kirillov's intention to commit suicide as an apocalyptic proclamation of the man–god makes the murder possible, since the conspirators act in the belief that he has agreed to take the blame for the crime.

Ultimately, however, the dimension of *Devils* that can be called "metaphysical drama" and that which can be called "political pamphlet" are not merely antithetical; like Stepan and Pyotr Verkhovensky, they share a kind of dialectical unity. The severance of *realiora*—or, more precisely, would-be *realiora*—from *realia* is apparent in both metaphysical drama and political pamphlet. What the reader constantly encounters both in the novel's political and social intrigues and in its philosophically oriented drama-dialogue is a disjunction between *realia* and the symbolic meanings that people attempt to impose on them. Thus, the other characters improbably elevate Stavrogin to the level of either a religious or a political messiah; Yulia von Lembke construes her provincial fete as "the proclamation of a great idea" (III, 1, ii), while Pyotr's cohorts act as though its disruption were all but the first step in the Russian Revolution; and the megalomaniacal Kirillov proclaims his suicide as the apocalyptic inauguration of a new metahistorical era. Time and again the novel presents such discrepancies between concrete reality and purported significance, between diminutive fact and improbably portentous interpretation. The behavior of characters in both the sociopolitical intrigue and the philosophical drama of *Devils* often resembles the issue of some hypertrophied head that is floating aloft like a gas-filled *vozdushnyi shar*: the product of a consciousness, whether nominally "idealistic" or "materialistic," that is in danger of losing all touch with the concrete and particular dimension of reality, the simple *realia* of human existence.

Although the novel locates the origins of this consciousness in Stepan Verkhovensky's idealist sensibility and gravitation toward an imagined "higher" reality, the cumulative indictment of Stepan is only one line of a complex dialectical argument in *Devils*. The counter line of argument, which is perhaps equally strong and developed with comparable thoroughness, suggests that people cannot orient themselves and make their way among *realia* without seeking the perspective of *realiora*, without the abstracting and generalizing power of the intellect and imagination, without some aspiration toward the ideal.

In the final analysis, Dostoevsky vindicates Stepan's idealist propensities in *Devils* and finds in him a redeeming potential for rebirth. Significantly, he allows him to pronounce the key interpretation of the novel's Biblical epigraph from Saint Luke, the story of the Garadene swine. After the Gospel seller Sofia Matveevna Ulitina reads the passage at Stepan's request, Stepan remarks: "But now an idea [*mysl'*] has occurred to me, *une comparaison*." And he goes on to compare the devils in the Biblical story to "all the miasmas, all the impurities" that have accumulated in Russia over the centuries. He speaks of these impurities and devils as leaving Russia and entering the swine, who, he says, are "we, we and those, and Petrusha—*et les autres avec lui*, and I perhaps the first one, at their head, and we shall all throw ourselves, mad and possessed, from the rocks into the sea and drown. . . . But the sick man [Russia] will be healed and will 'sit at the feet of Jesus' . . ." (III, 7, ii). One recognizes here Stepan's familiar inclination to see reality in terms of ideas and *comparaisons*. In this case, however, he draws on his idealist sensibility for real insight.

The two key moments of epiphany or resolution in the novel are given to the idealists Stepan and Shatov. These are moments of renewed contact with reality, experiences in which *realiora* and *realia* are at least briefly united. In his interpretation of the Gospel passage, Stepan, in effect, affirms the potential health of a Russia, a reality, that has been purged of his own destructive illusions. His interpretation is followed by a lapse into complete delirium and unconsciousness. But this final delirium and unconsciousness are purgative, and his subsequent awakening brings a sudden awareness of his immediate physical surroundings: *"Tiens, un lac,"* he exclaims, "Oh, my God, I had not even seen it before" (III, 7, ii).

Shatov's experience of insight occurs when fortuitous circumstances unexpectedly bring his estranged wife Marie to his door just as she is about to bear a child. For Shatov, too, the experience brings a kind of awakening to reality. Symptomatic of this awakening is the new thought that dawns on him when the nihilist midwife Arina Prokhorovna Virginsky proves willing to help in Marie's childbirth. " 'It seems that convictions and the person,' Shatov reflects, 'are two quite different things' " (III, 5, iii). This humble insight is precisely the one that has been missing in Shatov's earlier attempt to equate Stavrogin with his ideas. For Shatov it signals the emergence of human reality through a veil of ideas and ideals. The birth of Marie Shatov's child (juxtaposed, significantly, with the chapter in which Kirillov expounds the vision of eternal harmony that he believes will inspire people to cease bearing children) is one of the few unequivocally positive moments in *Devils* and, with Stepan's experience on his final journey, one of only two significant counterpoints to the negation of reality that so pervades the novel. Shatov, in his warmly comic enthusiasm, declares the birth to be "a great joy . . . the mystery [*taina*] of the appearance of a new being, a great and inexplicable mystery" (III, 5, vi). Having previously preached the *idea* of a God in whom he admitted he could not yet believe (II, 1, vii), Shatov now acknowledges God indirectly, not as an abstract concept but as the implicit source of this mysterious creation *ex nihilo*: "There were two, and suddenly a third person, a new spirit, whole and complete, such as cannot come from human hands; a new thought and a new love; it is even awesome." And finally Shatov says of this example of human life in its most humble and vulnerable state: "There is nothing higher in the world!" What he affirms, in essence, is the merging of *realia* and *realiora*. Without falsely becoming more than it is, the individual human infant becomes a general representative of his kind, embodying all the wonder, potentiality and contingency of human existence: "a small, red and wrinkled creature, so helpless it was almost terrifying, as precarious as a mote of dust that could be blown away by the first gust of wind, but crying and announcing itself as though it, too, had the fullest right to life." With Shatov, as with Stepan, the impulse to affirm a "higher" reality comes together here with the simple, redeeming affirmation of life itself.

In light of Dostoevsky's own intellectual biography, it is not surprising that he gives the self-styled "poet and thinker" Stepan the co-authorial role of interpreting the novel's central metaphor, or that he should later state, in the July–August issue of his *Diary of a Writer* for 1876: "Indeed, I love Stepan Trofimovich and respect him deeply." In his defense of art against the nihilists at the literary matinee, Stepan echoes ideas from Dostoevsky's own earlier defense of art against the nihilists in his 1861 article, "Mr. [Dobrolyu]–bov and the Question of Art." But this particular coincidence of Stepan's views and Dostoevsky's merely reflects the more general fact that Stepan embodies the essence of the idealist aesthetics that Dostoevsky had developed under Belinsky's influence in the 1840s, and that he continued to espouse long after he had renounced many other social, political, and philosophical views he associated with Belinsky.

Tunimanov has pointed out that Dostoevsky's professed initial willingness to sacrifice artistic quality [*khudozhestvennost'*] for polemical impact in *Devils* seems sharply inconsonant with the strong plea for artistic quality that Dostoevsky had developed earlier—precisely in "Mr. ——bov and the Question of Art."[7] Dostoevsky never entirely abandoned the polemical intention that had made him willing, at first, to forego artistic quality in *Devils*. In fact, he alluded to this aim in a letter that he wrote about the completed novel to Crown Prince Alexander III in February 1873, where he stressed the polemical point that "our Belinskys and Granovskys" were the "direct fathers of the

[7]Tunimanov, *op cit.*, p. 95.

Nechaevists." But to have sacrificed *khudozhestvennost'* in order merely to excoriate the "Belinskys and Granovskys" for fathering the Nechaevists and their politics would have belied both Dostoevsky's artistic credo and his own indebtedness for that credo to Belinsky and the intellectual milieu in which Belinsky was the dominant figure. It is appropriate, then, that the deeply ingrained commitment to *khudozhestvennost'* that ultimately took command in Dostoevsky's writing of *Devils* should have led him to a much deeper and more complex treatment of Stepan Verkhovensky's intellectual legacy. In this case, fidelity to artistic truth also meant fidelity to the ambiguities of Dostoevsky's own artistic roots.

The Art of Fiction
as a Theme in
The Brothers Karamazov

by Victor Terras

We know from Dostoevsky's theoretical writings that he was a believer in organic aesthetics who conceived of life and art as an inseparable unity. He took for granted that art is both a basic human need and a quintessential manifestation of the life force. Hence he also saw art as a key to the understanding of life's riddles. Throughout *The Brothers Karamazov*, aesthetic categories are unhesitatingly applied to the phenomena of life, for instance, when Dmitry thus describes the story of his romance with Katerina Ivanova: "You understand the first half: it is a drama and it took place there. But the second half is a tragedy, and it will happen here" (I, 3, iv).[1]

The excursions of the Karamazovs into the realm of aesthetics invariably lead to questions regarding the very essence and meaning of life. The antinomies and *aporiai* of the Good and the True encountered in the novel are not only paralleled by similar difficulties as regards the Beautiful, but actually emerge clearest in the aesthetic realm. Fyodor's assertion that it is "not only pleasant, but even beautiful at times to be insulted," so that a man would "feel insulted for the sake of aesthetics" (I, 2, ii). Dmitry's discourse on the ideal of the Madonna and the ideal of Sodom (I, 3, iii), Ivan's "anecdotes" on the delights of child abuse, Liza Khokhlakov's pleasurable daydreams of crucified children and pineapple compote—all these examples from the aesthetic realm show up the problematic nature of man even more

"The Art of Fiction as a Theme in *The Brothers Karamazov*," written for this collection by Victor Terras. Copyright © 1983 by Prentice-Hall, Inc.

[1]All quotations from *The Brothers Karamazov* will be in my own translation.

clearly than the respective examples regarding truth and justice, also present throughout the novel.

The Karamazovs are voluptuaries (*sladostrastniki*—the title of Book Three), aesthetes, and poets, whose true nature is revealed through the workings of their imagination. Fyodor's lubricious erotic fantasies, Dmitry's ardent declamations and "hymn of praise," Ivan's dreams of power, Alyosha's serene vision of "Cana of Galilee, and even Smerdyakov's utterly prosaic imagination reveal more about their nature than their actions or decisions do. Their characters are determined aesthetically as much as morally, and perhaps more so. Each of them is a different type of *homo aestheticus*.

In a sense, what is true of the characters of the novel is true of the novel as a whole. The impression created by many hundreds of literary digressions, quotations, and allusions is as important as plot line and philosophic argument. The role of quotations from and allusions to Pushkin may serve as an example.

The many quotations and reminiscences from the works of Pushkin draw the Karamazovs into the orbit of Dostoevsky's Pushkinian ideal of Russian man. Ivan's bittersweet confession that in spite of everything he still loves "those sticky little leaves" of springtime (II, 5, iii) is a reminiscence from Pushkin's poem "Cold Winds Still Blow" (*Eshche duiut kholodnye vetry*, 1828). There are several other reminiscences from Pushkin in the "Grand Inquisitor" chapter. A quotation from "The Stone Guest" ("The air is fragrant with laurel and with lemon," (II, 5, v) echoes the poet's nostalgia for the Mediterranean world. An allusion to the Beast of Revelations 13 and 17 blends into a reminiscence from Pushkin's "The Covetous Knight": "But then the Beast will crawl up to us, and lick our feet, and wet them with bloody tears from its eyes" (II, 5, v). Scene ii of Pushkin's play has: "Submissive, timid, bloodspattered crime / Comes crawling to my feet, licking my hand, / Looking me in the eye." The last line of the "Grand Inquisitor" has an explicit quotation from Pushkin: "And he releases Him 'into the dark squares of the city' " (II, 5, v). Like Pushkin, Ivan loves and understands Europe, even though—with Herzen, and with Dostoevsky, of course—he perceives it as a graveyard. But being a Russian and a Karamazov, Ivan loves life, and it is Pushkin who gives him the proper words to express his love of life.

Dostoevsky finds a way to connect Pushkin to Alyosha, too. The letter which Alyosha receives from Liza Khokhlakov is clearly derived, perhaps simply cribbed, from Tatyana's letter. Then, in Book Ten, Tatyana appears in person—through the back door, as is Dostoevsky's habit. Kolya Krasotkin, challenged by Alyosha as to whether he has actually read anything by "old Belinsky," says: "The spot about Tatyana, why she didn't go with Onegin" (IV, 10, vi). Kolya, who *has* read Belinsky, has not read Pushkin, however, and one senses Alyosha's pain as he establishes this fact. The implication is that Alyosha has read Pushkin and reveres him.

Dmitry is initially dominated by Schiller and that poet's lofty humanism. But as Fate strikes him down in Book Eight, he seems to move into Pushkin's orbit. His surprising refusal to become jealous of his Polish rival is explained in terms of an aphorism from Pushkin's *Table Talk* (III, 8, iii). Then, at a crucial juncture of chapter 4, "In the Dark," a line from *Ruslan and Lyudmila* flashes through his mind ("And nought but the whispering silence," (III, 8, iv). Half an hour later, he quotes Pimen's *Eshche odno poslednee skazan'e* ("One more last tale") from *Boris Godunov*. Dmitry's transfiguration into a willing martyr is highlighted by a convict's hymn of praise, which rises heavenward from a Siberian underground mine—clearly a reminiscence of Pushkin's "In the Depth of Siberian Mines" ("Vo glubine sibirskikh rud," 1827).

We know that all three brothers, as well as Fyodor, are great lovers and quoters of Schiller. All three brothers also quote Pushkin. Interestingly, Fyodor's contact with Pushkin coincides with an explicit quote from Schiller. When Fyodor challenges Dmitry to a duel "through a handkerchief," he is quoting—perversely, to be sure—from Schiller's *Cabal and Love* (I, 2, vi). But at the same time, an elderly Father's challenge to his son is a strong echo from Pushkin's "The Covetous Knight."

Pushkin was in the 1860s and 1870s a symbol—both rallying point and target of attack. To the nihilists, he stood for hedonism, *l'art pour l'art*, and the callous disregard of the upper class for the sufferings of the common people. To them he was the bard of "little feet," who would begin a poem on an apparent civic note, only to return cynically to these "little feet" ("City of Luxury, City of Poverty," 1828). The "civic" satirist D. D. Minaev had parodied this poem, attacking what he saw as its mindless frivolity. Dostoevsky comes up with a spirited anti-parody, Rakitin's *"Uzh kakaia zh eta nozhka"* ("What a little foot this is," [IV, 11, iv]). What do we see in it? Pushkin is properly put down, a social message is introduced, and there is a touch of "humor," seminarian style. The destruction of Rakitin and what he stands for was one of Dostoevsky's objectives in *The Brothers Karamazov*. Presenting him as utterly unworthy of Pushkin is one of the devices by which Rakitin is made into a hopeless vulgarian *(poshliak)*. In the semiotic system of *The Brothers Karamazov*, to be with Pushkin means to be on the side of life, hope, and whatever is genuine and Russian. Anything that is hostile to Pushkin is vulgar, shallow, lacking in life and vigor.

Schiller's "aesthetic education of mankind," the romantic conception of the "negative principle" (Goethe's Mephistopheles and romantic Satanism), Gogol's famous troika passage, and other highlights of Russian and world literature are taken up, challenged, manipulated, transformed, and sublated. A literary discourse consisting of quotations, allusions, polemic sorties, parody, paraphrase, and interpretation accompanies the plot of the novel and forms a subtext whose message complements that of the plot. With an erudite reader, it may in fact claim top attention, pushing the plot down into the position of a subtext.[2]

Dostoevsky's preoccupation with "fact" and "details of fact" is well known. The power of the simple, concrete fact often becomes apparent in *The Brothers Karamazov*. Dmitry struggles with the facts of life (he calls them *realizm*) from beginning to end. But then, too, the figure of fiction appears just as prominently, and with the same power.

The first illustration of the power of a "mere" fiction appears as early as in the first chapter of Book I: a young woman, without any factual reason, commits suicide only because in her imagination she sees herself as Ophelia (I, 1, iii). Dostoevsky was fascinated by the power of fiction no less than by that of a "simple fact." A notebook entry suggests that he was delighted to find an example of it in Tacitus, *Annals* 1: 22, where the story of one Vibulenus is told, who successfully incited his fellow soldiers to mutiny with an impassioned

[2]The role of quotation as a structural device is treated in detail by Nina M. Perlina, *Tsitata kak element poetiki v romane Brat'ia Karamazovy* (Brown University dissertation, 1977), to whom I owe some of the observations in this essay.

account of the cruel death of his brother—who later turned out to have been a mere figment of his imagination. And so it is the fiction of the open door as much as the fact of the brass pestle in the grass that convicts Dmitry.

An ironic *quid pro quo* of fact and fiction runs through the whole novel. An imaginary 3,000 rubles are as potent a factor in the plot as a real 3,000 rubles, or rather more so. In a display of ingenious as well as painstaking novelistic craftsmanship, Dostoevsky introduces a whole series of details which implant in the minds of several witnesses the erroneous notion that Dmitry was in possession of 3,000 rubles the night of his father's murder. One actually wonders if Dostoevsky is not polemicizing with Immanuel Kant's famous disquisition on the difference between an imaginary 100 Thalers and 100 real Thalers.

All this raises the question of what connection—if any—there is between truth on the one hand and "fact" or "fiction" on the other. Insofar as Dostoevsky was convinced that art is an avenue to truth, and art is of course part fact and part fiction, this question becomes directly relevant to Dostoevsky's philosophy of art.

In the very introduction to the novel, the narrator asserts that a strange and somewhat eccentric, rather than a familiar, "average" character, may carry "within himself the very heart of the whole." Then very early on in the novel, the narrator develops a curious notion of what makes a man a "realist." It would seem that a realist is a person who lives and thinks in terms of an immediately or intuitively given reality (I, 1, v). The opposite is, then, a "theoretician," who seeks to create and to realize a rational world of his own making. This makes Alyosha a "realist" and Rakitin a "theoretician."

Dmitry, after many trials and tribulations, comes to observe that, unlike in fiction, little accidents, not great events, destroy men in real life. He calls this "realism." Now, the contemporary theory of realism taught that the typical, rather than the fortuitous, should reign in fiction. Dostoevsky not only subscribed to this opinion but also believed that it was ultimately true of "real life" as well. So Dmitry is wrong when he sees himself as a victim of trivial accidents. He will realize this later in the novel. Similarly, the devil's suggestion that the truth is unhappily "almost always banal" (*pochti vsegda neostroumna*, [IV, 11, ix]) is another thesis advanced only to be refuted. Likewise, the notion that human life is a mere dream or illusion appears only as a warning to those of little faith: Mme. Khokhlakov is the case in point (I, 2, iii).

One thing is clear: those who pursue the truth rationally, confident of their human reason, are led into error. The truth will come to men through intuition or as inspiration. The distance from the truth of each character in the novel is measured by the power and quality of his—or her—imagination.

Fyodor's perverse mind and amoral character would suggest that he is far from the truth. But with the exception of Smerdyakov, he intuitively understands everybody and everything very well. In fact, while he is blind to Smerdyakov's murderous intentions, he correctly recognizes the lackey's basic flaw: the man lacks imagination (I, 3, vi), his sharp intelligence being entirely practical. Dostoevsky actually seems to have aimed at endowing Fyodor with an almost uncanny clairvoyance. He asks Alyosha to leave the monastery only minutes after Father Zosima did. He speaks the mysterious and prophetic words, "*Da, Dmitriia Fedorovich eshche ne sushchestvuet*" (I, 2, i). As so often, his verbal clowning (here, "Dmitry Fyodorovich does not exist as yet" instead of "Dmitry Fyodorovich isn't here yet") leads to the utterance of a deep truth. Fyodor's assessment of Ivan's personality is correct, within the limits of Fyodor's own mind. He may be predicting his own fate when he projects the image of von Sohn, old lecher and victim of an obscene murder, on the "landowner" Maksimov, clearly a "double" of Fyodor's.

Dmitry, a man of the senses and, like his father, a raconteur and lover of beauty, though of a finer mold, is gifted with intuition, empathy, and imagination. He is never too far from the truth. His marvelous gift of language lets him utter the most profound truths in palpable poetic form. He also has a sense of humor and a keen ear for any sort of dissonance. Dmitry intuitively senses the sterility and ugliness of Rakitin's positivism. He senses it immediately when Alyosha falls into "Jesuit" casuistry, repeating in effect an argument of Smerdyakov's, in trying to save his brother (Epilogue 2).

Alyosha is the author of Father Zosima's *Vita*. Throughout the novel he also echoes his teacher's words and teachings. It is surely significant that, more than Dmitry, he is susceptible to the temptations of reason, visited upon him through his brother Ivan and his friend

Rakitin. His teacher's shining example leads him back to the truth. Alyosha is a youth of delicate sensitivity and vivid imagination.

Ivan Karamazov, author of "The Grand Inquisitor," which he calls a "poem," also of an earlier poem "A Geological Cataclysm" and other works, is by far the most literate of the Karamazovs. His destruction as an author, which goes hand in hand with his downfall as a man, is one of Dostoevsky's main concerns in the novel. "The Grand Inquisitor" is undermined even from within through introduction of false notes, dissonances, melodrama, and inner contradictions, as well as by some telltale signs that the Grand Inquisitor is no prince of the Church or glamorous Miltonic Satan, but a "silly student, who never wrote two lines of poetry," as Ivan says himself (II, 5, v). The "poem" is, of course, totally demolished later by its parody in the ninth chapter of Book XI. Nor is this development unprepared. Many earlier hints act as fuses that will eventually explode Ivan's edifice. When the Grand Inquisitor develops his concept of a group of "clever people" (umnye liudi) who rule mankind by giving it bread, mystery, and authority (in fact, though, an unkept promise, magic, and tyranny), one is reminded of Fyodor's cynical comments on "us clever people who'll sit snug, drinking their brandy" (I, 3, viii). The chapter that concludes Book V is entitled "It's Always Worthwhile Speaking to a Clever Man." We know the definition of a "clever man" in all three instances: he is someone who has discovered that there is no God and uses his discovery to his advantage. Ivan, the "clever man," finds himself in the company of two other "clever people," Fyodor and Smerdyakov.

Like the Karamazovs, many characters of lesser importance are determined very largely by the products of their imagination: Grushenka by the fiction of her first love and by her tale of the onion, Katerina Ivanovna by her perverse dream of a life devoted to Dmitry, Liza by her fantasies, alternately sweet and cruel. Some characters we know virtually from their fictions only, such as Maksimov or Father Ferapont.

We know Dmitry's prosecutor, Ippolit Kirillovich, and his defender, Fetyukovich, almost exclusively through the products of their imagination. The former, a positivist and believer in psychology as an exact science, is an honest man and nobody's fool. But he has an ordinary imagination. He quickly creates a plausible account of the crime and an equally plausible image of the criminal. The prosecutor's version of what happened that fateful night is, however, based on two fictions: Grigory's honest mistake about the open door, which was really closed, and Smerdyakov's clever insinuations. The prosecutor also ignores a key fact that speaks in Dmitry's favor: the discrepancy between the amount of money found on Dmitry and the balance between 3000 rubles and the money spent by Dmitry.

Ippolit Kirillovich exposes each statement made by the accused as a clumsy fiction, which he demolishes by the logic of his own version. In fact, though, everything Dmitry says is the truth, while the prosecutor's version is false. In particular, the prosecutor fails to see that the screw of psychological analysis can always be given another turn: Dmitry's fumbling and "giving himself away" may be evidence of his guilt, but it also may be evidence of his innocence: an innocent man might blunder and fall into a trap that a guilty man, who would be on his guard, would see. Raskolnikov, who does not fall into Porfiry's trap, is a case in point. In fact, Dmitry's vivid imagination creates evidence against him, for instance, when he blurts out that the money was under his father's pillow—which he couldn't have known unless he was the murderer (III, 9, vi). Ippolit Kirillovich, a good man, simply underestimates the complexity of human nature. He is satisfied when he has proved Dmitry's story to be absurd, forgetting that the truth is sometimes absurd (IV, 12, viii).

The narrator's condescending attitude toward Ippolit Kirillovich suggests that he is believed by the townspeople to be a nice enough, but somewhat limited person. Yet, against all expectations, he triumphs over the redoubtable Fetyukovich. He never suspects that he has convicted an innocent man, certainly the last thing he would have wanted. It is somewhat of a surprise that Ippolit Kirillovich expresses many of the ideas which we know were Dostoevsky's own, as is readily demonstrated by comparing his speech to passages in Dostoevsky's *Diary of a Writer*. Dostoevsky, like Ippolit Kirillovich, was a believer in Holy Russia, "her principles, her family, everything she holds sacred" (IV, 12, ix). Ironically, these principles are upheld by the conviction of an innocent man.

The defender Fetyukovich is the exact opposite of Ippolit Kirillovich. He has his facts right. He can see through Smerdyakov. With perspicacity and intuition he reconstructs almost the entire course of events as they actually happened. He knows that he is skating on thin ice and skillfully slurs over the dubious steps in his argument. Fetyukovich says outright that the prosecutor's version of the events is open to the very same charge he had made against Dmitry's version, namely that it is a fiction: "What if you've been weaving a romance and about quite a different kind of man?" (IV, 12, xi). Fetyukovich reminds his opponent that one's image of another person is necessarily a fiction and that the real question is: how close is this fiction to the truth? He sarcastically calls the prosecutor's theory by which he had tried to prove premeditation on Dmitry's part "a whole edifice of psychology" (IV, 12, xii) and promptly demolishes it. He will not deny that his own version is a fiction, too. In fact, he will boldly admit that it is just that (IV, 12, xii). But the fact of the matter is that Fetyukovich's version happens to be true.

Fetyukovich is called an "adulterer of thought." His shallow liberalism is clearly odious to the narrator (and to Dostoevsky). Moreover, there is reason to believe that he thinks Dmitry is really guilty. When he swears "by all that is sacred" that he believes in Dmitry's innocence (IV, 12, xii), he is probably perjuring himself. And, last but not least, he loses his case, as the "jury of peasants" chooses to believe Ippolit Kirillovich.

In many ways the duel between Ippolit Kirillovich and Fetyukovich may be seen as a allegory of Dostoevsky's effort in *The Brothers Karamazov*. It was his swan song, much as Ippolit Kirillovich's oration was his. Like Fetyukovich, Dostoevsky pleads a difficult case in which the odds seem to be against the accused. The accused is God, the charge that He has created a world in which injustice and innocent suffering are allowed to prevail. Like Fetyukovich, Dostoevsky pleads his case with skill and eloquence, and is not above an occasional *argumentum ad hominem*, slurring over inconvenient details, and discrediting the witnesses for the prosecution. Especially the latter: Dostoevsky makes sure to destroy the reputation of every atheist in the novel.

Could it be that Dostoevsky, like Fetyukovich, does not believe in the truth of his version of the case? This is really immaterial: Fetyukovich certainly does his best to save Dmitry. Nor is it his fault that the accused is found guilty. A conscientious and unbiased jury should have found Dmitry innocent. Similarly, Dostoevsky certainly wants God to win and does his best to ensure that He does. Still,

Dostoevsky will lose his case with most readers. Like Fetyukovich's jury, they are biased, biased against God. Or, also like Fetyukovich's jury, they lack the imagination to follow Dostoevsky's intricate metaphysical argument.

In any case, Dostoevsky assigns the voice of truth to the man with the greater imagination, that is, to the artist (there is no question as to the great powers of Fetyukovich's imagination), and he does so regardless of the man's moral qualities. He also lets a jury of peasants reject the truth. The moral of the tale is then that an honest and well-meaning, but pedestrian man is prone to deep error and acts of grave injustice. It is Grigory, righteous and devout, but also obtusely unimaginative man who gives the false evidence that convicts Dmitry. To attain the truth, requires imagination, empathy, and inspiration.

Ippolit Kirillovich tries to put down Dmitry, saying: "To be sure, we are poets" (IV, 12, ix). The irony backfires, of course. Not only is Dmitry a poet, but he also knows more about the truth of life than the pedestrian prosecutor ever will. In the world of *The Brothers Karamazov*, everybody knows his or her measure of facts, and everybody must create his or her own fiction of the world. The poet's fiction is closest to the truth. The less a person is a poet, the farther removed is he or she from the truth. Significantly, it is Smerdyakov who advances the Russian nihilists' arguments against poetry, which Dostoevsky had combated all his life and which are thus denounced as a lackey's view of poetry (II, 5, ii). Rakitin's "polemic" with Pushkin serves the same purpose. All and sundry nonpoets and antipoets in *The Brothers Karamazov* are hopelessly removed from the truth as Dostoevsky sees it, as well as from seeing the truth in the Karamazov murder case.

Throughout *The Brothers Karamazov* we hear comments on the art of fiction in general, on various pieces of fiction introduced in the text, and on the novel at hand. The narrator's prefatory statement is quite characteristic in this respect. It suggests that "the main novel is the second," a novel yet to be written, which will deal with "the action of my hero in our day." While there is enough said in the text of *The Brothers Karamazov* to suggest that Dostoevsky did in fact intend to write a sequel, the reference to the "second novel" is, as far as the reader of *The Brothers Karamazov* is concerned, to an unknown and unknowable entity, to a fiction yet to be created and in effect as indeterminate as life itself. And yet the narrator refers to the "essential unity of the whole," suggesting that, somehow, the fiction yet to be created will grow organically from that which exists .

It seems odd that the narrator identifies his work as a "novel" (*roman*), thus abandoning the veracity topos used, for example, by the chronicler of *The Devils*. In fact, the narrator of *The Brothers Karamazov* occasionally presents himself to the reader as a novelist, the author of a work of fiction. Once in a while he will discuss novelistic strategy with his reader. His chapter titles, in particular, often remind the reader that he is reading a piece of fiction.

The narrator also provides the reader with bits and pieces of an internal commentary regarding the style of his narrative, or more often, the style of the various narratives introduced by him. Alyosha's summary of Father Zosima's last discourses to his disciples is said to be "incomplete and fragmentary" (II, 6, ii). Ivan's judgment of his own "poem" was quoted earlier. Dmitry's pathetic and funny effusions are accompanied by a continuous ironic commentary. Time and again, the inner commentary may be projected upon the novel as a whole. When the prosecutor says: "Perhaps I am exaggerating, but it seems to me that certain fundamental features of our educated class of today are reflected in this family picture" (IV, 12, vi), this is clearly a comment on the novel. In fact, when Ippolit Kirillovich exclaims: "But we, so far, only have our Karamazovs!" this may be read as a coded self-apotheosis of the novel, its message, and its author.

As the concept of a "novel" or "romance" (in Russian there is only one term for both: *roman*) advances to the foreground of the plot, a notion begins to emerge that the plot itself is a multiple fiction, beyond which only faint outlines of the truth are visible. As each and every step of Book VIII (and a good deal of what happened earlier) is retraced in Book Nine, Dmitry's version of the fateful events, which we know to be substantially true, now seems false, and the investigator's version, which we know to be false, becomes the "truth." Neither version accounts for what has really happened—this we shall hear from Smerdyakov in Book XI. In Book XII, and even more so in the Epilogue, the notion emerges that any form of temporal truth (legal, psychological, empirical) is irrelevant to God's truth. A flagrant miscarriage of justice reveals God's truth to Dmitry. In the Epilogue, if for a brief moment only, "a lie becomes the truth" even for Katerina Ivanovna, the person who, of all the main characters in the novel, is the least gifted to see the truth.

The key issue at hand is: Granted that every human effort to reach the truth is a work of fiction based on some highly insecure facts, which is more important in this effort—realistic detail or "grand invention as a whole," as the prosecutor puts it (IV, 12, ix)? The answer to this question, implicit in the entire text of the novel, is that both elements are inseparably linked. Fetyukovich states the resulting dilemma in his summation: "What troubles me and makes me indignant is that of all the mass of facts heaped up by the prosecution against the defendant, there is not a single one certain and irrefutable" (IV, 12, xii). According to an organic conception of the work of art—and of life—the whole is always more than the sum of its parts: thirty rabbits do not make one horse, as Porfiry puts it in *Crime and Punishment*. Dostoevsky certainly was a firm believer in the organic principle, which also suggests that if any part of the whole is flawed, the whole must be faulty, too. The prosecutor, who sincerely believes in this preconceived theory (or fiction), is an inferior artist. The flawed details of his fiction betray his whole work. Fetyukovich may not have a sincere belief in anything, but he is a gifted artist whose intuitive grasp of each detail produces the truth of the whole.

The inevitable corollary of this is that in his search for truth man needs to be not only sincere, but also gifted with an artist's imagination as well. The malodorous sinner Fyodor Pavlovich Karamazov has imagination and is therefore infinitely closer to the truth of God than the pedestrian Miusov. What makes Rakitin such a contemptible and worthless person is first and foremost the fact that he has no imagination and cannot even understand a joke. Katerina Ivanovna stumbles from one falsehood to another, betrayed by her total absence of real intuition. It also seems that the power of a person's imagination is proportional to his or her capacity for love, erotic or spiritual. But this is a different question.

I have tried to draw attention to what may be called a literary and aesthetic subtext of the novel. Analogously, and perhaps more persuasively, a biblical and religious subtext can be seen in *The Brothers Karamazov*. The novel contains literally hundreds of Biblical quotations and allusions, many of which form distinct patterns. With a shift of emphasis upon these elements, the novel might be viewed as a modern reaction to the challenge of Christian ethics and metaphysics.

Alyosha Karamazov
and the Hagiographic Hero

by Valentina A. Vetlovskaya

"The main narrative is the second," explains the narrator of *The Brothers Karamazov* in his introductory remarks, "—it is the action of my hero in our day, at the very present time. The first novel takes place thirteen years ago, and it is hardly even a novel, but only a period in my hero's early youth. I cannot do without this first novel, because much in the second would be unintelligible without it."[1]

Clearly Dostoevsky conceived of his work in the form of two novels, of which the second (not known to us) is the main one. It follows that without this second novel much in the first cannot be entirely comprehensible. It is essential, therefore, that we seek out and consider elements which might provide some clue to the overall structure of the two novels. In this way the balance of parts in our presentation will not be upset, and we shall avoid making secondary things primary and primary ones secondary.

We may note at the outset that Dostoevsky wrote his introductory remarks in 1878, that is, when beginning his work on *The Brothers Karamazov*. The idea of a continuation of the novel, then, was not an afterthought, the result of work already accomplished; rather, it preceded the writing of the part of the work we know. The elements of the work's overall structure, then, its foundation, must certainly be in

"Alyosha Karamazov and the Hagiographic Hero" [editor's title] by Valentina A. Vetlovskaya. From *Poetika romana "Brat'ia Karamazovy"* (Leningrad: Nauka, 1977), pp. 163–83. Copyright 1977 by Nauka, Leningrad, U.S.S.R. Reprinted with slight abridgement of the footnotes by permission of the author and VAAP (All-Union Association of Author's Rights) in the U.S.S.R. Translated from the Russian by Nancy Pollak and Susanne Fusso.

[1]*The Brothers Karamazov*, trans. by Constance Garnett, Modern Library, 1950, p. xviii. All subsequent references are to this edition. (Translator's note.)

place in the work as we know it—indeed, they must even be partially visible. Otherwise the reader would not have been informed in the introduction that the two novels have the "essential unity of the whole"; in fact, there would be no question at all of any essential unity. The introductory remarks provide some indication of the sense of the whole. The opening phrase of the introduction speaks of a biography: "In beginning the biography of my hero, Aleksey Fyodorovich Karamazov," etc. The narrator continues: "I have two novels and only one biography." What is important here, first, is that the narrator-author conceives of the whole as a biography, and, second, that Aleksey Fyodorovich Karamazov is the center of this biography. The preeminence of precisely this hero is emphasized throughout the entire story, in spite of the fact that the first novel is called *The Brothers Karamazov*.

The first line of the novel, closely related to the introduction, reads as follows: "Aleksey Fyodorovich Karamazov was the third son of . . . a landowner . . . in our district." The main hero is singled out. Further, the introductory story of Alyosha appears in a special chapter entitled, "The Third Son, Alyosha." By contrast, the more laconic and dry accounts of Dmitry and Ivan appear in chapters that seem to diminish rather than accentuate the importance of these heroes: "He Gets Rid of his Eldest Son," "The Second Marriage and the Second Family" (here Fyodor Pavlovich is in the foreground).

We may recall at this point that the word used for "biography," *zhizneopisanie*, signifies "*vita*." The narrator of *The Brothers Karamazov* emerges—not obtrusively, but clearly enough—as the narrator of a *vita*, with his "main" hero, Alyosha, as hero-saint.[2] The point deserves special emphasis. In this connection I. P. Eryomin has written about the life of Theodosius of Pechersk:

> From his first appearance in Nestor's Chronicle, Theodosius of Pechersk is presented to the reader in the "seraphic" image of the ideally positive Christian hero-saint. And he continues in the

[2]A. L. Volynsky, in connection with the portrait characterization of Alyosha in the novel, noted the latter circumstance: "His [Alyosha's—V. V.] quiet gaze, the longish . . . oval of his face, the animation of expression—all this merges into the sort of icon-like image found in old tsarist documents—an image in which there is nothing provocative, nothing sharply individual." A. L. Volynskii, *Tsarstvo Karamazovykh* (St. Petersburg, 1901), pp. 148–149.

same basic image through the entire *vita*, accompanied by prayerfully reverential epithets. . . . Even in early youth, he is "one of God's elect," an "earthly angel" and a "heavenly human being." "Drawn to God's love," even in childhood he reveals virtues not usually possessed by an ordinary person in such a totality; he performs acts that go beyond all norms of everyday human conduct: these acts—his spiritual exploits—evoke pious consternation in some people, in others, "unreasoning ones," reproaches and even derision.[3]

The basic motifs and, in part, the tone of the preliminary characterization of Alyosha remind the reader of the typical hagiographical tale. Thus, Alyosha has been living in the monastery "for the past year, . . . and seemed willing to be cloistered there for the rest of his life." "He was . . . an early lover of humanity," the narrator further explains, "and that he adopted the monastic life was simply because at that time it struck him, so to say, as the ideal escape for his soul, struggling from the darkness of worldly wickedness to the light of love." The narrator will return to this motif again.

The opposition of the "darkness of earthly malice" and the "light of love," and of (earthly) darkness and (heavenly) light in general, is a metaphor common to the *vita* narrative, and one that goes back to the evangelists' texts. (This opposition is consistently pursued up to the end of the novel.)

Like the typical hero of a hagiographic narrative, even in early youth Alyosha feels the urge to depart from the vain world, because earthly passions are alien to him.

The complex relations between the ideal hero of the *vita* and the surrounding world make this hero strange to ordinary people and ordinary perception. This is the way Alyosha is presented to the reader. The narrator speaks right away of a strangeness, a certain eccentricity in him, but at the same time explains that these qualities do not, nevertheless, signify isolation: ". . . on the contrary, it happens sometimes that such a person [the eccentric—V. V.], I dare say, carries within himself the very heart of the universal, and the rest of the men of his epoch have for some reason been temporarily torn from it. . . ." As a result Alyosha is both set off against other people (this is typical

[3]Eryomin, I. P., "K kharakteristike Nestora kak pisatelia," in his *Literatura drevnei Rusi* (Moscow-Leningrad, 1966), p. 30.

for the hero of a *vita*), and closely linked to them, because it is impossible to go far from the "heart," impossible to entirely break off from it. Such a twist is unusual for a *vita*.

The desire for seclusion, the unchildlike pensiveness and concentration of the young Alyosha, his alienation from the playfulness and joyfulness typical of children, pointed out by the narrator, develop the same idea of the hero's "strangeness" and "eccentricity." Such a development is also typical of the *vita* narrative.[4] But the "gift for arousing a special love for oneself," confirmed many times subsequently, is a sign of that side of Alyosha's character that, despite any strangeness (or, perhaps, because of that strangeness), makes him dear to all people.

"He never tried to show off among his schoolfellows" is the slightly altered expression of the motif of humility, the absence of pride typical of the hero of the *vita*. This motif is reiterated in the report that Alyosha "never resented an insult. It would happen that an hour after the offence he would address the offender or answer some question with as trustful and candid an expression as though nothing had happened between them" (I, 1, iv).

The absence of pride, along with the complete indifference to worldly goods (money, for example, both his own and that of others) is emphasized by the words: "Another feature characteristic of him—and very much so—was that he never worried about whose means he was living on. In this respect he was the complete opposite of his older brother Ivan Fyodorovich. . . ." With regard to this lack of the vain and sensitive pride with which his older brother is endowed, the narrator considers it necessary to note again the strangeness, the "apparent" holy-foolery of his "main" and "beloved" hero. (It is important that this holy-foolery comes not from indifference or incivility in relation to others but, on the contrary, from an extreme and perhaps naïve trustfulness and sympathy toward people.)

Alyosha's "wild fanatical modesty and chastity" also belongs to the obligatory attributes of the hero of the *vita*—another feature that makes him strange from an ordinary point of view and that, for

---

[4]See, for example, Nestor's account of the childhood of Theodosius: "Neither did he draw near to playing children, as is the habit of young people, but lo he abhorred their games." *Kievo-Pecherskii paterik*, introduction and notes by Prof. Dm. Abramovich (Kiev, 1931), p. 23.

example, makes "all his schoolfellows from the bottom class to the top want to mock at him" and to look upon him "with compassion" (I, 1, iv).

In general, the motifs that are enumerated here exhaust the preliminary characterization of Alyosha. They are all marked and coordinated with the usual representation of the hero of the *vita*, who, even in childhood, exhibits the uncommon characteristics of the future great ascetic and saint.

Other motifs, too, are heard, in a very muffled form, but nevertheless from the beginning—motifs that contrast with those just introduced and that are apparently intended to point not just to the future great ascetic, but also to the future (perhaps also great) sinner.[5] Rather than analyzing them, however, let us merely say that the motives that compel Alyosha to elect the monastery as the lot most congenial to him also make this choice rather flimsy. The hero aspires to "truth" and to "great deeds" and wants to achieve these things as hastily as possible but, starting from this same aspiration, others go the opposite road. Alyosha "was convinced of the existence of God and immortality" (I, 1, v), but after some time he could be "convinced" by something else (after all, he is only beginning to live). Alyosha encounters an extraordinary elder in the monastery and falls in love with him (I, 1, iv, v), but this encounter is fortuitous. Moreover, too strong a feeling of love for the elder alone is not such an unconditionally good thing as it might at first appear. These and similar considerations all arise in the reader's mind not at once, but only later, when the motifs of Alyosha's preliminary characterization begin to recur. Acquiring additional hints and associations, they take on an ambiguous character, leading the reader to contemplate the idea of turns for the worse in the fate of the main hero.

For example, the teachings of the elder make it clear that belief in God, which inspires the young hero, acquires the force of conviction only when it is the result of "the experience of active love" (I, 2, iv). This "active" love is "a harsh and dreadful thing," it is "labor and fortitude, and thus for some people, perhaps, a whole science." Such a love the elder contrasts with "contemplative" love, which "is greedy

---

[5]During the last period of his life, as is well known, Dostoevsky was extremely interested in the idea of writing a *Life of a Great Sinner*.

for immediate action, rapidly performed and in the sight of all" (I, 2, iv).

With the exception of the moment of self-admiration (which is in no way connected with Alyosha), everything in the characterization of "contemplative" love corresponds to the feeling with which Alyosha enters on the "monastic road." The hero is not yet ready for an "active" love, for the "harsh and dreadful," for "labor and fortitude." Therefore his choice, despite the fact that it is natural for this essentially saintly hero, has as yet the most hasty and preliminary character. It perhaps serves as a premonitory allusion to the future, but it is not very important in the present, for the hero begins directly from that with which he should have ended.

As a result the image of the main hero of the "biography" is presented as mobile, capable of further change, and lacking that schematic straightforwardness and fixity of form which burdens the typical hero of a *vita*. Let us stress that this changeability and mobility is indicated not so much in spite of the hagiographic canon, as within its boundaries, thanks to the ambiguity, created by the narration, of certain motifs originating in that canon.

It is precisely because Alyosha is not yet ready to serve God and the "truth," as he then imagined it, that the elder sends his "quiet boy" out of the monastery: "This is not your place for the time. I bless you for great service in the world. Yours will be a long pilgrimage . . . You will have to bear *all* before you come back. There will be much to do. But I don't doubt you, and so I send you forth . . . Work, work unceasingly . . ." (I, 2, vii). The fact that Alyosha is really still too young, unstable, and unconfirmed in his (still naïve) beliefs, is corroborated yet again by his reaction to the elder's words. "Alyosha started, when the elder said, '. . . leave the monastery. Go away for good.'" The hero is perplexed, confused, frightened. "But how could he be left without him [the elder—V. V.]? How could he live without seeing and hearing him? Where should he go? He had told him not to weep, and to leave the monastery. Good God! It was long since Alyosha had known such anguish" (I, 2, vii).

The above-cited motifs (on the one hand, the hero's uncommonness even in early youth, his decision to go into a monastery; on the other, his lack of inner preparation for this exploit, his dispatch into the world for such preparation) signify that in this case we are dealing with the organic combination in one character of the two usual types of hagiographic hero. The first type is the hero who senses, almost from infancy, his lofty calling, and subsequently follows it without swerving (like Theodosius of Pechersk or Sergius of Radonezh). The second type is the hero who turns to God and gives himself up to the same asceticism after many trials, mistakes and errors (Ephraim Sirin). Alyosha's dispatch from the monastery does confront him with this set of trials, for in relation to the hero of the *vita*, the world can only appear in its tempting aspect.

After the presentation of the main hero, a motif arises that links his name with that of Aleksey the Man of God. This motif is at first heard obliquely. The hero of the *vita*, widely known in its time, is only recalled to the reader's mind. The occasion for this reminder is the elder's conversation with one of the devout women, who is wasting away with grief over her dead boy. To the elder's question as to what her son was called, the mother answers:

> "Aleksey, Father."
> "A sweet name. After Aleksey, the Man of God?"
> "Of God, Father, of God, Aleksey the Man of God!"
> "What a saint he was! I will remember him, mother . . ." (I, 2, iii)

Since the name of the main hero has already been mentioned and he himself has been presented to the reader in a hagiographic halo, the reminder of Aleksey the Man of God brings to mind certain details of the "biography" that support the idea of Alyosha's closeness to the hagiographic hero mentioned here.

Aleksey the Man of God was born in Rome; his parents were rich and distinguished Romans: "Under the emperors Arcadius and Honorius, at the end of the fourth century, there lived in Rome a distinguished man by the name of Euphimian, and his wife Aglaida. . . ."[6]

---

[6]*Izbrannye zhitiia sviatykh, kratko izlozhennye po rukovodstvu Chetikh Minei*, 2nd ed., revised and supplemented, (Moscow, 1860), March 17. This edition was in Dostoevsky's library. See L. Grossman, *Biblioteka Dostoevskogo* (Odessa, 1919), p. 154. Especially interested in the *vita* of Aleksey the Man of God, Dostoevsky undoubtedly did not limit himself to the short exposition of it in this edition. The *Lives of the Saints* by Dimitrius of Rostov and the *Prologue*, quite authoritative and accessible in their time, were well known to him.

In the version of the life found in the *Lives of the Saints* by Dimitrius of Rostov, we read: "There was in ancient Rome a pious man by the name of Euphimian, at the time of the pious emperors Arcadius and Honorius, great among the nobles and exceedingly wealthy. . . ." In the *Prologue* version of the life of Aleksey the Man of God we read: "He was from ancient Rome, the son of Euphimian the patrician, his mother was Aglaida. . . ."[7]

Clearly it is not by chance that it is precisely in the chapter, "The Third Son, Alyosha," that the portrait of Fyodor Pavlovich is given, which ends with the words: "He was fond indeed of making fun of his own face, though, I believe, he was well satisfied with it. He used particularly to point to his nose, which was not very large, but very delicate and conspicuously aquiline. 'A regular Roman nose,' he used to say, 'with my goitre I've quite the countenance of an ancient Roman patrician of the decadent period' " (I, 1, iv). To be sure, the evident resemblance between Fyodor Pavlovich and the father of the ancient hero of the *vita*, who was by habit quite pious, is confined to this casual remark.

Of course, this remark is important in general as well: it likens the present to the past, gives the "particular" a broad significance, because the "confusion," decay, and "fall" of present-day Russian life is related here to the "fall" of ancient Rome. If the analogy is continued, however, then a rebirth out of this "fall," like the rebirth of ancient (pagan) Rome, must appear on the paths of Christianity. Moreover, because Rome was unable to deal with this problem in its own time, since, as Ivan explains, "Rome . . . retained too much of pagan civilization and culture" (I, 2, v), then clearly the problem stands now before the "fallen" and also decaying Russia. All this is in accordance with Slavophile ideas and the Slavophile conception of the history of the West and Russia, with which Dostoevsky sympathized. If one believes the testimony of Vladimir Solovyov, these themes should have been strongly heard in the second novel.[8] In the first novel they are

---

[7]Both the *vita* in the edition of Dimitrius of Rostov and the *Prologue* redaction are cited according to the texts included by V. P. Adrianova-Perets in the appendix to her *Zhitie Alekseia cheloveka bozhiia v drevnei russkoi literature i narodnoi slovesnosti* (Petrograd, 1917), pp. 501, 512.

[8]Vl. Solov'ev, *Tri rechi v pamiati Dostoevskogo (1881–1883 gg.)*, (Moscow, 1884), pp. 20–21.

only hinted at, and they are not the themes that are important for us now. We are interested in Alyosha and his connections with the hero of the ancient *vita*. It is likely that Fyodor Pavlovich's claim to resemblance to the ancient Roman is, in this respect, a significant detail.

One would think that one of Alyosha's recollections, which originated in his infancy, has the same significance—a circumstance over which the narrator lingers with a degree of conscientiousness that is strange, it would seem, for such a trifle, and to which he subsequently returns. Alyosha "remembered one still summer evening . . . ; in a corner of the room the holy image, before it a lighted lamp, and on her knees before the image his mother, sobbing hysterically with cries and moans, snatching him up in both arms, squeezing him close till it hurt, and praying for him to the Mother of God, holding him out in both arms to the image as though to put him under the Mother's protection . . ." (I, 1, iv).

The mother's prayer for her son, presented here as Alyosha's most vivid recollection, is clearly a modification of a motif in the life of Aleksey the Man of God, in which the prayer originates either from the mother alone, as here (and as, for example, in the redaction of Dimitrius of Rostov), or from both parents (as in the edition in Dostoevsky's library), and where it precedes the miraculous birth of the future saint. Thus in both cases the hero's later career is linked with an anticipatory parental supplication, anguish over the son and tears.[9] Also important is the fact that the prayer of Alyosha's pious mother appeals precisely to the Mother of God and to her protection.

In various redactions of this *vita* the saint, for whose sake God has been implored, leaving home, gives himself up to an ascetic life on the porch (or in the vestibule) of the temple of the Mother of God. After a certain time the Mother of God orders her servant to bring Aleksey into this temple, "for his prayer rises to God, and like a crown on the royal head, so does the Holy Spirit rest upon him."[10]

In the sacred poem about Aleksey, which Dostoevsky knew as well

---

[9]This motif is encountered not only in the *vita* of Aleksey the Man of God. It is generally diffused in *vita* literature.

[10]*Izbrannye zhitiia sviatykh* . . . , March 17.

as he knew the *vita*, the Mother of God also sends the saint back to his former home, to his father, mother, and spouse.[11]

In the novel, the sending of Alyosha from the monastery back into the world and also back to his relatives corresponds to this sending of the saint back to his relatives—by God's will (in the *vita*), or by the command of the Mother of God (in the sacred poem). Alyosha is sent back into the world by his spiritual father, Father Zosima. It is subsequently pointed out by Ivan that this is a "divine" elder, a "Pater Seraphicus," and consequently his will is the will of God. Not by chance, the Mother of God is also linked to the elder from the very beginning; among the few trifling, briefly noted objects in his elder's cell, the icon of the Mother of God is singled out and emphasized twice: "The cell was not very large and had a faded look. It contained nothing but the necessary furniture, of course and poor quality. There were two pots of flowers in the window, and a number of icons in the corner—among them, one of the Mother of God, of enormous dimensions and painted, apparently, long before the schism. Before it a lamp was burning. Near it were two other icons in shining settings, and, next to them, carved cherubims, china eggs, a Catholic cross of ivory, and a Mater Dolorosa embracing it . . ." (I, 2, ii).

Clearly, the combination of the Orthodox and Catholic images of the Mother of God in the elder's cell, like the fact that the elder is at once a Russian ascetic and a Pater Seraphicus, is accorded particular

[11]An analysis of the artistic text points definitively to Dostoevsky's close familiarity with this sacred poem. I am grateful to G. M. Fridlender for kindly drawing my attention to a letter of February 13, 1873, from T. I. Filippov to Dostoevsky, which contains one of the variants of the sacred poem about St. Aleksey. Concluding this variant, partly transmitted word for word, partly retold, Filippov writes: "Here, dear Fyodor Mikhailovich, are the verses you need, with a little appendage which won't bother anything, and which might even be useful in illuminating the whole epos" (Pushkin Institute of Russian Literature, 29883.SSXb.12). The composition of the poem has been altered in T. I. Filippov's variant. First come the laments of the parents over the deceased Aleksey (it was precisely the laments that apparently interested Dostoevsky). Then comes the little "appendage"—the beginning of the poem and everything that precedes the laments. Filippov's variant was not complete and was not the only one known to Dostoevsky.

significance here. After all, the life of Aleksey the Man of God is a very ancient *vita*. The events described in it date back to the end of the fourth and beginning of the fifth centuries, i.e., to the time when the division of the Christian church had not yet occurred. This life is familiar to Orthodox and Catholics alike.[12] The Mother of God, at whose temple the saintly youth appears, is, as it were, at once the Orthodox Mother of God and the Catholic Mater Dolorosa. Father Zosima, who sends Alyosha into the world, to his relatives, being at once a Russian Orthodox ascetic and a Pater Seraphicus, reduplicates this same motif.

Dostoevsky, though not overly concerned with formal matters (the precise reproduction of the sequence of hagiographical motifs and their literal transmission), nonetheless has adhered to the hagiographic outline in the most important points of Alyosha's story. The elder, for example, sends Alyosha back not only to his father and brothers (Alyosha himself recalls his deceased mother and upon arrival seeks out her grave), but also to his (here, it is true, future) bride.

The complexity of Alyosha's relations with Liza Khokhlakova is noted from the very beginning: Alyosha's attachment to Liza countervails his lofty goals.

> "Why do you make fun of him [Alyosha—V. V.] like that, naughty girl?" the elder says to her. Liza suddenly and quite unexpectedly blushed. Her eyes flashed and her face became quite serious. She began speaking quickly and nervously in a warm and resentful voice:
> "Why has he forgotten everything, then? ... No, now he's saving his soul! Why have you put that long gown on him? If he runs he'll fall."
> And suddenly she hid her face in her hands and went off into terrible, uncontrollable ... laughter. The elder listened to her with a smile, and blessed her tenderly. ...

[12]D. Dashkov gives a detailed exposition, comparative analysis, and criticism of several Latin redactions of the *vita*. See D. Dashkov, "Stikhi i skazaniia pro Alekseia bozhiia cheloveka," in *Besedy v obshchestve liubitelei rossiiskoi slovesnosti pri imp. Moskovskom universitete*, No. 2, (Moscow, 1868). Dostoevsky was possibly familiar with this work. Other sources were probably also known to him. For example, at the end of the 1870s, the *Gesta Romanorum* were published, in Vol. 2 of which (St. Petersburg, 1878) there is one of the redactions of the *vita* of St. Aleksey.

"I will certainly send him," the elder decided (I, 2, iv).

Let us note that it is hardly by chance that Alyosha's future bride and spouse is called Liza. In the Russian versions of the life of Aleksey the Man of God, the name of the bride and spouse of the saint is not mentioned, but several variants of the sacred poem speak either of Katerina or of Lizaveta:

> The father permitted him to wed
> A princess renowned and promised to him,
> Lizaveta by name.[13]

In the elder's conversation with the devout women, where the name of Aleksey the Man of God is heard for the first time, the name of Lizaveta is heard as well:

> "Is that your little girl?"
> "My little girl, Father, Lizaveta."
> "May the Lord bless you both, you and your babe Lizaveta . . ."
> He blessed them all and bowed low to them (I, 2, iii).

The chapter "A Lady of Little Faith" (following "Devout Peasant Women") involves four characters: elders (Alyosha's spiritual father, Father Zosima; Liza's mother, Mme Khokhlakova) and minors (Alyosha, Liza). In view of the consistency of motifs, Alyosha's link with Aleksey the Man of God and Liza's with Lizaveta, the bride and spouse of the saint in the Russian sacred poem, can be assumed, while the elder's firm intention to send Alyosha to Liza after her mother's words and her own takes on the character of a betrothal. Subsequently this betrothal is confirmed. Alyosha says to Liza: "I shall be leaving the monastery altogether in a few days. If I go into the world, I must marry. I know that. *He* [the elder, Dostoevsky's emphasis—

---

[13]*Kaliki perekhozhie. Sbornik stikhov i issledovanie P. Bessonova*, (Moscow, 1861) var. No. 28 (hereinafter the variants of the sacred poem about Aleksey the Man of God from the collections of Kireevsky, Bessonov and Varentsov are indicated in the text of the book). We basically rely on the texts of Bessonov, because Dostoevsky could not have missed them: the collection was widely known. Dostoevsky was apparently also familiar with the editions of P. Kireevsky (*Russkie narodnye pesni sobrannye Petrom Kireevskim*, Part 1 (Moscow, 1848) and V. Varentsov (*Sbornik russkikh dukhovnykh stikhov, sostavlennyi V. Varentsovym* (St. Petersburg, 1860), in each of which there is also a variant of the poem that interests us. . . .

V. V.] told me to marry, too. Whom could I marry better than you—
and who would have me except you? I have been thinking it over" (II,
5, i).

Aleksey the Man of God, the hero of the hagiographic narrative
and of the sacred poem, is mentioned a few more times later in the
novel. Thus, ordering his monks and devotees to read the sacred
writings to the people, the elder also speaks of the *Lives of the Saints*
and advises them to choose therefrom, at least "the life of Aleksey, the
Man of God" (II, 6, i). Later, in the scene at Grushenka's, in response
to Alyosha's request that he not grow angry and condemn others,
Rakitin, in irritation, replies directly: "You were so primed up with
your elder's teaching last night that now you have to let it off on me,
Alyoshenka, Man of God!" (III, 7, iii). The seminarian Rakitin could
not casually call Alyosha by the name of the saint. The diminutive
form used by Rakitin, entirely alien to the *vita*, is known, however, to
the sacred poem, in which it is, of course, uttered in a different spirit:

> He [the father of the saint—V. V.] calls the
>   holy men to his house
> And gives a name to the baby,
> He gave him a sacred little name,—
> Lekseyushko, little Man of God. (Bessonov, var. no. 32)

The epithet "prince," which Grushenka accords to Alyosha in the
same scene, comes either from the *vita*, where this word is encountered extremely rarely, to be sure, or (what is much more likely) from
the sacred poem, where it arises quite naturally against the background of the usual folk appellations, and is to be found pretty much
everywhere.

Later Mitya once again connects his younger brother with Aleksey
the Man of God: "Damn ethics. I am done for, Aleksey, I am, you
Man of God! I love you more than anyone. It makes my heart yearn to
look at you" (IV, 11, iv). Thus a motif (Alyosha–Aleksey the Man of
God) that is introduced at first tentatively and as though in passing, is
heard at the end of the novel in full force.

As for the significance of this chain of motifs in the system of the
entire novel, let us first of all emphasize the fact that, in connecting his
hero with Aleksey the Man of God, Dostoevsky selects the central
figure of the most popular *vita*. "One may say without exaggeration,"

writes V. P. Adrianova-Perets in her study devoted specifically to this *vita*, "that not one of the ascetics of the Russian land provoked such interest, aroused such sympathy for his life, as did Aleksey the Man of God."[14] In particular, the scholar sees the reason for such popularity in the fact that this *vita* absorbed many beloved motifs of Russian hagiography (such motifs are also heard in *The Brothers Karamazov*, and several of them are enumerated above).

> Combined ably into a single artistic story . . . they were associated in the consciousness of the Russian reader with a large number of familiar images and ideas, and thus they favored the popularity and the durability of this *vita*, which gave an impetus to further treatments both in literature and in popular poetry, in Russia as well.[15]

The sacred poem about Aleksey which Dostoevsky had in mind as well as the *vita* is just such a popular poetic reworking.

The basic features of the *vita* of Aleksey the Man of God and of the sacred poem about him are Aleksey's departure from home to perform the exploits customary for the hero of a *vita*, and his life in his parents' home upon his return.[16] It is precisely from the time when the saint, unrecognized, lodges in his parents' home, that a grave temptation begins: the saint is faced not with a rejection of the world

---

[14]V. P. Adrianova, *Zhitie Alekseia cheloveka bozhiia v drevnei russkoi literature i narodnoi slovesnosti*, p. 127.

[15]*Ibid.*, p. 144.

[16]In contrast to the *vita*, the poem sometimes emphasizes Aleksey's desire, in his departure from home, to serve not only his own salvation but that of his relatives:

. . . I went to an alien land,
to pray for papa's sins,
to work for mama's sins! (Var. of Kireevsky)

See also Bessonov, var. Nos. 29, 30. An echo of this motif (which is omitted by T. I. Filippov's variant) appears in *The Brothers Karamazov*, in Fyodor Pavlovich's reply to his son's request to allow him to go back to the monastery: "After all I'll miss you, Alyosha . . . However, here's a good opportunity: pray for us sinners; sitting here, we've sinned too much. I've been thinking all the time about this: who's ever going to pray for me? Is there such a person in the world?" (I, 1, iv).

in order to save himself and, perhaps, others, but with a sojourn in the world for those same goals.

In accordance with the spirit and meaning of the *vita* and the poem about Saint Aleksey, Alyosha Karamazov's rapprochement with the world and his relations at first turns out to be a trial for him. The narrative is constructed so that after the scene in the monastery, which serves as the starting point of the action, Alyosha is sent on errands by first one, then another character; he listens to others' stories, usually filled with perturbation and grief, that cast doubt on the affirmation of God's endless love, charity, and beneficence. The tempting character of these encounters, commissions, and confessions is conveyed through various motifs.

Among these motifs, the indication of Alyosha's suffering (in contrast to his joyful sojourn in the monastery and his communion with the elder) is one of the most constant and important ones. "This request [of Katerina Ivanovna—V. V.] and the necessity of going had at once aroused an uneasy feeling in his heart, and this feeling had grown more and more painful all the morning . . ." (I, 3, iii). So begins Alyosha's ascetic life in the world and his "ordeals." On the way to Katerina Ivanovna, Alyosha's brother Mitya stops him:

> "I might have sent anyone, but I wanted to send an angel. . . ."
> "Did you really mean to send me?" cried Alyosha with a distressed expression (I, 3, iii).

Alyosha's suffering, which reveals the gravity of others' appeals and commissions for this "quiet boy," is contrasted with the joy of those who, voluntarily or not, tempt Alyosha: " 'Oh, gods,' exclaims, again, Mitya, 'I thank you for sending him to me by the back way, and he came to me like the golden fish to the silly old fishermen in the fable!' " (I, 3, iii). " 'Here he is! Here he is!' yelled Fyodor Pavlovich, highly delighted at seeing Alyosha. 'Join us. Sit down. Coffee is a lenten dish, but it's hot and good. I don't offer you brandy, you're keeping the fast. But would you like some? No; I'd better give you some of our famous liqueur. . . . Now we've a treat for you, in your own line, too. It'll make you laugh. Balaam's ass has begun talking to us here . . .' " (I, 3, vi). "Alyosha left his father's house," the narrator further recounts, "feeling even more exhausted and dejected in spirit than when he had entered it. . . . He felt something bordering upon despair, which he had never known till then" (I, 3, x).

The world into which Alyosha is sent by the elder disturbs and torments the young hero.

> Why, why, had he gone forth? Why had he sent him "into the world"? thinks Alyosha, returning to the monastery the very first day of his "travels." Here was peace. Here was holiness. But there was confusion, there was darkness in which one lost one's way and went astray at once . . . (I, 3, xi).

The day after this sorrowful return Father Paisy, again seeing Alyosha off "into the world," pronounces unexpected parting words: "Remember, young man, unceasingly . . . that worldly science, which has become a great power, has . . . analyzed everything divine handed down to us in the holy books. After this cruel analysis the learned of this world have nothing left of all that was sacred of old" (II, 4, i). Hastening to "protect the young soul entrusted to him," Father Paisy speaks words that are of the utmost important for an understanding of subsequent events: ". . . you are young," he addresses Alyosha, "and the temptations of the world are great and beyond your strength to endure" (II, 4, i).

Alyosha's meeting with his father, then with the schoolchildren, then the "lacerations," of which the gravest is the last (the confession of Captain Snegiryov, in which the theme of the innocently suffering child is heard), continues the grave series of "temptations" of Alyosha. The gloomy impressions from his first days of acquaintance with the world, even before the conversation with his brother Ivan, behind whom stands "worldly science," make Alyosha let slip a phrase expressing something that was "already undoubtedly tormenting him": "And perhaps I don't even believe in God" (II, 5, i).

Alyosha's sudden confession, on the one hand, and Father Paisy's warning, on the other, uttered on the same day as the brothers' meeting in the tavern, both have a very direct relation to that meeting. Ivan's tempting speech, which comes along with the other temptations but is stronger than they are, is addressed to the hero, who is already disturbed by the world's "darkness." Here the suffering child, familiar to the reader and to Alyosha through the captain's confession, arises once more on the lips of the "learned" Ivan, now as a kind of "emblem" and basic argument of "worldly science," which has left "nothing . . . of all that was sacred of old." Having told Alyosha about the general and the persecuted child Ivan asks:

"Well—what did he deserve? To be shot? To be shot for the satisfaction of our moral feelings? Speak, Alyosha!"

"To be shot," murmured Alyosha, lifting his eyes to Ivan with a pale, twisted smile.

"Bravo!" cried Ivan, delighted. "If even you say so . . ." (II, 5, 4).

The delight of the atheist Ivan, in accordance with the author's conception, must not only indicate temptation, as did earlier the delight of Mitya or Fyodor Pavlovich, but also compromise Alyosha's words in the eyes of the reader: this delight signifies that here Alyosha proves to be too close to his older brother. Ivan continues thus: "You're a pretty monk! So there is a little devil sitting in your heart, Alyosha Karamazov!" In the author's opinion, the reader must guess that if even the atheist Ivan perceives no sanctity in Alyosha's reaction ("Shoot him!"), and begins to speak of a "devil," then it must be that there is no such sanctity.

Fulfilling others' requests, listening to others (above all his brother Ivan), Alyosha gives way to temptation. The "darkness" of the world does not remain alien to this hero's heart, and not only because he is too young, but also because Alyosha, as he himself explains more than once, is a Karamazov. Notwithstanding his strangeness, Alyosha is the same sort of man as everyone else (in contrast to the *vita* and the poem, in the novel this motif is carried out quite definitely). The very deep affinity of the "angel" Alyosha for the other "sinners" presumes, for the young and inexperienced hero, the possibility of committing the same errors as the others. "Yes, yes, it is he, it is Pater Seraphicus, he will save me—from him and forever!" (II, 5, v)—races helplessly through Alyosha's mind when he hurries to the monastery after the conversation with Ivan.

The death of Father Zosima and everything that follows it is a trial that makes Alyosha's heart overflow with suffering, and provokes his reproaches and indignation. Speaking of these events, the narrator distinguishes two circumstances that "exerted a very strong influence on the heart and soul of the main . . . hero of the story" (III, 7, i). The first is Ivan's pernicious influence on Alyosha. "Oh, it was not that something of the fundamental, elemental, so to speak, faith of his soul had been shaken. . . . Yet a vague but tormenting and evil impression left by his conversation with Ivan the day before, suddenly revived again now in his soul and seemed forcing its way to the surface of his consciousness" (III, 7, ii). Outraged by the injustice of Heaven in relation to the deceased elder, Alyosha repeats Ivan's words: "I am not rebelling against my God; I simply 'don't accept His world.'" The blasphemy of these words on the lips of the young ascetic is obvious. "... This is a jolly fine chance and mustn't be missed ..." Rakitin immediately decides (III, 7, ii). The second circumstance that the narrator emphasizes (both justifying and condemning Alyosha) is that Alyosha loved his spiritual father, Father Zosima, too much: "The fact is that all the love that lay concealed in his pure young heart for everyone and everything had, for the past year, been concentrated—and perhaps wrongly so—on one being, now deceased. It is true that that being had for so long been accepted by him as his ideal, that all his young strength and energy could not but turn towards that ideal, even to the forgetting at the moment of everyone and everything" (III, 7, ii). These explanations by the narrator are extremely important.

Growing indignant and grumbling, Alyosha, like Ivan, demands "supreme justice," which, in the young hero's opinion, has been "violated." Instead of the glory and triumph of the deceased righteous man, whom he loved with an exceptional love, Alyosha sees this righteous man "degraded and dishonored" (III, 7, 2). The narrator insistently strives to show that Alyosha's error (his grumbling and indignation) is rooted in the exceptional nature of his love, which—in its own way, of course, but essentially the same as with Ivan—destroys the living connection between things. Alyosha involuntarily forgets that his elder belongs entirely to the world, "sinful" and "stinking" in its sins, and thus bears the guilt for its ugliness along with everyone else. According to the logic of the narration it emerges that the elder bears this guilt to an even greater degree than do others: remitting others' sins, he takes them upon his own soul and, consequently, answers for them, for it is clearly only under such a condition that he has the right to forgive others.[17] The idea of the connection between each person

[17]N. Kostomarov retells a legend, communicated to him by F. I. Buslaev and known here and in the West in many variants, about a sinner who killed his father and seduced his mother. He seeks a priest who could remit his sin: "The sinner went to several priests to beg forgiveness, but *since not one could bring himself to forgive him and take responsibility for such a sin, he killed them....*"

and everyone else, and the responsibility of each for everyone, repeated many times by the elder himself during his life, underlies the artistic narrative here as well. But it is precisely this idea that Alyosha has forgotten in his grief.

If Alyosha had loved the elder more "correctly," that is, not with an exceptional love but in the same way that he loved others, he would not have found grounds in the righteous man's "shame" for the condemnation of "God's world." Everything in this world is connected. And just as there are none who are completely righteous, so there are none who are completely sinful. For this reason the scene of Alyosha and Grushenka, coming after the scene of the young hero's bitter suffering, harmoniously complements the story about the righteous man's "shame." Here the sinful woman unexpectedly reveals a degree of love, reverence for sanctity, and compassion for her dispirited brother that, considering her "incorrect" view of things, would not be supposed of her. Thanks to this, Grushenka is able to encourage Alyosha: the loftiness of her soul, made manifest "at that moment," is the essential link in the chain of phenomena that, according to the author's conception, makes their entire relationship not frightfully incongruous but comforting and harmonious.

Alyosha's dream ("Cana of Galilee") naturally concludes these scenes. The boundlessness of God's love for all people and the joy of those who are united by this love are manifested here to the young ascetic as if before his very eyes. The link of everyone with each other,

---

(N. Kostomarov, "Iz mogil'nykh predanii. Legenda o krovosmesitele," *Sovremennik*, 1860, Vol. LXXX, Section I, p. 223). In the apocryphal "Voprosy Ioanna Bogoslova Avraamu na Eleonskoi gore," to the question whether the priest takes the sins of the confessor upon himself, the following answer is given: "If a son steals with his father, do they not bind him together with his father, and lead them both to trial, and don't they both pay for that theft? Child, *those also, the sin of the confessor and the priest, the sin is common to both, doing that he answers for him and takes his sins upon himself.*" N. S. Tikhonravov, *Pamiatniki starinnoi russkoi literatury, izdavaemye grafom Gr. Kushelevym-* p. 210; cf. "Voprosy sv. Ioanna Bogoslova o zhivykh i mertvykh . . . ," in *Pamiatniki starinnoj russkoj literatury, izdavaemye grafom Gr. Kushelevym-Bezborodko*, Issue 3 (St. Petersburg, 1862), p. 116. In the light of these parallels, the "breath of corruption" revealed after Zosima's death signifies that the "stink of sins," his own and others', no longer burden the elder. The italics in the quotations are mine.

salutary and joyful when God is among people (a circumstance which must be construed in a broad sense), staggers Alyosha's soul with ecstasy. The idea of the primordial beauty and purity of "God's world," and of the responsibility of all people for the fact that they make this beautiful world vicious, is what the author tries to emphasize in "Cana of Galilee." It is just this idea that Alyosha suddenly grasps, "for the rest of his life and forever and ever": "What was he weeping over? Oh! in his rapture he was weeping even over those stars, which were shining to him from the abyss of space . . . He longed to forgive everyone and for everything, and to beg forgiveness. Oh, not for himself, but for all men, for all and for everything. 'And others are praying for me too,' echoed again in his soul. . . . He had fallen on the earth a weak boy, but he rose up a resolute champion, and he knew and felt it suddenly at the very moment of his ecstasy" (III, 7, iv).

Thus the young ascetic's passionate and exceptional love for his spiritual father yields, at this important moment, to a just as passionate love for the world and for all people without exception. "He who loves everyone alike in compassion and indifferently," reasons Isaak Sirin, mentioned and quoted in *The Brothers Karamazov*, "has achieved perfection."[18] Alyosha (not intellectually, but emotionally) finds a way out of suffering in the joyful acceptance of "God's world," and in union with everything and everyone. This loving union with people, the intimate inclusion of them all (including the most sinful) in his soul eliminates the contradiction between love of God and love of people—the basic contradiction overcome by the hero of the ancient *vita*, Aleksey the Man of God. For such an unqualified love, the possibility of which is indicated by the moment of Alyosha's ecstasy, is itself, in the author's conception, divine love. " 'Someone visited my soul in that hour,' Alyosha would say afterwards, with firm faith in his words" (III, 7, iv). " 'Brothers,' the elder used to teach, 'have no fear of men's

[18]Isaak Sirin, *Slova podvizhnicheskie* (Moscow, 1858), p. 60. This idea is repeated: "When [a man—V. V.] sees all people . . as good, and no one seems to him impure or defiled, then he is truly pure in heart" (*ibid.*, p. 141). Among the surviving notes for the novel we read: "Elder: The main thing is not to lie. Not to store up possessions, to love (Damaskin, Sirin).' " F. M. Dostoevsky, *Polnoe sobranie sochinenii v tridtsati tomakh*, vol. XV (Leningrad, 1976), p. 320. He probably had in mind the discussions of genuine love by Ioann Damaskin and Isaak Sirin.

sin. Love a man even in his sin, for that is the semblance of Divine Love and is the highest love on earth. Love all God's creation, the whole and every grain of sand in it. . . . Love the animals, love the plants, love everything. If you love everything, you will perceive the divine mystery in things. Once you perceive it, you will begin to comprehend it better every day. And you will come at last to love the whole world with an all-embracing love' " (II, 6, iii).[19]

If the moment of Alyosha's ecstasy is prolonged (as the words of the elder prophesy) or if this moment really acquires the greatest significance in the hero's life (as the narrator foretells), the world will cease to play its tempting role for the young ascetic. When this world is revealed to the hero in the beauty and harmony of all its relations, and not in an ugly conglomeration of absurdities, when it evokes an ecstatic rapture, then there is no place for the condemnation of its creator. Dostoevsky clearly tries to carry out this idea.

True, it is possible that the moment of Alyosha's ecstasy before "God's world" is only an anticipation. It is possible that subsequently Alyosha will turn from the "correct road" once more. All this is possible. But if Alyosha does turn from this road, then it would certainly be in order for him to enter onto it later, once and for all. It is precisely this outcome that the logic of the artistic narrative demands.

A person who joyfully takes into his soul the entire world ("both the whole, and every grain of sand") without exception, accepting all people in spite of their "stinking sin," loving it all with an equally deep love, in other words, a person who comprehends the beauty and blessing of God's creation and along with it the beauty and blessing of the creator, is, of course, a "man of God." The world and God are harmoniously reconciled in the soul of this hero.

So Alyosha emerges (or must emerge) from the grave trial to which the "divine" elder sends him. And thus Dostoevsky interprets the central figure and the central confrontation of the *vita* of Aleksey the Man of God against a new background. In the continuation of the novel about Alyosha this interpretation would, it is likely, appear more clearly, but even now it is sufficiently obvious.

[19]Zosima's words, like the concluding scene of "Cana of Galilee," particularly rely on Isaak Sirin's discussion of higher perfection, included in the "passion of a man's heart for all creation, for men, for birds, for animals, for demons and all creatures" (Isaak Sirin, *Slova podvizhnicheskie*, p. 299).

Memory in
The Brothers Karamazov

Robert L. Belknap

During Dostoevsky's lifetime, memory became a respectable subject for experimental enquiry, after centuries as the object of religious or physiological speculation or of practical brochures on how not to forget names, books, speeches, etc. The new mnemonics came to Russia at the hands of two competing schools of psychology, the neurologists and the alienists. Each group had its eighteenth-century antecedents, its nineteenth-century clinical and theoretical achievements, and its special techniques for investigating the mind. For Dostoevsky's purposes, most scholars find the beginnings of the neurological approach in a famous passage in the *Dialogue between d'Alembert and Diderot*:

Diderot. Could you tell me what is the existence of a sentient being, with respect to itself?

D'Alembert. It is the consciousness of having been itself, from the first·instant of its thinking to the present moment.

Diderot. And on what is this consciousness based?

D'Alembert. On the memory of its actions.

Diderot. And without this memory?

D'Alembert. Without this memory, it would have no self at all, for feeling its existence only in the moment of the impression, it would have no account of its life. Its life would be an interrupted series of sensations linked by nothing.

Diderot. Well, what is memory? Whence comes it?

D'Alembert. From a certain accretive system which grows strong or weak and sometimes is altogether lost.

"Memory in *The Brothers Karamazov*" by Robert L. Belknap. From *American Contributions to the Eighth International Congress of Slavists*, vol. 2., *Literature*, edited by Victor Terras. (Slavica Publishers, Inc., Columbus, Ohio, 1978), pp. 24–40. Reprinted by permission of the publisher.

Diderot. So if a sentient being with this system appropriate for
memory links the impressions it receives, and by this linkage
forms an account which is that of its life, and acquires the consciousness of itself, then it denies, affirms, concludes, and
thinks?

D'Alembert. It seems so to me; I have just one more problem.

Diderot. You're wrong; you've lots more.

D'Alembert. But one principal one; it seems to me that we can only
think of a single thing at a time and that in order to form a
simple proposition, not to speak of these enormous chains of
reasoning which embrace in their orbit thousands of ideas, it is
necessary to have at least two things present, the object which
seems to fall under the eye of predication, and the quality which
is affirmed or denied with reference to it.

Diderot. I agree; and that has sometimes made me compare the
fibres in our organs to sentient vibrating strings. The sentient
vibrating string oscillates, resounds for a long time after being
plucked. This oscillation, this sort of inevitable resonance is what
keeps the object present while the predicating understanding is
occupied with the qualities appropriate to it. But vibrating
strings have still another quality; they make others tremble and
this is how a first idea recalls a second, the two a third, all three a
fourth, and so on without our being able to set limits to the
awakened, enchained ideas of a philosopher meditating or listening to himself in silence and darkness. This instrument makes
astounding leaps, and an idea once awakened can make an har-
monic tremble at an incomprehensible interval from it. If the
phenomenon is observed among sounding strings, inanimate
and separated, how would it fail to occur among points that are
animate and linked, among continuous and sentient fibres.[1]

Diderot's generating analogy in this passage resonates through the
history of thought from Pythagoras's strings to Pavlov's bells, but in
the 19th century it took on a special connection with positivism and
materialism all over Europe. While *The Brothers Karamazov* was gestat-
ing, Hippolyte Taine published his article on *Cerebral Vibrations and
Thought*, which can exemplify the approach taken by the many pro-
ponents of neurology whom Dostoevsky knew, ranging from Sechenov,
to Chernyshevsky, to Claude Bernard.

[1]Diderot, "Entretien entre Diderot et d'Alembert," in *Oeuvres* (Paris: Bib-
liothèque de la pléiade, 1951), p. 879.

Since mental phenomena are only more or less deformed or transformed sensations, let us compare a sensation with a molecular movement of the nervous centres. Let us take the sensation of the yellow of gold, of a sound like *ut*, that which the emanations of the lily produce, the taste of sugar, the pain of a cut, the sensation of tickling, of heat, of cold. The necessary and sufficient condition of such a sensation is an intestine movement in the grey substance of the annular protuberance, of the tubercula quadrigemina, perhaps of the thalamus opticus—in short, in the cells of a sensory centre; that this movement is unknown is of little consequence; whatever it be, it is always a displacement of molecules, more or less complicated and propagated; nothing more. Now what relation can we imagine between this displacement and a sensation. Cells, formed of a membrane and of one or several nuclei, are scattered through a granular substance, a sort of pulp or greyish jelly composed of nuclei and innumerable fibrils. . . .[2]

When juxtaposed to the Diderot passage, the Taine passage shows what had happened to vibrational neurology in a century and a half. For Diderot, the vibrations constitute an elaborated and illuminating simile for the retentive and associative powers of the mind. Taine realizes the trope; the microscope and the scalpel have anatomized the fibers, and Taine is certain that the movements are there merely awaiting discovery. Diderot is exploring the nature of thought through memory, which distinguishes beings which have a self from others. Taine is exploring it through sensation, which blurs any such distinction. Most important of all, from Dostoevsky's point of view, Diderot is working on a genuine puzzle with his intellectual equal. Taine's unselfconscious scientism is as patronizing as Bazarov's. The creator of Fyodor Karamazov could respect the creator of Rameau's nephew for his psychological insights, although Fyodor himself might mock Diderot as the emblematic unbeliever; but the detestation with which the underground man approached piano keys and organ stops, or with which Mitya Karamazov approached Claude Bernard were borrowed from Dostoevsky's own attitude towards the psychological

[2]Hippolyte Taine, "Cerebral vibrations and thought," *Journal of Mental Science*, No. 7101, April 1877, p. 1 (tr. from *Revue Philosophique de la France et de l'étranger*).

reductionism of the neurologists. The purest example of this attitude is probably his obsessively angry series of references in the 1877 notebooks to the sentence, "He is not a man but a lyre," which had been intended as praise for a public speaker.[3]

When Dostoevsky needed expert advice on a psychological question, he therefore wrote not to a neurologist, but to an alienist.[4] The eighteenth-century forerunners had also developed the underlying metaphor for this group, which was hydraulic rather than vibrational, and which persists in Freudian thinking to this day. By mid-century, Russian journals were comparing hallucinations to outbursting artesian waters, discussing the pressure of unfulfilled needs, and so on. This way of thinking came more from Mesmer's thin magnetic fluid than from the older doctrines of the humors or the still older Epicurean flux among the atoms of spirit. In the 1820s James Braid had divorced the practice of hypnotism from the suspect doctrines of magnetism, and Eliotson and others in England had begun using hypnotism for anesthesia and therapy, and accounts of amputations under hypnosis began to appear in the medical journals until superseded by ether. By the 1870s, Liébault and Bernheim at Nancy were working to separate the phenomena of suggestion from those of hypnotic sleep, or "somnambulism," as they called it. This distinction opened the way for Charcot, already a leading neurologist, to adopt hypnotism as one of his tools, and Charcot's work helped produce the Freudian synthesis which eventually drove both reflex conditioning and hypnotism out of most therapy for half a century. The central technique of these hypnotists focussed on the direct power of the repeated word. As one of its best practitioners, Jules Liégeois described it in the 1890s:

> I place myself facing the subject, seated or standing, and I invite him to look fixedly at me, without any extraordinary effort; after a few moments, I say to him, "You are going to feel a drowsiness; and imperious need of sleep is taking possession of you; your eyelids are becoming heavy. They are coming down. Your eyes are closing. You are going to sleep, sleep." Then a light pressure is brought to bear on the eyeballs, covered by the

---

[3]*Literaturnoe Nasledstvo*, Vol. 83 (Moscow, 1971), p. 426 and *passim*.
[4]E.g., F. M. Dostoevskii, *Pis'ma*, Vol. IV (Moscow, 1959), p. 190.

lowered eyelids, and the above suggestion is repeated several times as needed, or else a similar one.[5]

These techniques of suggestion through repetition gave the hypnotists the tool they needed to explore memory through amnesia and to correct the opinion Diderot had ascribed to d'Alembert, that a memory may be "altogether lost." In the 1850s it was already accepted doctrine that "every sleeper remembers things far more exactly than when he is awake. What he has once known he recovers in somnambulism."[6] Although these hypnotists and alienists and their intellectual descendants have examined and generalized this problem of latency up until the present time, their efforts to explain it have tended to remain in the domain of analogies. In 1919 for example, Henri Bernheim's book *Automatism and Suggestion* contained the following passage:

> In all these states, the amnesia is neither constant nor absolute . . . Even in the case of memories apparently erased, one can always, as I have determined, revive them by verbal suggestion. I tell the subject to shut his eyes and to recollect: I concentrate his attention in this way, I say to him "You are going to recollect everything," and the memories reappear sometimes instantly or quickly; other times more slowly, through gradual evocation. One would say that the impressions from a state of sleep or of somnambulism, produced in a special state of consciousness where the attention is concentrated like a nervous light, are no longer illuminated in the normal state of consciousness, when the light is no longer concentrated upon them; they have become latent; they again become luminous, conscious, if suggestion again concentrates on these dim impressions the light of cerebral attention . . .
>
> [He rejects a neurological explanation, and continues:] The evocation of a memory would therefore not be the revival of a localized imprint, but the reproduction of the special cellular modality which created the impression or the idea in the first place. The latent memory does not exist as long as it is latent. It can be awakened by the cellular modality the same way a re-

[5]Jules Liégeois, *De la suggestion et du somnambulisme* (Paris, 1899), p. 89.
[6]Karl Freiherr von Reichenbach, *Der sensitive Mensch* (Stuttgart, 1855), II, 693-4.

membered motion does not exist but can be awakened by a muscular contraction.[7]

This formulation that in amnesia, natural or hypnotic, memories are latent, not lost, was available to Dostoevsky long before he undertook *The Brothers Karamazov*. In an article on current psychological developments, he would have read the following statement in the *Fatherland Notes* for 1861, CXXXVI, as a part of his regular reading: "In somnambulism, memories not only appear with great liveliness; they even pass from one session of sleep to another, so that somnambulists sometimes continue in one session activities that were begun in another; in the waking interval of consciousness, the memory of these actions is lost." He need not, however, have read articles on science in the 1860s to learn about the need to revive a situation in order to revive a memory. His favorite English author, Dickens, had Jasper refer to this need in Chapter III of *The Mystery of Edwin Drood*: "If I hide my watch when I am drunk, I must be drunk again before I find it." Dickens was enormously interested in hypnotism, and his friend Wilkie Collins made the regeneration of a latent memory the climactic episode in *The Moonstone*. In short, long before *The Brothers Karamazov* Dostoevsky had as a part of his intellectual background the doctrines of persistent latency and of recovery triggered by parallel circumstances in real life or in a state suggested through elaborated repetition.

Quite apart from its current appeal to Dostoevsky's scientific, literary, and journalistic contemporaries, memory concerned him personally for two reasons. The first reason was his worry about his own memory, his dread of the effect upon it of each epileptic fit. He told his wife about the lost feeling during the period of recuperation, before the memories were restored. In short, he went agonizingly through his own investigation of amnesia many times a year. He talked about the feeling of rereading *Crime and Punishment* after having quite forgotten it, or of unconsciously using the hero of Anna Korvin-Krukovskaya's book as a source for Alyosha Karamazov, and told Vsevolod Solovyov:

> Everything that happened to me before this first [epileptic] seizure, every minutest event of my life, every face I met, all that I

[7]Henri Bernheim, *Automatisme et suggestion* (Paris, 1919), p. 61.

read or heard, I remember down to the most trivial detail. Everything that began after the first seizure I often forget; I sometimes quite forget people whom I have known well; I forget faces. I have forgotten all that I have written after the prison camp; when I was finished *The Possessed*, I had to reread it all from the beginning, because I had forgotten even the names of the characters.[8]

Dostoevsky's second reason for being concerned with memory involved his deep personal concern with immortality. In the life of a man or a nation, he attached great importance to the "opportunity to utter one's own word," not so much to make one's mark on the world as to enter into the community of mankind. In his 1863–4 notebook, he meditates as follows on this problem:

Is there a future life for every "I"? People say a man collapses and dies *altogether*. We already know it isn't altogether, because just as a person giving physical birth to a son transmits to him a part of his identity, so in the moral world, he leaves a memory of himself to people, that is, he enters into the future development of mankind with a part of his former identity that had been alive on earth. (N.B. The desire for eternal memory in the funeral service is indicative of this.)[9]

This rather trite sense of one's survival in the memory of others led later to Dostoevsky's interest in Fyodorov's projects for the resurrection of one's ancestors. In his letter about Fyodorov, however, Dostoevsky sees a likely contradiction between the church's teaching and Fyodorov's kind of resurrection, whereas in the notebook entry, he had seen the church's funeral service of eternal memory as a link between the two kinds of immortality.[10]

With this background and these concerns of Dostoevsky's in mind, I should like to examine *The Brothers Karamazov* as an essay on remembering and forgetting. The book is many other things, of course,

[8]Vsevolod Solov'ev, "Vospominaniia o Dostoevskom" (St. Petersburg, 1881), p. 10, cited in *Literaturnoe nasledstvo*, Vol. 83, p. 357.
[9]Ibid., p. 174.
[10]*Pis'ma*, op. cit., p. 10, March 24, 1978. Robert Lord makes the connection between Fedorov's teachings and *The Brothers Karamazov*, in his *Dostoevsky, Essays and Perspectives* (Berkeley, 1970), Chapter X.

but the other important ones have received more scholarly attention. The theme of memory emerges in the first sentence of the first chapter with the statement that Fyodor Karamazov's death was still recollected after thirteen years. It recurs until the last chapter of the novel, which begins with a service of eternal memory for the dead Ilyusha, and ends with a speech about childhood memories. Book One of the novel sets up a careful opposition between the way old Fyodor forgets and the way Alyosha remembers. In Chapter II, Fyodor had cast off his son Mitya, "not out of cruelty towards him, nor from any insulted conjugal feelings, but simply because he forgot about him altogether." (I, 1, ii)[11] A little later, the narrator states, "If papa should remember him (and he couldn't actually fail to know about his existence) then he would himself send him off to [Grigory's] hut." When Fyodor's second wife dies, Alyosha is only four, "but strange though it is, I know he remembered his mother all his life, as if through a dream, of course. After her death, it happened with [Ivan and Alyosha] just the same as with the first child, Mitya. They were altogether forgotten and cast out by their father" (I, 1, iii). Later Alyosha admits that he has returned to his father's house in order to find his mother's grave, but his father has already forgotten where they buried her. (I, 1, iv) Later still in the novel, when Fyodor describes in disgusting detail how he had reduced Alyosha's mother to hysterics by spitting on her icon, Dostoevsky carefully marks a mysterious lapse in Fyodor's memory:

> Something very strange occurred—only for a second, it's true. The realization had actually, apparently, escaped the old fellow's mind that Alyosha's mother was Ivan's mother too.
> "How do you mean, your mother?" he muttered. (I, 3, ix)

For contrast to Fyodor's forgetting, Alyosha's remembering appears most elaborately in another passage:

> I have already recalled that although [Alyosha] had lost his mother when only four, he remembered her from then on, for his whole life, her face, her caresses, "just as if she stood before me alive." Such recollections (as we all know) can be remembered from an even earlier age, even from two years, but only emerging all one's life as bright spots from the murk, as if they were corners torn from a great picture which is extinguished

[11]All quotations from *The Brothers Karamazov* will be in my own translation.

and lost except for just that corner. Just so it was with him: he remembered one quiet summer evening, an open window, the slanting beams of the setting sun (these slanting beams were what he most remembered), in a room, in the corner, an image, a lamp lighted before it, and before the image his mother, on her knees, sobbing as if in hysterics, shrieking and wailing, clasping him in both arms, embracing him tightly, till it hurt, and praying to the Virgin for him, stretching him from her embrace with both hands towards the image as if for the Virgin's protection. Suddenly the nurse runs in and snatches him from her in terror. There's the picture! In that instant Alyosha also remembered his mother's face: he said it was ecstatic but beautiful, judging by as much as he could remember. But he seldom liked to confide this memory to anyone. (I, 1, iv)

The passage not only distinguishes Alyosha, the rememberer from his father the forgetter, but also links remembering with two other central businesses of Book One, the abandonment and the blessing of children.

Out of these early encounters with the theme of memory comes a secondary, moral association with memory. Dostoevsky is conditioning his reader to connect memory with love, attention, and family, while forgetting is connected with neglect and debauchery. This particular associative loading of memory is by no means automatic for Dostoevsky. In *The Devils*, for example, the vindictive whim of a spoiled eccentric leads Madame Stavrogina to tell Stepan Verkhovensky, "I will never forget this." But in *The Brothers Karamazov*, where this key passage has given memory a rich meaning at the start, Ivan can later use the established associations to load other elements with beauty or horror. In discussing those sinners immersed so deeply in the burning lake that they cannot emerge, Ivan cites "an expression of extraordinary profundity and power." This is the sentence, "These, God is already forgetting." (I, 5, v) In contrast to this forgetting, Ivan has already made a comment that links exploits with memory:

I treasure that certain human exploit in which you may long since have even stopped believing, but still honor in your heart for old memory's sake.... I want to go to Europe, Alyosha; I'll leave from here; and I know, of course that I'm just going to a graveyard, but to the most, the most precious graveyard, that's the thing. Precious are the dead that lie there; every stone above them proclaims such a burning past life, such a passionate belief in their exploit, in their verity, in their struggle and their science, that I know in advance I shall fall upon the ground and kiss those stones and weep over them. . . ." (I, 5, iii)

This association between ecstatic joy and an exploit whose life resides not in any validity but merely in being remembered shapes our whole understanding of the legend of The Grand Inquisitor. At the end of the legend, when Alyosha says that the Grand Inquisitor does not believe in God, Ivan portrays the Inquisitor's whole life as an exploit:

> Suppose that should be true. You've finally solved the problem. And actually the whole secret is just that, but isn't that suffering, for such a man as he, who has destroyed his whole life on an exploit in the desert and not cured his love for humanity.

This double exploit, sacrificing one's life first for salvation, and then for humanity, embodies that romantic beauty which Dostoevsky often ascribed to the great Russian radicals, and makes the tremendous power and appeal of the Grand Inquisitor in some sense a commentary on Herzen, Belinsky, and the others whose beauty and whose language are incorporated into his makeup. By involving such exploits with memory earlier, and by involving memory with families and blessings earlier, Dostoevsky has manipulated his readers' instincts into a sympathy with the Grand Inquisitor which he then sets about destroying.[12]

The association of memory with the good things and forgetting with evil ones prevails when Alyosha mysteriously forgets his brother Dmitry after the legend, although Ivan has mentioned his name three times on the preceding page, but the next rich and vivid collection of memories occurs when Zosima discusses his dying brother Markel:

> I remember, once I went into him alone when no one was with him. It was in the evening, clear; the sun was setting and illuminated the whole room with a slanting ray. He beckoned to me; I saw and went to him; he took me by the shoulders with both

---

[12]I have described the manipulative process in "The Rhetoric of an Ideological Novel," in Wm. Todd, ed. *Literature and Society in Imperial Russia, 1880-1914* (Stanford, 1977).

hands, looked me in the face ecstatically, loving; he said nothing, just looked thus for a moment or so, "So," he said, "go now, play, live for me." I went out and went to play. And since then in my life I have recollected many times with tears the way he ordered me to play for him. (II, 6, ii)

This childhood memory of a laying on of hands is followed by twelve sentences which bracket a chapter break and deal with plot, not memory. The first two of these sentences treat Markel's death, and the next five describe the impact of this death on the neighbors and on Zosima, immediately and later. The five sentences in the next chapter begin with Zosima's mother, who responds to the urging of neighbors and sends him to the Cadets School in St. Petersburg. The last of these twelve sentences records her death, and is followed by a rather abrupt return to the subject of memory.

From my father's house, I carried only precious memories, for men have no more precious memories than those from their first childhood in the parental home, and this is almost always so, if the family contained even a little bit of love and unity. And even from the worst of families, precious memories can be preserved, if only your spirit is willing and able to seek the precious. Among my memories of home, I reckon also memories about sacred stories which I was curious to get to know in my parental home, while still a child. I had books then, sacred stories with beautiful pictures, called "A Hundred Sacred Stories from the Old and New Testament," and I even learned to read from it. It is still lying now on my shelf; I keep it as a precious memento. But even before I began to read, I remember how I first was visited by the influence of the spirit, when I was still eight years old. My mother took me alone (I don't remember where my brother was) into the temple of the Lord, in holy week, on Monday for the Mass. The day was clear, and recollecting it now, I seem to see again the way the incense rose from the censer, and from above in the dome, through a little window, there poured upon us in the church the rays of God, and rising up to them in waves, the incense seemed to melt into them. I gazed in holy wonder, and for the first time in my life, received the seed of God's Word consciously into my heart. (II, 6, ii)

This passage reintroduces the theme of memory in its full vividness, with the same collection of associations as in Alyosha's early recollections—a mother with a child, a consecration, slanting sunlight, etc. But here, instead of an icon there are holy scriptures, and instead of an essay on the dreamlike vividness and isolations of early memories, there is an essay on their moral importance.

Memory is not confined to passages of high seriousness in the novel, but its presence as a theme can shape our awareness of sentimental or misleading comfortable passages. At Mitya's trial, when Dr. Herzenstube reminisces about Mitya's childhood, he clearly remembers the lad's behavior, but takes several lines of text in his effort to remember the Russian word for "nuts." He tells of giving Mitya a pound of nuts and instructing him in the formula of consecration at baptism, *"Gott der Vater, Gott der Sohn, und Gott der Heilige Geist."* Next time Mitya sees him, he remembers the beginning of the formula, but has forgotten the Holy Ghost, and has to be retaught.

> Twenty-three years later, I am sitting one morning in my office, my hair already white, and suddenly a blooming youth comes in whom I can't recognize at all, but he raised his finger and said, "Gott der Vater, Gott der Sohn, und Gott der Heilige Geist! I've just arrived and came to thank you for a pound of nuts, for no one had ever bought me a pound of nuts at that time, and you alone bought me a pound of nuts." And then I recollected my happy youth and the poor boy outdoors with no shoes, and my heart was moved, and I said, "You are a noble young person, for you have remembered all your life that pound of nuts which I brought you in your childhood." And I embraced him and blessed him. And I wept. He was laughing, but he was weeping too. (IV, 12, iii)

This passage can be taken as a splendid piece of tear jerking at a moment in the novel which has been rather dry of emotion, and a moment when relief is necessary before the catastrophe. But it is more interesting to treat the passage as a minuet about the themes of remembering and forgetting. Both Herzenstube and Mitya begin by forgetting words. Herzenstube begins by reminiscing about Mitya's childhood, and ends with a sentence whose crucial word is the conjunction "for." "You are a noble person, for you have remembered all your life the pound of nuts which I brought you in your childhood." This "for" can mean either that the remembering is evidence of nobility or that the remembering led to the nobility, but in either case, it enacts the principle which Zosima had enunciated concerning the importance of even a single precious childhood recollection, if one's spirit is willing and able to seek the precious. The themes of childhood, abandonment and consecration are brought together again, this time in the mood of sentimental nostalgia rather than of inspirational teaching or narrative exposition, but here again the moral importance of memory as such emerges centrally.

This collection of passages raises an interesting question—what is the connection between memory, consecration, and suffering children? Ivan Karamazov linked the suffering of children to the question of the theodicy—how does one justify a God who permits innocent suffering? Zosima's answer to this question is ingenious, essentially rhetorical and, I believe, original.

> My brother used to ask the birds for forgiveness. That, however mindless it may be, is also true, for everything is like an ocean; everything is interflowing and in contact; you touch it in one place and it gives at the opposite end of the world. Suppose it is insane to ask birds for forgiveness; still it would be better for the birds and for the child, and for every living thing around you if you yourself were better than you are now, even just one drop better. Everything is like an ocean, I say unto you. (II, 6, ii)

Zosima takes the first creature one can think of that is more innocent than a child, and blames its suffering not on God but on Zosima's interlocutors, using the doctrines of universal determinism which the materialists of Dostoevsky's day could hardly deny. The argument is ingenious, but it is abstract and mystical as expressed here, and conflicts with the evidence of our own experience; we have all done good deeds that did no visible good to bird, beast, or fish. Zosima must therefore adduce a second doctrine to handle good deeds that are lost:

> Even if you have given off light but see that people are not saved even in the presence of your light, still, remain firm in the power of the light of heaven; believe that even if they have not been saved now, they will be saved; and if they are not saved, their sons will be saved, for the light will not die, although you may be dead. The righteous departs, but his light remains. The salvation always comes after the death of the savior. (II, 6, ii)

This denial that good deeds are ever lost has nothing of the mystical about it. It relates to the practical efficacy of good on earth. It therefore is subject to the questions of mechanism which Zosima's more mystical insights bypass because they come from direct experience. Dostoevsky had to deal with practical, skeptical readers who would ask, "Just how does a good deed of mine ever help if it affects a child who dies, or who later commits murder—and if my good deeds can be lost, just how can I be guilty of a sparrow's fall." In this way a rational opponent of Dostoevsky's could challenge only half of the determinist position and say that every good or evil deed is socially determined, as is argued at times in *Crime and Punishment*, but that while its causes are determined, its moral effects may be lost. Dostoevsky has to confront this problem of lost good in order to make his essentially rhetorical attack on the problem of evil cogent among a rationalist readership. But in saying that good deeds were latent, not lost, he had to name a repository for good while it is not visible in a child, or after the child has died. The repository he names is intuitively acceptable, and anything but original. He could have drawn it from the fifty-fourth chapter of one of his favorite books, *The Old Curiosity Shop*.

> There is nothing . . . no, nothing innocent or good, that dies, and is forgotten. Let us hold to that faith, or none. An infant, a prattling child, dying in its cradle, will live again in the better thoughts of those who loved it; and play its part, through them, in the redeeming actions of the world, though its body be burnt to ashes or drowned in the deepest sea. . . . Forgotten! Oh if the good deeds of human creatures could be traced to their source, how beautifully would even death appear; for how much charity, mercy, and purified affection would be seen to have their growth in dusty graves.

In this passage, Dickens names the repository of good that appears to be lost. He makes the same connection between memory and immortality on earth, and the same connection between memory and a dying child. Taking this familiar linkage, Dostoevsky introduced a series of children into *The Brothers Karamazov*, including Alyosha, Markel, Zosima, and Mitya. Each of these went through a consecration in a passage cited in this paper; Markel died, and in each of the others, the good to which he was consecrated became latent. But latency, as Dostoevsky knew from the psychology of his times, was not loss, and the memory of Markel, the figure of Zosima appearing in a dream after death, and Alyosha's ability to help Ilyusha, Kolya, and the boys, all are examples of the persistence and indeed the enhanced contagiousness of good beyond its apparent death. Dostoevsky indicated his biblical source for this pattern in his epigraph to *The Brothers Karamazov* which equates this good with a seed. "Except a corn of wheat fall into the ground and die, it abideth alone, but if it die, it bringeth forth much fruit."

This formula begins with Alyosha's insemination with grace, and it ends with his effort to implant a memory in the boys in his funeral oration after the service of eternal memory:

> We are about to part, gentlemen. Let us agree right here at Ilyusha's stone, that we shall never forget—first of all, Ilyushechka, and second, one another. And whatever may happen to us after this in life, though we might not meet for twenty years after this, we will still remember how we buried this poor boy at whom we had thrown stones earlier, do you remember by the bridge, there, and after that all came to love him so. He was a wonderful boy, a good, brave boy, he had a sense of honor and of the bitter insult to his father, against which he rebelled. So first, we will remember him, gentlemen, all our life. And though you may be busy with the most important matters, may have attained repute or fallen into the greatest misfortune, never forget the way it once was well with us here, all in communion.
>
> What I say to you may be unclear, but you still will remember it, and sometime after this will agree with my words. Know, then, that there is nothing higher or stronger or healthier, or more useful for the life ahead than good memories of any sort, and especially those carried out of childhood, from your parents' home. People will tell you a lot about your education, but maybe this sort of beautiful, holy memory is the best education of all. If a person can take such memories along through life, then he is saved for life. And even if but one good memory remains with us in our heart, that may someday serve as our education. We may grow vicious after this, but still, however vicious we may be, which God forbid, yet as we remember how we buried Ilyusha . . . the most savage and mocking person among us will not be able

to laugh inwardly at his kindness and goodness at this current moment. Moreover, maybe just this memory alone will hold him back from some great evil (Epilogue 3).

In this final speech in *The Brothers Karamazov*, Dostoevsky presents memory as an actual moral force, latent for years, perhaps, as science, literature, and personal experience had taught him it could be, but offering the immortality on earth which had concerned him early in his career, and at the same time offering a rationally acceptable repository for the good whose preservation was indispensible to his theodicy.

But rational answers never sufficed for Dostoevsky. As a moral and manipulative novelist, he was not content to describe precious memories. He was setting out to create them in his readers, and one technique he used calls to mind the works on hypnotism I have sampled earlier. The hypnotists had learned repetition produces suggestion, and in the sixty sentences from *The Brothers Karamazov* in this paper, Dostoevsky used words directly relating to memory, permanance, or clarity sixty times.

The Paradox of
the Legend of the Grand Inquisitor
in *The Brothers Karamazov*

by Jacques Catteau

All novelistic techniques refer back to a metaphysical theory. Thus, our analysis of structures and the creative process in Dostoevsky's work has led us to a metaphysical theory of creation.[1] Starting out with the central unrealized design of "The Life of a Great Sinner," we have defined the metaphysics of Dostoevsky's creative work as a poetics that seeks to reconcile four opposing freedoms that occurs in two parallel pairs: in writing—the freedom of the character and of the novelist; in the realm of thought—the freedom of man and of God.[2]

The latter two constitute the heart of the Legend of the Grand Inquisitor, one of the high points in *The Brothers Karamazov*. They had been central also to the rejected utopia of the Crystal Palace and the sterile and devitalized utopia of the Golden Age. The debate on utopia—one which Dostoevsky mounts through his atheistic, or at least agnostic, characters—is the atheistic side of that supreme reflection on divided freedom. The Legend of the Grand Inquisitor, narrated by an atheist, paradoxically constitutes a bridge to the Christian side.

In both cases Dostoevsky deals with a question that is crucial to our time: the question of Hope. The Crystal Palace seems to him an illusory hope; the Golden Age, a hope that has been found again but is internalized and remains a purely moral one. Could the Legend of

"The Paradox of the Legend of the Grand Inquisitor in *The Brothers Karamozov*" was written for this collection by Jacques Catteau. Copyright © 1983 by Prentice-Hall, Inc. Translated by Françoise Rosset.

[1] Jacques Catteau, *La Création littéraire chez Dostoievski* (Paris, Institut d'études slaves, 1978).

[2] *Ibid.*, 315–16.

the Grand Inquisitor be the eclipse of hope, the imprisonment of hope, or does it leave the door open to some ray of hope?

> After the *Eclipse of God* (Martin Buber), after the *Eclipse of Reason* (Horkheimer) some prophets would place us now on the threshold of a third great eclipse at the level of civilization, an eclipse as disquieting and tragic as the two preceding ones: the Eclipse of Hope.

Thus writes Jacques Le Goff in *Le Monde*, April 3, 1979. Yet more than a century ago in 1879, in *The Brothers Karamazov*, Dostoevsky foresaw the three eclipses simultaneously. Placing in parentheses God and creative human reason, the Grand Inquisitor would imprison the hopes of men and Jesus Christ himself. Has he not resolved to save mankind in spite of itself, and without Christ—an interloper come to disrupt his pious work! "Why have you come to interfere with us now?" he repeats three times. Everything has been transferred to the Pope, let us do our work. The prisoner remains silent. If he were to speak up, he would deprive mankind of the freedom he so defended while on earth. This divine logic, based on the primacy of freedom, the freedom to distinguish between good and evil, free choice or free love, the Grand Inquisitor counters with his own logic, one firmly grounded in the three forces of miracle, mystery, and authority. Why imagine Christ's response? One might as well read the Gospel. Their two logics work in parallel ways. They do not struggle; they sink into the infinity of human history: they are the eternal libertarian line of Christ and the no less eternal authoritarian line that runs through the Inquisition and proliferates in the totalitarian cancers of the twentieth century. Yury Dombrovsky, in his *Department of Useless Things*, comments on Christ and Dostoevsky in a way that curiously crystallizes this idea of two parallel categories of logic, the libertarian and the authoritarian:

> —. . . All gentleness [*krotost'*] is a terrible force. Don't you remember who said that?
> —Tolstoy, probably?
> —No. Dostoevsky. In his last years he often thought of Christ, only he did not know how to deal with him and he conducted various experiments. Sometimes he left Christ gentleness and love and took from him the superflous wrath and sword: this would produce Lev Nikolaevich, Prince Myshkin, a figure who from all evidence was not only not viable, but frankly destructive

to those who loved him. At other times, he returned the sword to Christ and threw the rest away: this produced the Grand Inquisitor, or in other words, Christ chastising Christ.[3]

The Legend of the Grand Inquisitor is indeed part of a long tradition where, side by side with those who despise the Inquisition, we find poets whose natural heresy and powerful love have often rebelled against the Church hierarchy. Let us mention only those which Dostoevsky may have read. In 1847, the *Carmina Burana* were published from an anonymous manuscript discovered in 1803 in the convent of Benediktbeuren. A wandering poet, a distant forebear of Ivan Karamazov, had written in it: "Then the Pope said to the Romans: If the son of Man comes to our Holy See, ask him: Friend, why have you come? And if he insists on entering without giving you anything, cast him out into the darkness." Some poets of the Reformation imagine a new trial of Christ come back to earth and his condemnation by the Church. In the nineteenth century, Goethe follows in their footsteps with his *Voyage to Italy* (1816–1817): if Christ came back to earth, he would again be crucified. Balzac has a similar motif in his notes, in addition to his *Jésus-Christ en Flandre:* a meeting between Christ and the Pope. *Le Christ au Vatican*, an anonymous work attributed to Victor Hugo despite his protestations, is a variation on the same theme. Dostoevsky, a onetime Fourierist, was probably familiar with the works by the socialists Cabet and Desamy, in which Christ, come back into the middle of the nineteenth century, is condemned again by civil or military courts. To this theme of the recrucified Christ is added that of the Grand Inquisitor, a motif which the Russian author, as a great admirer of Schiller, knew from Don Carlos; he knew it also from the poem by his friend A. N. Maikov, "The Legend of the Spanish Inquisition," published in 1861 in *Vremia*, the first journal edited by the Dostoevsky brothers. The same theme was to be found in W. Prescott's two-volume *History of the Reign of Philip II, King of Spain*, translated in 1858, which occupied a prominent place in Dostoevsky's library.[4]

[3]Jurii Dombrovskii, *Fakul'tet nenuzhnykh veshchei* (Paris, YMCA Press, 1978), p. 272.

[4]For the numerous possible sources of the Legend of the Grand Inquisitor, see the commentary and bibliographical references in F. M. Dostoevskii, *Polnoe sobranie sochinenii v 30 tomakh* (Leningrad: Nauka, 1976), vol. 15, pp. 462–66. [hereafter cited as "Coll. Works"]

Dostoevsky's original contribution over that of his predecessors is the confrontation between Christ and the Grand Inquisitor in sixteenth century Seville. The great dates of Church history are correct, witness the reference to the year 756 when Stephen II saw his temporal power over the church estates confirmed by Pepin le Bref ("Exactly eight centuries ago, we took from *him* [Satan] what you had rejected with indignation, the last gift *he* offered you as *he* showed you all the kingdoms on earth; we accepted Rome and Caesar's sword . . ." [II, 5, v])[5] Historical details, however, are treated casually. The Grand Inquisitor's face is not veiled, as was the rule. Moreover, Ivan shamelessly ignores the fact that the Inquisition was carried out mostly by Dominicans, and not by the Jesuits, whose motto he cites: *Ad majorem Dei gloriam.*

Who is the Grand Inquisitor? For the last century, answers have varied, interpretations have multiplied. And each man sees in the parable a weapon to dispatch his own personal enemy. Anything is possible if one forgets to question Dostoevsky himself. Yet upon questioning Dostoevsky and the witnesses in whom he confided, one finds that the Russian author's intent may be illuminated in several ways, all tied to a central theme.

A first reading and the writer's comment to Putsykovich confirm that the Legend is directed against Caesaro-papism and Catholicism, especially against "the dreaded era of the Inquisition, which had such a nefarious effect on Christianity and on all mankind."[6] This is a consequence of the battle Dostoevsky waged against the papacy in his novels *The Idiot* (1873), *The Devils* (1876), and particularly in his *Diary of a Writer* (1877). The papacy was both arrogant (proclamation of papal infallibility) and vulnerable in its temporal power (hence the appeal to France to preserve the Papal Estates, as in 756). It would be absurd to deny Dostoevsky's hatred of Catholicism and of the "black army," the Jesuits, the spearhead of papism.

A second reading, and letters to Pobedonostsev, Procurator-General of the Holy Synod, and to Lyubimov, who was in charge of publishing *The Brothers Karamazov*, suggest another interpretation.[7]

---

[5]All translations are directly from the Russian [ed.].

[6]*Novoe vremia*, Jan. 16, 1902, No. 9292.

[7]Letters from Dostoevsky to Lyubimov, May 10, 1879; to Pobedonostsev, May 19; to Lyubimov, June 11, etc. F .M. Dostoevskii, *Pis'ma* (Moscow: Gosizdat, 1959), IV, pp. 52–59.

The Legend is a full-scale attack on the "future socialist kingdom" preached by Russian nihilist youth. This is fully confirmed by the motifs of "bread" and of the "Tower of Babel." By enslaving freedom of conscience, atheists like Ivan and his creature, the Grand Inquisitor, violate human conscience and reduce mankind to the rank of cattle.

A third reading, and a more refined synthesis, was given by Dostoevsky himself on December 30, 1879, before a student audience. This is how he presented his Legend of the Grand Inquisitor.

> An atheist suffering from his lack of faith goes through one of his wrenching moments to compose a weird, fantastic poem, staging a confrontation between Christ and one of the foremost Catholic prelates, the Grand Inquisitor. The suffering of the poem's author comes precisely because in the image of this prelate of Catholic faith, one so far removed from the true faith of the first apostles, he really sees a true servant of Christ. Yet his Grand Inquisitor is at bottom an atheist. The meaning here is that, once we distort Christ's faith by tying it to the goals of our world, the whole significance of Christianity is lost at once, the spirit inevitably ceases to believe, and instead of Christ's sublime ideal, there is erected a new Tower of Babel. Christianity's lofty conception of mankind is practically reduced to a view of mankind as a herd of wild animals, and under the guise of a *social* love for mankind we can already detect a hidden contempt for it.[8]

There is no contradiction in these three readings if we recognize that Dostoevsky views materialist socialism as the child of the Roman idea, perpetrated by Catholicism. One must recall Prince Myshkin in *The Idiot* thundering against the infamous temporal power of the Pope and making a complete amalgam of Catholicism, atheism, and socialism. One must recall also Shatov's declarations in *The Devils*; and especially the *Diary of a Writer* where Dostoevsky the publicist relentlessly reiterates the blood relationship between Catholicism and communism and harps on their alliance under the leadership of the Pope and his Jesuit cohorts, following in the footsteps of Marx and Bakunin. As early as 1863–1864, Dostoevsky was elaborating his theme in a piece that has only recently been published: "Catholic

[8]Coll. Works, vol. 15, p. 198.

christianity has given birth to socialism alone, ours will bear brother-hood."[9]

The third reading is without doubt the most fruitful one. Ivan is no longer a self-assured atheist. He suffers from his "lack of faith." The church in question is not just the Catholic Church but a church alien-ated from the true faith of the first apostles. Even if Dostoevsky seems to make an exception of the Orthodox Church (in Russian, the church of the true faith, *pravoslavie*), nonetheless the fact remains that the danger he exposes could very well affect the whole Christian church with its excessive concern with its "social" role in organizing society, and even the church "in general" (this is what Dostoevsky allegedly told Lyubimov, though one cannot fully accept the latter's word).

Here we find ourselves at the heart of the believers' dilemma. The issue agitates the souls of those seeking greater equality and justice in our lowly world. The Inquisition, presented in the Legend more as a force organizing society than as a guardian of dogma, poses the prob-lem of the church's authoritarian intervention in the social sphere. Should it save mankind in spite of itself? Should the church organize society in an authoritarian manner? One must read between the lines for Dostoevsky's answer, as his Christ keeps significantly silent. The answer is a clear rebuke to the Church and *a fortiori* to any attempt to impose on man a system of totalitarian organization for the sake of his own happiness.

Dostoevsky's indictment of his Grand Inquisitor would indeed seem grave and without appeal. The utopia of human happiness at any cost rests on three definitive denials that kill all hope: the denial of man, of human society's ability to construct itself, and of God. This ninety-year-old man, despite the wound of his ardent love, drives the universe back into ice. He has lost all faith in life, liberty, or culture. He takes the place of God and exhibits all the vices that he gratui-tously and impudently heaps upon God: pride, presumption, heed-lessness. Faith in Christ is too costly for man, he says through Ivan who shares his belief: the ideal is inaccessible. God, he says, gambled too heavily, we must lower the stakes. Hope is dead. For the painful, thorny game of freedom of good and evil, for unacceptable suffering,

[9]*Neizdannyi Dostoevskii, Literaturnoe nasledstvo* (Moscow, 1971), Vol. 83, p. 176.

we should substitute—and he is in such a hurry, as impatient as Belinsky[10]—balsamic care and anesthetizing labor.

To begin with the Grand Inquisitor, descending further than the Underground Man in his pessimistic analysis of the human creature, renders man infantile and denies him the status of an adult. Look at him, he says to Christ, is this God's image—this puny runt, "weak," "depraved," "rebellious," "ungrateful"? This is a "scruffy kid," a "schoolboy" in need of the discipline of a father who loves and chastises him well. Look at him; he keeps asking for his freedom but prefers the happiness of bread and a peaceful conscience. Give him his freedom, he will voluntarily put it down at the feet of those before whom his eternal anxiety leads him to bow. For not only is freedom too much to bear, though free will is always seductive, but, once sated, man thirsts for mystery. This is the paradox of love through contempt—an old theme in Dostoevsky's work. Murin, a character in *The Landlady* (1847), comments ironically: "Man is weak. Alone, he will never make it. Give the weakling his cherished freedom, he will bind it himself and bring it back to you." The Inquisitor says the same to Christ: "Man has no more tormenting need than the need to find someone to whom he can hand over the gift of freedom with which the unfortunate creature was born." And he adds: "Only to the one who can appease their conscience and take possession of their freedom!" The Inquisitor is a thorough pessimist—he does not believe in man. Let us organize his happiness, he decides.

The Grand Inquisitor, then, detects not the slightest capacity in social man to organize universal harmony, to construct a society that is more or less egalitarian and just. Every time he mentions the tower of Babel, past or future, the implacable old man posits inevitable failure:

> Centuries will pass and mankind will proclaim through its men of wisdom and science that there is no crime, that there is therefore no sin either, that there are only hungry people. 'Feed us, and then ask virtue from us!'—that is what they will write on the banners which they will raise against Thee and with which they will destroy Thy temple. In place of Thy temple they will erect a new edifice, erect anew the terrible tower of Babel, and . . . they won't finish this one as they did not finish the one before . . .

[10]Coll. Works, vol. 21, p. 12.

After suffering a thousand years with their tower they will come to us again! They will seek us out again hidden under the earth in the catacombs. . . . And then we shall finish building their tower (II, 5, v).

Later in the Legend, the same motif recurs:

Oh, centuries are yet to come, [full of] the disorder of the free mind, of their science and cannibalism, for having begun the tower of Babel without us, they will end with cannibalism. But then the beast will come crawling to us and will lick our feet and bespatter them with tears of blood from their eyes. And we shall mount the beast and raise the cup, and on it will be written: 'Mystery!' (II, 5, v)

The Grand Inquisitor, like his disciple, Shigalyov, the totalitarian theoretician of *The Devils*, does not believe in reason, in science, or in talent. Like the nihilist Pyotr Verkhovensky, he will tear out Cicero's tongue, put out Copernicus's eyes, and stone Shakespeare. He will replace man's education and science with mystery, the fear of prisons, and the dread of *autos-da-fé*. He will abandon their freedom. He is essentially echoing Shigalyov who presumably had read the article by the student Raskolnikov. Shigalyov proposed that

. . . mankind be divided into two unequal parts. One tenth will receive freedom of person and unlimited power over the other nine-tenths. The latter will have to give up their individuality and be turned into something like a herd of animals; through their boundless obedience and through a series of regenerations they will attain to a primeval innocence, something like a primeval paradise, although, of course, they will have to work. (II, 7, ii)

Shigalyov and the Grand Inquisitor worship these crystal palaces where the bird Kagan *(khan)*, which is the absolute Master, reigns supreme.[11] In reading the Grand Inquisitor's bland and paradisiacal project for a society, one has failed to notice that it was nothing more than a picture of a totalitarian universe, one constructed by a *nomenklatura*, an elite, who denied the science of economics, concep-

---

[11]For a discussion of the path from the crystal palace to the utopia of the Grand Inquisitor, see Catteau, "Du palais de cristal à l'Age d'or ou les avatars de l'utopie," *Dostoievski* (Paris, l'Herne, 1973), pp. 176–95. (*Cahier* No. 24).

tual thinking, and productive intelligence. The Grand Inquisitor declares in advance that socialism with a human face, or even liberal societies, simply cannot be realized. He preaches totalitarian obscurantism while impudently waving the flag of the mystery of Christ, though he does not really believe in it and wants to keep the Messiah in darkness. At this point Christ, who is listening attentively, must have thought that his church had perhaps followed the Grand Inquisitor for too long.

At last, having closed all the roads open to man, the Grand Inquisitor rejects God who, rather than gathering the flock, has scattered men over unknown byways. He renounces immortality. Can one ponder enough this dreadful statement near the end of the fanatical monk's speech: "And for their happiness we will allure them [men] with the reward of heavenly eternity. For even if there is something in that other world, it surely will not be for beings such as these." In his mind salvation for all means renunciation of immortality for all. This terrible confession calls to mind the "Discourse of the dead Christ from the top of the universe, that there is no God," in Jean Paul Richter's *Siebenkäs:*

> Then a tall and noble silhouette of eternal pain
> descended from on high upon the altar,
> and all the dead cried out:
> "Christ! Is there no God?"
> He answered, "There is none. . . ."
>
> "Jesus! Have we no father?"
> And he answered, bathed in tears:
> "We are all orphans, you and I,
> we have no father."[12]

Jean Paul Richter's character wakes from this terrifying nightmare, but the Grand Inquisitor topples the nightmare into reality. Christ is supposed to have "invented God"—thus reads a grave comment in the notebooks to *The Brothers Karamazov*, to be spoken by the Grand Inquistor.[13] The image takes on fantastic dimension without parallel.

---

[12]Jean Paul [Richter], *Siebenkäs* in Werke (Munich: Carl Hanser, 1959), vol. 2, p. 269.
[13]"Secret—that there is no truth, no god, that is, the god that you preached." Coll. Works, vol. 15, p. 320.

What if God had indeed died? What if the church was nothing more than a grand imposture? Never has doubt delved so deeply into Richter's "eternal midnight."

Ivan does not have the audacity to follow his own logic nor the blasphemous grandeur of the Grand Inquisitor. He dares not imagine a world without God, even a fake one. He does send his ticket back to God, but he is like Versilov in *A Raw Youth*. Though Versilov paints a picture of mankind having lost the great idea of immortality, he nevertheless ends his evocation with the appearance of Christ on the Baltic from Heine.[14] Similarly, Ivan raises Christ against his Torquemada.

Alyosha, who understands this well, says to Ivan, "The poem is in praise of Jesus, it is not a disparagement," adding hesitantly, "as you had wished." This is truth itself. Christ stands there, in silence, light flowing from his eyes; the people recognized him at once, and the crowd saw miracles follow upon miracles. And what is the meaning of that kiss of Christ's on the bloodless lips of the inflexible ninety-year-old? Forgiveness? Absolution, because the Inquisitor's sin is motivated by an excess of love? It could in no way signify approval, as some nostalgic crusaders seem to hold. But it is certainly a refusal to judge, to condemn, and thus a brilliant acknowledgment of that freedom of good and evil which makes men like the gods. Christ seals with a kiss the freedom he has brought. Alyosha understands this: in a gesture of spontaneous imitation that is typical of him, he kisses Ivan on the lips. Doubt, be it a dreadful blasphemy, is a sign of the painful freedom Christ bestowed upon man. With his Grand Inquisitor, Ivan grips the world in the cold rings of despair. With his Christ, before whom the doors to the dungeon open, Ivan creates a breath of hope.

However, what can Christ do? Is he but a witness, silent and "bathed in tears," watching as man is being torn apart by his inability to completely love his neighbor as he, Jesus, knew how to do—a cruel thought often repeated by Dostoevsky? Will Christ remain the inaccessible ideal that brought the sword and spread the storm? His silence embraces. In the same manner in *The Idiot*, Myshkin, who is a Christ figure, as confirmed by Dostoevsky's letters and notes, remains speechless in the face of a terrifying revolt by the atheist Ippolit, a

---

[14][See Heine's poem, "Frieden" from the cycle *Die Nordsee*—ed.]

brother to Ivan Karamazov. The other guests insult the despairing young man. The Grand Inquisitor spits his bitterness in Christ's face. There is nothing to say. There is nothing to say to an unbeliever, especially when the denial of God is an ethical one and comes from the heart, as it does in Ivan who is shattered by the suffering of children, and in the Grand Inquisitor who burns with love for these weak human creatures. The only thing to do is to keep on loving forever, while restoring to the Other his soul and his personality. This is what Dostoevsky, who could not find a direct rebuttal to Ivan's Legend, tried to do in the chapter "A Russian Monk." Here love for the Other is no longer domineering, contemptuous, or haughty, but restores to each being his *self*, or at least attempts to restore it.

The moral message of the Legend of the Grand Inquisitor is none-theless vigorously asserted: man's freedom is absolute and cannot be evaded; even misguided, it is sealed by God.

What is difficult is to hope, especially when hope dies in the servant of Christ and seeks refuge with the atheist. Emmanuel Mounier, a believer, speaks of tragic optimism. Ernst Bloch, an atheist, proposes a paradoxical formula in his work *Atheism in Christianity:* "Only a true Christian can be a good atheist; only a true atheist can be a good Christian." This is not a play on words. Ivan stands on the divide where the Christian and the atheist sides meet. He decides nothing; on the contrary, he restores things to what they were at the beginning of the Legend. The Grand Inquisitor frees Christ, the bearer of freedom. All is tragically renewed, all becomes possible again in a new legend: hope is both extended and released.

Hope, no matter how threatened by "eternal midnight," is a sign of spiritual life. In *Notes from the House of the Dead*, Dostoevsky makes a curious remark about the character Akim Akimych: "He was not par-ticularly religious either, as the rules of good behavior seemed to have swallowed up everything else in him, all human talents and idiosyn-crasies, and all passions or desires, good or bad" (I, 10). It is clear that for the author, a religious spirit necessarily implies the existence of passions and desires, even of bad ones. *Accidie* is deadly to spiritual life. Thus he always grants the gift of faith to those who, atheists or believers, do not despair of man, and this occasionally leads to as-tounding reversals. An example of this is an experiment attempted and abandoned by Dostoevsky in the notebooks to *A Raw Youth*. The novelist creates a character who is unique and original in his thought: Fyodor Fyodorovich. His name and patronymic mark him as the messenger of a secret predilection of Dostoevsky's. He is a kind of Prince Myshkin, an "idiot," a grown-up child, heart full of intuition and naive shrewdness, soul brimming with a violent love for childhood. Only, unlike Myshkin, this Christ-like being is an atheist and a fanatic revolutionary. Another character (later to become Versilov), also an atheist but a despairing one, tries to prove to him that Christ took freedom as the foundation of society and that there is no other freedom than that of Christ. Our atheistic and communist Myshkin, Fyodor Fyodorovich, contests the argument, but transformed suddenly by the love of an abandoned child, he becomes a Christian.[15] That is a daring conception of Dostoevsky; he entrusts the defense of Christ's gift of freedom to an atheist suffering, like Ivan, from lack of faith, while he bestows upon another atheist, the fanatic socialist Fyodor Fyodorovich, the privilege of Christian grace!

Hope decided the outcome. Faith in man does not necessarily lead to faith in God, but faith in God, for Dostoevsky, must absolutely go through faith in man. Therein lies the paradox of the Legend of the Grand Inquisitor. Ivan is an atheist first because he has lost his faith in man, and he subsequently denies human creative reason and God himself. And yet he invites Christ into his Legend and acknowledges him. Though he heaps bitter reproaches upon him through the Grand Inquisitor, Ivan manages ultimately to record man's essential freedom and to let Christ go for another experiment— perhaps a happier one, but at any rate one to be realized *through* freedom and *in* freedom.

[15]Coll. Works, vol. 16, pp. 14–15.

Chronology of Important Dates

1821 Fyodor Mikhailovich Dostoevsky born October 30 (Julian calendar), in Moscow.

1837 His mother dies.

1838 Enters military engineering school in St. Petersburg.

1839 Father killed by his own serfs.

1843 Finishes the engineering course and enters government service in a military department in St. Petersburg.

1844 Leaves government service.

1846 Publishes *Poor Folk (Bednye liudi)* and *The Double (Dvoinik)*.

1847 "The Landlady" *(Khoziaika)*. *Petersburg Chronicle (Petersburgskaia letopis')*

1848 "The Faint Heart" (Slaboe sertse), "An Honest Thief" (Chestnyi vor), "White Nights" (Belye nochi).

1849 Arrested for participation in Petrashevsky Circle; tried and sentenced; led to execution, but pardoned; sentenced again to four years of prison and four years in army as a private; put in irons and taken to Siberia by sled.

1857 "The Little Hero" (Malen'kii geroi) published anonymously. Marries Marya Dmitrievna Isaeva.

1859 Allowed to resign from Army and return to Russia and St. Petersburg. *Uncle's Dream (Diadiushkin son). The Friend of the Family (Selo Stepanchiko i ego obitateli)*.

1861 Begins publishing *Notes from the House of the Dead (Zapiski iz mertvogo doma). The Insulted and Injured. (Unizhennye i oskorblyennye)*.

1862   "An Unpleasant Predicament" ("Skvernyi anekdot"). First trip abroad.

1863   *Winter Remarks on Summer Impressions (Zimnie zametki o letnikh vpechatleniiakh).* Second trip abroad.

1864   Becomes editor of *Epokha*, successor to his brother's journal *Vremia* (Time). *Notes from the Underground (Zapiski iz podpol'ia).* Death of his wife in Moscow.

1865   *Epokha* ceases publication. Third trip abroad.

1866   *Crime and Punishment (Prestuplenie i nakazanie). The Gambler (Igrok).*

1867   Marries Anna Grigorievna Snitkina. The couple leaves Russia for Europe where they remain for four years.

1868   *The Idiot (Idiot).*

1870   *The Eternal Husband (Vechnyi muzh).*

1871–72 Publication of *The Devils [The Possessed] (Besy).*

1873–74 Editor of *The Citizen (Grazhdanin).* Begins *Diary of a Writer.*

1874   Trip to Bad Ems (Germany) and Geneva.

1875   Begins publication of *The Raw Youth (Podrostok).* Trip to Ems.

1876   Continuation of *Diary of a Writer (Dnevnik pisatelia);* in November number: "A Gentle Creature" ("Krotkaia").

1877   *Diary of a Writer;* in April number: "The Dream of a Ridiculous Man" ("Son smeshnogo cheloveka").

1878   Death of son Aleksey (Alyosha). Visits Monastery Optina with Vladimir Solovyov.

1879   Begins publishing *The Brothers Karamazov (Brat'ia Karamazov).* Trip to Ems.

1880   Completion of publication of *The Brothers Karamazov.* Pushkin speech in Moscow. Publishes a single number of *The Diary of a Writer.*

1881   Dies January 28 in St. Petersburg. Buried February 1 in cemetery of Alexander Nevsky Monastery.

Notes on the Editor and Authors

ROBERT LOUIS JACKSON (born 1923), American scholar, the editor of this volume, is Professor of Russian Literature at Yale University. He is the author of *Dostoevsky's Quest for Form: A Study of His Philosophy of Art; The Art of Dostoevsky: Deliriums and Nocturnes*; and other studies on Russian and comparative literature.

MIKHAIL M. BAKHTIN (1895–1975), Russian scholar and critic, is the author of *Problems of Dostoevsky's Poetics; Rabelais in the History of Realism*; and numerous other studies on aesthetic and literary themes.

JOSEPH FRANK (born 1918), American scholar and critic, is Professor of Comparative Literature at Princeton University. He is the author of *The Widening Gyre, Dostoevsky: The Seeds of Revolt*, and other works on Russian and comparative literature.

GARY SAUL MORSON (born 1948), American scholar, is Professor of Russian Literature at the University of Pennsylvania. He is the author of *The Boundaries of Genre: Dostoevsky's* Diary of a Writer *and the Traditions of Literary Utopia* and other critical essays.

ROBIN FEUER MILLER (born 1947), American scholar, has taught at Columbia University and is a postdoctoral fellow at Harvard University Russian Research Center. She is the author of *Dostoevsky and* The Idiot.

ADELE LINDENMEYR (born 1949), American scholar, is an Assistant Professor of History at Carnegie–Mellon University. She is the author of essays on various problems in Russian social history.

D. S. SAVAGE (born 1917), British poet, critic, and scholar, is the author of *A Time to Mourn* (poems), *The Withered Branch, Hamlet and the Pirates*, and other works.

MICHAEL HOLQUIST (born 1935), American scholar, is Professor of Russian Literature at Indiana University. He is the author of *Dos-

sky and the Novel and other essays on literature and criticism, as well the editor of *The Dialogic Imagination: Four Essays by M. M. Bakhtin.*

VLADIMIR A. TUNIMANOV, (born 1937), Russian scholar, is a senior research fellow at the Pushkin Institute of Russian Literature in Leningrad. He is the author of *Tvorchestvo Dostoevskogo 1854–1862*, a study on Dostoevsky's *Diary of a Writer*, as well as other essays on Russian literature.

GORDON LIVERMORE (born 1942), American scholar, taught Russian literature at Dartmouth and is currently an editor and translator for the *Current Digest of the Soviet Press* in Columbus, Ohio.

VICTOR TERRAS (born 1917), American scholar, Professor of Russian Literature at Brown University. He is the author of *The Young Dostoevsky, 1846–1949*, *The Heritage of Organic Aesthetics: Belinskij and Russian Literary Criticism*, and other essays in Russian and comparative literatures. He is the editor of *A Karamazov Companion: Commentary on the Genesis, Language, and Style of Dostoevsky's Novel*.

VALENTINA A. VETLOVSKAYA, Russian scholar, a senior research fellow at the Pushkin Institute of Russian Literature in Leningrad, is the author of *Poetika romana 'Brat'ia Karamazovy* and other essays on Dostoevsky.

ROBERT L. BELKNAP (born 1929), American scholar, is Professor of Russian Literature at Columbia University. He is the author of *The Structure of* The Brothers Karamazov and other essays on Russian literature and criticism.

JACQUES CATTEAU (born 1935), French scholar, is Professor of Russian Literature at the Sorbonne in Paris. He is the author of *La Création littéraire chez Dostoievski* and other essays on Russian literature.

Selected Studies on Dostoevsky

Bibliography

Bulletin of the International Dostoevsky Society, Nos. 1-9 (1972–1979) and its continuation, *Dostoevsky Studies*. See also the annual bibliographies put out by PMLA.

Rice, Martin P., *F. M. Dostoevsky. A Bibliography of Non-Slavic Critical Literature About Him: 1900–1980*, Knoxville, Tenn., University of Tennessee, 1984.

Critical and Biographical

Bakhtin, M. M., *Problems of Dostoevsky's Poetics*, Caryl Emerson, trans., Minneapolis, University of Minnesota Press, 1983.

Belknap, Robert L., *The Structure of* The Brothers Karamazov, The Hague-Paris, Mouton & Co., 1967.

Berdyaev, N., *Dostoevsky*, Donald Attwater, trans., New York, 1957.

Catteau, Jacques, *La Création littéraire chez Dostoïevski*, Paris, Institut d'études slaves, 1978.

Cox, Roger L., *Between Earth and Heaven: Shakespeare, Dostoevsky, and the Meaning of Christian Tragedy*, New York-Chicago, Holt, Rinehart and Winston, 1969.

De Lubac, S. J. Henri, *The Drama of Atheist Humanism*, Edith M. Riley, trans., Cleveland-New York, World Publishing Co., 1967.

Fanger, Donald L., *Dostoevsky and Romantic Realism*, Chicago, Liveright, 1967.

Frank, Joseph, *Dostoevsky: The Seeds of Revolt, 1821–1881*, Princeton, N.J., Princeton University Press, 1976.

———*Dostoevsky: The Years of Ordeal, 1850–1860*, Princeton, N.J., Princeton University Press, 1983.

Gerigk, Horst-Jürgen, *Versuch über Dostoevskijs "Jüngling": ein Beitrag zur Theorie des Romans*, Munich, Wilhelm Fink, 1965.

Gibian, George, (ed.), *Dostoevsky*, Crime and Punishment, *The Coulson Translation, Backgrounds and Sources, Essays on Criticism*, New York, W. W. Norton, 1964.

Gibson, Boyce A., *The Religion of Dostoevsky*, London, SCM Press Ltd., 1973.

Girard, René, *Dostoïevski. Du Double à l'unité*, Paris, Plon, 1963.

Goldstein, David I., *Dostoevsky and the Jews*, Austin, Tex., University of Texas, 1981.

Grossman, Leonid, *Dostoevsky: His Life and Work*, Indianapolis–New York, Bobbs-Merrill Co., 1975.

Guerard, Albert J., *The Triumph of the Novel: Dickens, Dostoevsky, Faulkner*, New York–London, Oxford University Press, 1976.

Holquist, Michael, *Dostoevsky and the Novel*, Princeton, N.J., Princeton University Press, 1977.

Ivanov, Vyacheslav, *Freedom and the Tragic Life: A Study in Dostoevsky*, Norman Cameron, trans., S. Konovalav, ed., New York, Noonday Press, 1960.

Jackson, Robert Louis, *The Art of Dostoevsky: Deliriums and Nocturnes*, Princeton, N.J., Princeton University Press, 1981.

———*Dostoevsky's Quest for Form: A Study of His Philosophy of Art*, (2nd ed.), Bloomington, Ind., Physsardt, 1978.

———*Dostoevsky's Notes from the Underground in Russian Literature*, (2nd ed.), Westport, Conn., Greenwood Press, 1981.

———(ed.), Crime and Punishment: *A Collection of Critical Essays*, Englewood Cliffs, N.J., Prentice-Hall, Inc., 1974.

Jones, Malcolm V., *Dostoevsky: The Novel of Discord*, London, T. Elek, 1976.

Kabat, Geoffrey C., *Ideology and Imagination: The Image of Society in Dostoevsky*, New York, Columbia University Press, 1978.

Linnér, Sven, *Dostoevskij on Realism*, Stockholm, Alquist & Wiksell, 1967.

———*Starets Zosima in* The Brothers Karamazov: *A Study in the Mimesis of Virtue*, Stockholm, Alquist & Wiksell, 1981.

Magarshack, David, *Dostoevsky*, New York, Harcourt Brace, 1961.

Matlaw, Ralph E., The Brothers Karamazov: *Novelistic Technique*, The Hague, Mouton & Co., 1957.

———(ed.), *Dostoevsky*, The Brothers Karamazov, *The Garnett Translation, Background and Sources, Essays in Criticism*, New York, W. W. Norton, 1976.

Miller, Robin Feuer, *Dostoevsky and* The Idiot: *Author, Narrator, and Reader*, Cambridge, Mass., Harvard University Press, 1981.

Mochulsky, Konstantin, *Dostoevsky: His Life and Work*, Michael A. Minihan, trans., Princeton, N.J., Princeton University Press, 1967.

Morson, Gary Saul, *The Boundaries of Genre: Dostoevsky's* Diary of a Writer *and the Traditions of Literary Utopia*, Austin, Tex., University of Texas, 1981.

Natova, Nadezhda, *Dostoevskij v Bad Emse*, Frankfurt am Main, 1971.

Neuhäuser, Rudolf, *Das Frühwerk Dostojewskijs: literarische Tradition und gesellschaftlicher Ausbruch*, Heidelberg, Wilhelm Fink, 1979.

Peace, Richard A., *Dostoevsky: An Examination of the Major Novels*, Cambridge, England, Cambridge University Press, 1971.

Rozanov, V., *Dostoevsky and the Grand Inquisitor*, Spencer I. Roberts, trans., Ithaca, N.Y., Cornell University Press, 1972.

Sandoz, Ellis, *Political Apocalypse. A Study of Dostoevsky's Grand Inquisitor*, Baton Rouge, La., Louisiana State University Press, 1971.

Schmidt, Wolf, *Der Textaufbau in den Erzählungen Dostoevskijs*, Munich, Wilhelm Fink, 1973.

Seduro, Vladimir, *Dostoevski in Russian Literary Criticism, 1846–1956*, New York, Columbia University Press, 1957.

————*Dostoevski's Image in Russia Today*, Belmont, Mass., Nordland Publishing Co., 1975.

Shestov, Lev, *Dostoevsky, Tolstoy and Nietzsche*, Bernard Martin and Spencer Roberts, trans., Athens, Ohio, Ohio University Press, 1969.

Simmons, Ernest J., *Dostoievski: The Making of a Novelist*, New York–London, Oxford University Press, 1940.

Steinberg, Aron, *Dostoievsky*, London, Bowes, 1966.

Steiner, George, *Tolstoy or Dostoevsky: An Essay in the Old Criticism*, New York, Alfred Knopf, 1959.

Terras, Victor, *A Karamazov Companion: Commentary on the Genesis, Language, and Style of Dostoevsky's Novel*, Madison, Wis., University of Wisconsin Press, 1981.

————*The Young Dostoevsky, 1846–1849*, The Hague, Mouton & Co., 1969.

Van der Eng, J., *Dostoevskij romancier*, The Hague, Mouton & Co., 1957.

Vladiv, Slobodanka B., *Narrative Principles in Dostoevskij's* Besy: *A Structural Analysis*, European University Papers, Series 16 (Slavic Languages and Literatures), Vol. 10 (1979), Berne, et al, Peter Lang.

Wasiolek, Edward, *The Major Fiction*, Cambridge, Mass., M.I.T. Press, 1964.

————(ed.), Crime and Punishment *and the Critics*, San Francisco, Wadsworth, 1961.

Wellek, René, (ed.), *Dostoevsky: A Collection of Critical Essays*, Englewood Cliffs, N.J., Prentice-Hall, Inc., 1962.

Index